CONTENTS

ENVIRONMENTAL LAW IN SCOTLAND

Second Edition

Edited by

Colin T. Reid
Professor of Environmental Law, University of Dundee

W. GREEN/Sweet and Maxwell
EDINBURGH
1997

First published 1992
Reprinted 1994
Second edition 1997

© 1997
W. GREEN & SON LTD AND CONTRIBUTORS

ISBN 0 414 01182 1

No natural forests were destroyed to make this product;
only farmed timber was used and replanted

A CIP catalogue reference for this book is available from the British Library

Typeset by Trinity Typesetting, Edinburgh
Printed and bound in Great Britain by the Cromwell Press, Wiltshire

PREFACE

Environmental law continues to become increasingly important in many aspects of legal and commercial life. In the five years since the first edition of this book was published, the law has become no less complex, and it is no easier for those trying to discover what the law says to find their way through the ever-increasing mass of detailed regulations. There appears still to be a need for a book which will introduce people to the subject, and present an overall picture of the most important areas of environmental control. Our aim remains as stated in the original title: to offer a guide to environmental law in Scotland.

As in the first edition, the contributors were asked to provide a short introduction to their topic, to offer a sketch-map presenting the general outline and structure of the law, and to indicate where more information can be found. This they have done, with, perhaps, greater diversity than in the first edition. We have not attempted to provide a comprehensive statement or critical assessment of the law, but rather an introduction for those who are not familiar with the areas of law covered. We hope that the book will provide a starting-point for legal practitioners and a useful guide for all those who need to understand something of the range of legal measures designed to regulate our impact on the environment.

Environmental law continues to develop rapidly, with new legislation emerging every year. The previous edition was produced while we were waiting for significant parts of the Environmental Protection Act 1990 to come into force. This edition comes as the Environment Act 1995 is coming into effect. In such circumstances it is virtually impossible (and not necessarily particularly helpful) to state the law as at one particular date, thereby guaranteeing that the book will be out of date when it is bought. Again, therefore, we look forward rather than back, and throughout the book it has generally been assumed that the recent legislation has been or will be brought into force as scheduled, in order to present a guide to the law as it is developing, rather than as it was in the past. There is a risk that this will be a "fantasy law book", describing laws which never take effect (as with the first edition's coverage of the 1990 Act's provisions on contaminated land), but taking that risk seems preferable to providing an outdated account of the law on a single day some months before publication.

The new legislation has resulted in many amendments to older statutes and regulations, sometimes changes of major importance, but frequently only consequential amendments arising from the reorganisation of public bodies or from amendments to the law in related fields. The long-overdue consolidation of the planning legislation is a relief to all who have to use the law in that area, but other areas, perhaps most notably water pollution, cry out for similar treatment. Listing every amendment to every piece of legislation mentioned in this book would fill pages by itself (some have been amended almost a dozen times, with no fundamental alterations) and, again bearing in mind the aim of this book, as a general rule we have mentioned specifically only those amendments of particular significance. In all cases the statutory references should be read as references to the relevant provisions as amended.

One significant development in the years since the first edition has been the growth in the literature on environmental law. A note of further reading is given, at the end of the book rather than at the end of each chapter, but the list is not comprehensive and concentrates on books and some key government papers, as opposed to providing a full bibliography.

As editor, my thanks go to all of the contributors for the skill and effort they have applied in providing their chapters. The two who actually met the original deadline have my special thanks, but the patience of all the early contributors is gratefully acknowledged. I am grateful also to those who have allowed their work for the first edition to form the basis of new chapters. Where there have been changes to the contributors from the first edition, these are all the result of the original authors having other commitments which prevented them from revising their contributions (albeit in one case this became apparent to me only at a very late stage). My thanks also go to all of the staff at Greens who contributed to the final production and appearance of the book.

Colin T. Reid
May 1997

TABLE OF CASES

TABLE OF STATUTES

TABLE OF STATUTORY INSTRUMENTS

TABLE OF EUROPEAN MATERIAL

Decisions

TABLE OF ABBREVIATIONS

AQMA	Air Quality Management Area
BATNEEC	Best available techniques not entailing excessive cost
BPEO	Best practicable environmental option
BPM	Best practicable means
CAA	Civil Aviation Authority
CAA 1993	Clean Air Act 1993
CFC	Chlorofluorocarbon
CLC	International Convention on Civil Liability for Oil Pollution Damage 1969
CLC 1992	International Convention on Civil Liability for Oil Pollution Damage 1992
COPA 1974	Control of Pollution Act 1974
CRISTAL	Contract Regarding an Interim Supplement to Tanker Liability for Oil Pollution
DSA 1996	Deer (Scotland) Act 1996
EA 1995	Environment Act 1995
EEA	European Environment Agency
EMAS	Eco-Management and Audit Scheme
EP(AAR)R 1991	Environmental Protection (Applications, Appeals and Registers) Regulations 1991
EP(PPS)R 1991	Environmental Protection (Prescribed Processes and Substances) Regulations 1991
EPA 1990	Environmental Protection Act 1990
HMIPI	Her Majesty's Industrial Pollution Inspectorate
HNS	Convention on Liability and Compensation in Connection with the Carriage of Hazardous and Noxious Substances by Sea 1996
IMO	International Maritime Organisation
IPC	Integrated pollution control
IPPC	Integrated pollution prevention and control
LAPC	Local air pollution control
LOF	Lloyds Open Form
MARPOL	International Convention for the Prevention of Pollution from Ships 1973
NPPG	National Planning Policy Guideline
OPRC	Convention on Oil Pollution Preparedness, Response and Co-operation 1990
PAN	Planning Advice Note
RPA	River purification authority

SDD	Scottish Development Department
SODD	Scottish Office Development Department
SEPA	Scottish Environment Protection Agency
SNH	Scottish Natural Heritage
SOEnvD	Scottish Office Environment Department
SSSI	Site of special scientific interest
TAC	Total Allowable Catch
TOVALOP	Tanker Owners' Voluntary Agreement Concerning Liability for Oil Pollution
WCA 1981	Wildlife and Countryside Act 1981

CHAPTER ONE

INTRODUCTION

HISTORY AND DEVELOPMENT

Although environmental law is thought of as being a new subject, the law in 1.1.1
Scotland has long been concerned with such matters. Looking simply at the
legislation from the Scottish Parliament, the main concern at first was with
the preservation of natural resources for exploitation by the community (or
often by certain privileged members of the community), *e.g.* there are many
provisions concerned with protecting the King's forests[1] and regulating the
taking of game,[2] including a partial moratorium on hunting at a time when a
shortage of game had developed.[3] Protecting people and their property from
the risks of the natural world was another aim, *e.g.* in laws encouraging the
destruction of birds viewed as agricultural pests,[4] and prohibiting the pulling
of vegetation on sand dunes to prevent erosion causing harm to inhabited
areas.[5] Other laws fit more closely the modern conception of environmental
law, *e.g.* prohibitions on water pollution resulting from the washing of green
lint in lochs and streams,[6] and regulations on where and how offensive and
hazardous trades could operate in Edinburgh.[7]

However, other than the game laws, these provisions have left little trace 1.1.2
in the modern law, which is essentially a response to the problems of the
industrial age. The law of nuisance developed at the end of the eighteenth
century,[8] and during the nineteenth century there was considerable legislative
intervention to protect the living and working conditions of the population:
the Factory Acts from 1833, the Nuisances Removal and Diseases Prevention
Act 1848 and its successors, the Alkali Acts from 1863, and the Public
Health (Scotland) Act 1897, parts of which remain in force. During the

---

[1] *e.g.* APS II 343 c.9 (1535); III 560 c.35 (1592); IV 67 c.20 (1594); and *Leges Forestarum*;
see, generally, Gilbert, *Hunting and Hunting Reserves in Mediaeval Scotland* (1979).
[2] *e.g.* APS I 576 (1400); II 52 c.36 (1457); II 107 c.15 (1474); II 483 c.3 (1551).
[3] APS II 486 c.15 (1551).
[4] APS II 51 c.32 (1457).
[5] APS IX 452 c.54 (1695).
[6] APS IV 287 c.12 (1606).
[7] APS IV 632 c.29 (1621).
[8] Whitty, *"Nuisance"*, in *The Laws of Scotland: Stair Memorial Encyclopaedia* (1988), Vol.
14, paras. 2007–2016.

twentieth century the authorities responsible for administering such provisions have been transformed, and environmental regulation has increased dramatically in scope and detail. The Clean Air Acts of 1956 and 1968 and the Control of Pollution Act 1974 established frameworks for a broad range of controls, supported by volumes of delegated legislation, while the Environmental Protection Act 1990 (EPA 1990) and the Environment Act 1995 (EA 1995) mark the start of a new chapter in our environmental law.

1.1.3   Recent developments in the law reveal a number of trends. First, it is possible to detect the emergence of a number of principles which may help to give shape to the discussion and future development of the law. Three perhaps stand out — sustainable development, the polluter pays principle and the precautionary principle — but in each case there is uncertainty over the precise meaning of the concept and argument over how it should be applied in practice.

1.1.4   The most quoted definition of sustainable development is that taken from the Brundtland Commission: "Sustainable development is development that meets the needs of the present without comprising the ability of future generations to meet their own needs".[9] It is seen as an attempt to reconcile the conflicting goals of economic development and environmental protection, ensuring that the benefits of any development outweigh its costs, including its environmental costs.[10] However, exactly how these costs should be assessed and how they should be balanced against other costs and benefits remains a difficult and frequently controversial issue, especially as it can be argued that a true commitment to sustainability would require a massive change in many aspects of our industrial, commercial and economic life. Nevertheless, sustainable development is now firmly enshrined in U.K. policy,[11] and in the law to the extent that both Scottish Natural Heritage[12] (SNH) and the Scottish Environmental Protection Agency[13] (SEPA) have obligations to have regard to sustainable development. It remains to be seen how far the oft-stated commitment to sustainable development will, in fact, produce significant changes in policy.

1.1.5   That a polluter should pay for the harm which has been caused to others has traditionally been part of our law where the polluter has been at fault. This one, narrow manifestation of the polluter pays principle is now being

---

[9]   World Commission on Environment and Development, *Our Common Future* (1987), p. 43. This definition is adopted in *Sustainable Development: The U.K. Strategy*, Cm. 2426 (1994), but it should be noted that the passage in the Brundtland Commission's report continues with a reference to "the essential needs of the world's poor, to which overriding priority should be given".

[10]   *Sustainable Development: The U.K. Strategy*, Cm. 2426 (1994), Chap. 3.

[11]   *ibid.*

[12]   Natural Heritage (Scotland) Act 1991, s. 1(1).

[13]   EA 1995, s. 31(2).

augmented by others. The law is increasingly imposing strict liability,[14] and liability to pay for general clean-up costs, rather than merely to compensate the legally recognised harm suffered by others.[15] Polluters (or, rather, potential polluters) are asked to pay for the costs of the regulatory regimes which seek to ensure that their activities do not, in fact, cause environmental harm.[16] There are, however, difficulties in determining how far the principle should extend. To what extent, and through what mechanisms, should polluters be made to pay not just for the direct harm they cause, but for the more diffuse and indirect environmental costs of their activities? How are these costs to be assessed? Who, indeed, is to be identified as the polluter — the producer, the retailer or the consumer?

The precautionary principle states that the absence of conclusive scientific proof is not a good reason for failing to take preventive action once a risk of environmental damage has been identified. The global measures which address the issue of climate change are a clear example of this principle in operation.[17] Again, however, there are many different ways of formulating the principle, each reflecting a different emphasis on the various elements. What level of scientific opinion is necessary before a risk is taken seriously? How are the likelihood of the risk, the seriousness of the harm and the costs of preventive action to be balanced? The formulation favoured by the Government refers to taking preventive action "if the balance of likely costs and benefits justifies it",[18] but that, of course, leaves open the further question of how the costs and benefits are to be assessed and then weighed against each other. As with the other principles, the precautionary principle can therefore act as only the most general of guidance when it comes to taking particular decisions.

1.1.6

A second trend is that the international scale of modern environmental problems has meant that our law is increasingly influenced by developments at a European and global level. Pollution does not stop at national frontiers, and states have become increasingly aware of the need for concerted action to ensure that the environment is adequately protected. Their willingness to co-operate in such matters has been enhanced by the realisation that differing environmental standards can considerably distort the international market-place. Thus, although the law continues to be structured and enforced within a national framework, the substantive rules contained in the law are increasingly the product of international agreement at some level, whether

1.1.7

---

[14] *e.g.* EPA 1990, s. 73(6).
[15] *e.g.* Control of Pollution Act 1974, s. 46 (as substituted by Water Act 1989, Sched. 23, para. 5).
[16] EA 1995, s. 42(3).
[17] *e.g.* United Nations Framework Convention on Climate Change, 1992; see *Climate Change: The U.K. Programme*, Cm. 2427 (1994).
[18] *This Common Inheritance: Britain's Environmental Strategy*, Cm. 1200 (1990), para. 1.18.

broad declarations from global conferences,[19] specific international treaties[20] or detailed European legislation.[21]

1.1.8 A third trend has been towards integration of the legal approaches to environmental matters. In the same way that it has been realised that national environments cannot be treated separately, it has been appreciated that it is also impossible to isolate the various elements of the environment and deal with each separately. The traditional approach was to deal with air pollution separately from water pollution and waste disposal, but the need for a more integrated approach has been realised, to ensure that pollution is not merely transferred from one medium to another and that the best environmental option can be chosen. This is reflected in various recent changes to the law, *e.g.* integrated pollution control under EPA 1990, whereby many of the environmental consequences of a process are considered at once,[22] and environmental assessment in the planning system, where all aspects of the environmental impact of a proposed development are considered.[23] Similarly, the duty of care in relation to waste ensures that those producing and handling waste must consider all stages in its processing "from the cradle to the grave",[24] and the growing use of environmental auditing[25] aims to encourage industrial concerns to assess all the consequences of their activities.

1.1.9 The desire for an integrated approach is also reflected by the reduction in the number of authorities with responsibilities for environmental matters. Scottish Natural Heritage has been created as a single body concerned with nature conservation, landscape preservation, amenity and recreation in the countryside, merging the functions previously split between the Nature Conservancy Council for Scotland and the Countryside Commission for Scotland.[26] More significantly, SEPA was created to take over the environmental responsibilities of local authorities, the river purification boards and Her Majesty's Industrial Pollution Inspectorate (HMIPI).[27] By uniting the main functions in the hands of one body, a fully integrated approach can be taken to much environmental regulation, and the body can concentrate on its environmental responsibilities, free from the potential conflicts of interest which arose from the range of functions carried out by local authorities.

---

[19] *e.g.* the Rio Declaration on Environment and Development (1992).
[20] *e.g.* the Vienna Convention for the Protection of the Ozone Layer (1985) and the Montreal Protocol on Substances that Deplete the Ozone Layer (1987). See paras. 2.1.4–7.
[21] See Chap. 12.
[22] See Chap. 5.
[23] See paras. 7.4.17–20.
[24] See paras. 4.5.1–8.
[25] Not yet a legal requirement, but a voluntary scheme exists within the European Community; Regulation 1836/93.
[26] See para. 10.1.3.
[27] EA 1995, Pt. I; SEPA came into operation in April 1996. See para. 1.4.6.

Greater emphasis on a strategic approach to environmental issues is a 1.1.10 fourth trend which is apparent. The appreciation that environmental problems cannot be addressed on a local and fragmented basis has led to the development of strategies and programmes to direct the overall response to such issues. The broad sweep of the Government's White Paper, *This Common Inheritance: Britain's Environmental Strategy*,[28] and the programmes developed as a result of the Rio Summit,[29] bring together policy and legal issues from many fields, with a growing awareness of the need for a wide range of issues to be tackled together. The role of development plans in the town and country planning system has been enhanced,[30] and national strategies are required for air quality[31] and waste.[32] All these developments reveal a move towards dealing with environmental issues on a longer term and more co-ordinated basis.

A fifth trend has been to increase the potential for public involvement in 1.1.11 environmental regulation. One of the features of the past reliance on regulatory authorities was the very limited opportunities for members of the public to become involved in matters of environmental control. In the absence of legal title deriving from some direct consequences on individual health or property rights, it was not possible for individuals to take action to enforce environmental standards, or even discover the basic information on which assessments of the health of the environment and the level of pollution could be made. Everything was left to the wide discretion of the regulatory bodies.

Now, largely prompted by European developments,[33] much more 1.1.12 information is available. This is provided primarily through public registers which are a feature of the regulatory schemes,[34] and through the general obligation on public bodies to provide environmental information to the public.[35] This obligation is of potentially great significance in ensuring that important information comes into the public domain, although there remains uncertainty over its exact scope, *e.g.* in relation to what information "relates to the environment", which bodies have "public responsibilities for the environment" and the precise limits of the many exceptions, and there is no mechanism short of judicial review to challenge the withholding of any information. Information is also made available through access to the

---

[28] Cm. 1200 (1990).
[29] *Sustainable Development: The U.K. Strategy*, Cm. 2426 (1994); *Climate Change: The U.K. Programme*, Cm. 2427 (1994); *Biodiversity: The U.K. Action Plan*, Cm. 2428 (1994).
[30] See para. 7.3.9.
[31] EA 1995, s. 80. See paras. 2.3.2–5.
[32] EPA 1990, s. 44B. See para. 4.2.5.
[33] Directive 90/313 on freedom of access to information on the environment.
[34] See, *e.g.* EPA 1990, ss. 20–22, 64–66, 78R, 95, 122–123.
[35] Environmental Information Regulations 1992 (S.I. 1992 No. 3240).

environmental assessment statements for certain new developments,[36] and initiatives such as eco-labelling,[37] energy labelling[38] and eco-audits.[39]

1.1.13 The issue today is what the public can do with the information which has become available. With better knowledge about the state of the environment and the causes of harm to it, those who are concerned should be able to apply pressure much more effectively to the Government and the regulatory bodies. They should also be able to participate more effectively when there are opportunities to make representations before decisions are taken, *e.g.* when applications for integrated pollution control authorisations[40] are advertised. Such public involvement is already well-developed in the planning system, but it remains to be seen whether it will, in fact, become a major feature of other regimes, where the issues may be more technical and any harmful effects may be less immediately apparent and diffused over a much wider area.

1.1.14 Whether a citizen armed with information will also be able to take legal action against the regulators or polluters in order to enforce compliance with the prescribed standards has not yet been fully explored in Scotland. Private prosecutions are not available, and anyone seeking to use judicial review to ensure that an authority is properly meeting its obligations faces the hurdle of establishing title and interest to sue. As nobody has a legal right to a perfectly clean environment, and nobody owns wild birds or fish in the sea, this may be a significant hurdle, especially for pressure groups which may be the parties most likely to have the determination, expertise and resources to sue. Recent Scottish authority, *Scottish Old People's Welfare Council, Petitioners,*[41] denied standing to a pressure group, but the English courts have now permitted such groups to sue,[42] emphasising the importance of the rule of law and the fact that if the pressure group was not allowed standing there was nobody else in a position to challenge the legality of the governmental action.[43] These arguments could provide a basis for allowing such actions in Scotland; whereas in the *Scottish Old People's Welfare Council* case the individual claimants for social security benefit had a stronger connection with the issue than the pressure group, in many environmental disputes there will be no individuals with a greater claim to standing than a pressure group.

[36] See paras. 7.4.17–20.
[37] Regulation 880/92; *e.g.* Decision 93/430/EC on eco-label criteria for washing-machines.
[38] Directive 92/75; *e.g.* Energy Information (Refrigerators and Freezers) Regulations 1994 (S.I. 1994 No. 3076).
[39] Regulation 1836/93.
[40] See para. 5.4.2.
[41] 1987 S.L.T. 179.
[42] *R. v. Inspectorate of Pollution, ex p. Greenpeace (No. 2)* [1994] 4 All E.R. 329.
[43] *R. v. Secretary of State for Foreign Affairs, ex p. World Development Movement Ltd* [1995] 1 W.L.R. 386 at 395.

LEGAL APPROACHES

A variety of methods are used in the regulation of human impact on the 1.2.1
environment. The law of delict, especially nuisance, still has a role to play
in imposing liability for harm caused to other people and their property.[44]
The common law is, however, limited, primarily because only a pursuer
whose legal rights have been damaged can raise an action. This means,
first, that the law cannot be invoked in response to some forms of
environmental harm (*e.g.* chemical pollution killing wild animals, since
these are not the subject of any property rights) or can be activated only
when the harm reaches a fairly serious level at which property rights or
individual health are affected. There is no general legal right to insist on
wholly clean air or a clean environment, the only right of action being to
protect one's health and the value and quiet enjoyment of one's property.

The second limitation of the common law arises from the limited class 1.2.2
of pursuers. There must be a pursuer whose rights have been affected and
who is willing to raise the action. If activity on a piece of land is causing
severe environmental damage, but only to the same proprietor's land, there
is no possibility of third parties intervening, and in many situations the
personal or economic relationship between the potential pursuers and the
defender may be such that legal action is unlikely. On the other hand, the
protection of an aggrieved neighbour's private rights may be allowed to
stand in the way of works which may inevitably cause some nuisance, but
are very much in the public interest. Neither is the common law good at
ensuring that appropriate preventive steps are taken. It may be possible to
obtain an interdict where there is a clear risk of harm being caused, but
something more is needed to ensure that proper safeguards are taken at all
stages of the construction and operation of potentially polluting plant etc.

There is therefore a need for legal intervention in the public interest, 1.2.3
which can take several forms. The most common is to create some form of
administrative regulatory system. Before an activity can lawfully be carried
out, official permission is required from a regulatory agency. Within the
broad framework set by legislation, the agency will have considerable
discretion in deciding whether and on what conditions permission should
be granted, and, in the event of a breach of control, in deciding what sanction,
if any, should be applied. This model allows for a flexible system of control,
taking account of all the local and particular factors affecting individual
sites.

In terms of determining the standards to be applied there is also a range 1.2.4
of possibilities. In the past, the British tendency has been for the flexible
approach which flows from a requirement that any factory, etc., adopt the

---

[44] See Chap. 9.

"best practicable means" to avoid pollution, allowing the environmental context and other considerations, including the costs of reducing pollution, to be taken into account, rather than insisting on fixed and measurable limits. This flexible approach has now been refined into the concept of best available techniques not entailing excessive cost (BATNEEC), which will entail a greater commitment to achieving the minimum environmental harm, but still leaves some room for flexibility.[45]

1.2.5   The alternative of establishing fixed limits can be applied in various ways. For example, quality standards can be set for the river or local atmosphere into which emissions are being made, limits can be set for emissions from particular sites, standards can be prescribed for particular processes or for particular products.[46] Each of these will influence in different ways the conduct of the processes likely to cause pollution, but will provide objective tests against which performance can be tested.

Enforcement

1.2.6   A common feature of the legislation in this area is the attention given to the enforcement of the law. The authorities are given powers of entry, search and seizure to ensure that they are not thwarted by unco-operative operators.[47] The law usually includes offences of strict liability, and where this is modified by the existence of defences the onus is commonly on the accused to establish that the exculpatory features do, in fact, exist. Such an approach encourages those concerned to take the utmost care to avoid breaches of the law, whilst relieving the enforcement authorities of the often impossible task of proving exactly how and through whose fault a particular polluting incident occurred.

1.2.7   The reliance on strict liability does, however, allow a considerable element of discretion to the authorities. Every infraction of the law, however minor or blameless, could result in a prosecution, but the authorities do not seek to prosecute in every case, often relying on persuasion and co-operation rather than the strict enforcement of sanctions to ensure future compliance with the law. The reluctance to prosecute stems from a variety of reasons, including the costs in terms of time and labour in preparing cases for the courts (*e.g.* in gathering proof to the legal standard), the problems of persuading the busy prosecution authorities to devote their energies to cases which may be seen as marginal to their main work, and the limited results achieved — penalties in the past have tended to be low, leaving the stigma of conviction as the only real penalty.[48]

---

[45]   See paras. 5.4.11–19.
[46]   See paras. 2.8.1–12.
[47]   *e.g.* EA 1995, s. 108.
[48]   Rowan-Robinson, Watchman and Barker, *Crime and Regulation* (1990).

Recent developments suggest that the position may be changing. The 1.2.8
fine of £1 million imposed in February 1990 for oil pollution of the Mersey[49]
remains an exceptional case, but there are signs that the courts are now
willing to impose significant fines in some cases.[50] Recent legislation,
particularly the Environmental Protection Act 1990, provides substantial
maximum penalties for many offences, including terms of imprisonment.
Moreover, there is the increased possibility of personal liability for directors,
managers and other senior officers of companies through whose neglect
the company commits an offence.[51]

ECONOMIC FACTORS

Environmental controls inevitably entail costs for industry in terms of both 1.3.1
compliance costs and the fees charged by regulatory authorities.[52] As
environmental controls become stricter, and as liability in various forms is
imposed for harm caused, these costs become more significant, prompting
a close examination of how materials are used and wastes produced.
However, there is also the possibility of using economic or pricing
mechanisms more directly as a means of achieving environmental goals.
Examples in the present law include the lower duty levied on lead-free
petrol,[53] landfill tax,[54] and the use of management agreements[55] whereby
sums are paid to landowners in return for their agreement to manage their
land in ways which may not achieve the maximum economic return, but
which are beneficial to nature conservation.

Ambitious schemes could be used to play a more major role in 1.3.2
environmental controls. Rather than imposing limits on emissions, taxes
could be levied on the amount of pollution emitted. In addition to providing
an economic incentive for reducing pollution, such a scheme may encourage
industry to minimise emissions, not merely reduce emissions to meet the
prevailing legal standard. Marketable pollution permits could be introduced,
the total volume of emissions to be permitted in an area being set and then
divided between polluters; those able to reduce their emissions could sell
an unused quota to other concerns, while environmental groups could buy
quotas but not use them, thereby reducing the overall volume of emissions.

---

[49] *National Rivers Authority v. Shell U.K. Ltd* [1990] *Water Law* 40.
[50] *e.g.* fines of up to £12,000 for a single offence in a series of water pollution cases during
the construction of the M74; (1995) 49 S.P.E.L. 45.
[51] EPA 1990, s. 157.
[52] The fees charged are to be set so as to ensure that the regulatory schemes are self-financing;
EA 1995, s. 42(3).
[53] Hydrocarbon Oil Duties Act 1979, s. 13A.
[54] See paras. 4.7.1–3.
[55] See para. 10.3.2.

The perceived advantage of this approach is that the burden of meeting the desired standard is divided between the polluters in an economically efficient way — not by imposing a uniform standard but by allowing each concern to choose its response according to the practicality of cleaning up its own processes. Other possibilities include the introduction of a carbon tax — a tax charged on fuels according to the amount of carbon dioxide produced in their use.

1.3.3   Such radical innovations would probably be feasible only in conjunction with some form of regulatory scheme, and their effects are difficult to predict: if the financial incentives are set too low, the impact may be minimal; if they are set too high, there may be a disruptive effect on industry and unforeseen and inequitable consequences for groups unable to adjust their conduct. It is likely, however, that there will continue to be interest in developing economic means of influencing our impact on the environment, both as incentives for "good" conduct and to penalise those causing unacceptable pollution.[56]

AUTHORITIES

1.4.1 The administration of environmental matters was transformed in 1996 by the creation of SEPA, but other bodies are still involved. Beyond our shores, the work of international bodies, such as the Commission on Sustainable Development, established after the Rio Summit, will have an effect on overall policy. Major legal initiatives come from the European Community, which in this field has been able to benefit from the varied experiences of the Member States on environmental matters.[57] There may be years of argument and many fundamental amendments before proposals made by the European Commission are accepted and take any legal form, but anyone wishing to look into the future for environmental law in this country must examine what is being discussed in Brussels. The role of the European Environment Agency may also be important, at present as the source of "objective, reliable and comparable information",[58] but with the potential to develop further.[59]

1.4.2   In this country, central government becomes involved in many ways. The details of the law are directly in the hands of the Government because so much of the law in this area is to be found in delegated legislation. The statutes themselves offer merely a framework within which the detailed legal regimes are constructed. The need to implement E.C. law also leads

---

[56] See, generally, Economic Instruments for Environmental Protection, Annex A to *This Common Inheritance*, Cm. 1200 (1990); Bándi, "Financial Instruments in Environmental Protection" in *European Environmental Law: A Comparative Perspective* (Winter ed., 1995).
[57] See Chap. 12.
[58] This phrase is taken from the Agency's mission statement.
[59] See para. 12.3.8.

to much delegated legislation, the European origins of the rules sometimes being hidden by the fact that the rules take the form of domestic legislation.

The powers of government to issue guidance to environmental bodies is of increasing importance. In some areas this is well established, *e.g.* the role of national planning guidelines, circulars and planning advice notes in the planning system,[60] but a notable feature of much recent legislation is the extent to which the way in which the regulatory powers are to operate depends not on any legal rules but on guidance in many forms. Thus, SEPA is required to have regard to guidance from the Secretary of State with respect to the aims and objectives which he considers it appropriate for SEPA to pursue, including its contribution to sustainable development.[61] More striking still is the position with regard to contaminated land, where virtually every feature of the proposed regime, from the definition of contaminated land to the allocation of liability for its remediation, is to be controlled by guidance from the Secretary of State, some of which *must* be followed.[62] Such guidance must be laid before Parliament,[63] but does not fit within any recognised form of delegated legislation. It is therefore to the guidance rather than to the words of the legislation that one must look to find out what the law will actually mean in practice. 1.4.3

As well as determining the general rules, central government can become involved in particular issues as individual cases may be referred to the Secretary of State and his staff, either where there is a requirement for official consent or approval, or where there is an appeal from the decisions of other bodies.[64] The importance of central government is increased by the number of indirect controls at its disposal, such as its influence over the membership (and often funding) of public bodies such as SEPA and Scottish Natural Heritage. Such issues generally fall under the ambit of the Scottish Office Agriculture Environment and Fisheries Department, or the Scottish Office Development Department in relation to planning matters, but on many issues there must be close liaison with the Department of the Environment south of the border, while the influence of other departments (especially the Treasury) must also be remembered. 1.4.4

In the past, local government was heavily involved through its responsibilities for sewerage and water supply, the control of waste, and aspects of air pollution. The reorganisation in 1996 removed these tasks from local authorities, which do, however, still retain some environmental functions. The town and country planning system remains a matter for local councils, as do public health and statutory nuisance, including responsibility 1.4.5

---

[60] See paras. 7.3.1–6.
[61] EA 1995, s. 31.
[62] See paras. 6.4.1–2.
[63] EPA 1990, s. 78YA.
[64] See, *e.g.* paras. 4.3.44–47.

for most contaminated land under the proposed new regime.[65] Local authorities' wide powers in relation to recreation and amenity may also be exercised with a view to environmental considerations.

1.4.6   The most important body now is SEPA, which has responsibility for most areas of pollution control, taking over from local authorities, HMIPI and the river purification boards. SEPA's pollution control powers are to be exercised "for the purpose of preventing or minimising, or remedying or mitigating the effects of, pollution of the environment",[66] and other factors to be taken into account include the social and economic needs of any area of Scotland, maintaining freedom of public access to land, buildings and sites, and the desirability of protecting the natural heritage and buildings and sites of archaeological, architectural, engineering or historic interest.[67] Guidance from the Secretary of State must be taken into account, including guidance on how SEPA can contribute towards attaining the objective of sustainable development.[68] SEPA is also under an obligation to take into account the likely costs and benefits of the exercise or non-exercise of its powers in each particular case, but only to the extent that it is not unreasonable for it to do so and that there is no conflict with its legal duties — qualifications which, when added to the vagueness of the main obligation, render this a difficult provision to give real meaning to.[69]

1.4.7   The activities of many other bodies can also affect the environment, and, increasingly, regard for environmental consequences is being included within the general aims and functions of public bodies. The Forestry Commission must endeavour to seek a reasonable balance between the promotion of commercial forestry and the conservation of nature and natural beauty,[70] and Scottish Enterprise is required to have regard to the desirability of safeguarding the environment.[71] Only in the most blatant instances where environmental factors are wholly ignored is it likely that any court would hold a body in breach of such vague obligations. Nevertheless their presence does ensure that public bodies must at least give some consideration to the environmental impact of their actions and listen to arguments from those expressing environmental concern.

1.4.8   Mention should also be made of the important role played by a large number of non-governmental organisations. In relation to the protection of the countryside and wildlife, much practical work is carried out by charitable

---

[65] See Chap. 6.
[66] EA 1995, s. 33(1).
[67] *ibid.* s. 32.
[68] *ibid.* s. 31.
[69] *ibid.* s. 39.
[70] Forestry Act 1967, s. 1(3A) (added by Wildlife and Countryside (Amendment) Act 1985, s. 4).
[71] Enterprise and New Towns (Scotland) Act 1990, s. 4(4).

bodies such as the National Trust for Scotland,[72] the Scottish Wildlife Trust and the Royal Society for the Protection of Birds. The role of these and other bodies in conserving aspects of our natural heritage and in drawing attention to environmental issues has been of great importance, especially in the decades before environmental matters became a matter of significant official concern.

OTHER TOPICS

The topics covered in this book are those which play the most obvious part 1.5.1 in regulating our environment, but by no means exhaust those which may be relevant. Many other areas of law are concerned with environmental matters, and some of the more significant are noted below, in each case the law being very heavily influenced by developments at E.C. level. However, it is important to stress that wherever one attempts to draw the boundary, environmental law cannot exist as an isolated area of law, set apart in a compartment on its own. Since all kinds of human activity can affect the environment, for good or ill, all forms of law may be relevant to environmental issues. For example, the present rural landscape has been affected more by the laws on landownership and by the nature of the financial support for agriculture and forestry than by any other legal or administrative factor. A good environmental lawyer must be prepared to make use of all aspects of the law which may be relevant to the task in hand.

Hazardous substances

The control of hazardous substances falls between environmental law and 1.5.2 the law on health and safety, and is generally under the supervision of the Health and Safety Commission and Executive. The risks posed by the transport, storage and use of such material have led to a broad range of legal controls, aiming to protect both the working environment of those involved with the materials and the environment in general. Hazardous substances consent must also be obtained from the planning authority where more than the prescribed amount of certain prescribed substances are to be kept.[73] There are controls on the transport of hazardous substances by road, rail, air and sea,[74] and the relevant authorities must be notified of installations

---

[72] The Trust enjoys some special legal status under a series of private Acts of Parliament.

[73] Planning (Hazardous Substances) (Scotland) Act 1997; Town and Country Planning (Hazardous Substances) (Scotland) Regulations 1993 (S.I. 1993 No. 323).

[74] *e.g.* Carriage of Dangerous Goods by Road Regulations 1996 (S.I. 1996 No. 2095); Carriage of Dangerous Goods (Classification, Packaging and Labelling) and Use of Transportable Pressure Receptacles Regulations 1996 (S.I. 1996 No. 2092); Carriage of Dangerous Goods by Rail Regulations 1996 (S.I. 1996 No. 2089); Air Navigation (Dangerous Goods) Regulations 1994 (S.I. 1994 No. 3187); Merchant Shipping (Dangerous or Noxious Liquid Substances in Bulk) Regulations 1996 (S.I. 1996 No. 3010).

using and storing such substances.[75] More detailed controls over the importation and use of certain materials exist, and there are rules designed to secure the monitoring of their usage and to protect those working with hazardous materials from harmful exposure.[76]

1.5.3 The Secretary of State has a general power to prohibit or restrict the importation, use, supply or storage of any substance or article where necessary in order to prevent pollution of the environment or harm to the health of humans, animals or plants.[77] Wide powers exist to make emergency orders to prohibit or restrict the distribution of food which may have become contaminated at any stage in the food chain.[78] More generally, the basic obligations under the Health and Safety at Work etc. Act 1974 to protect employees and others from dangers to their health should also achieve a degree of environmental protection.[79]

Radioactive substances

1.5.4 The particular hazards of radioactive substances have produced a further set of legal controls. The Nuclear Installations Act 1965 requires that all sites using significant quantities of radioactive material be licensed, imposes a duty to prevent injury or damage to property and provides a statutory right to compensation for injury caused, with an extended limitation period of 30 years to take account of the particular nature of radiation-related illnesses. The Radioactive Substances Act 1993 lays down a registration scheme for the use and storage of radioactive material, while any disposal or accumulation of radioactive waste requires an authorisation from the Secretary of State. There are also regulations controlling the transport of such material.[80] The domestic rules are closely linked with those drawn up by Euratom (the European Atomic Energy Community) and the International Commission on Radiological Protection.

Pesticides

1.5.5 The sale and use of pesticides are strictly controlled under Part III of the Food and Environment Protection Act 1985 and regulations made under it.

---

[75] Notification of Installations Handling Hazardous Substances Regulations 1982 (S.I. 1982 No. 1357); Control of Industrial Major Hazards Regulations 1984 (S.I. 1984 No. 1902).

[76] Control of Substances Hazardous to Health Regulations 1994 (S.I. 1994 No. 3246).

[77] EPA 1990, s. 140; *e.g.* Environmental Protection (Controls on Injurious Substances) Regulations 1992 (S.I. 1992 No. 31).

[78] Food and Environment Protection Act 1985, Pt. I (as amended by the Food Safety Act 1990, s. 15).

[79] Health and Safety at Work etc. Act 1974, ss. 2–6.

[80] *e.g.* Radioactive Material (Road Transport) (Great Britain) Regulations 1996 (S.I. 1996 No. 1350); the power to make such regulations is contained in the Radioactive Material (Road Transport) Act 1991.

Before a pesticide can be advertised, sold, supplied, stored or used it must gain ministerial approval, which will be granted subject to conditions, including a duty to take all reasonable precautions to safeguard the environment,[81] and limits are set for the permissible levels of pesticide residues in food.[82] The use of other chemicals for similar purposes is also controlled in some circumstances.[83]

Genetically modified organisms

A new area of environmental law which is likely to become of increasing importance as technology develops and its applications are expanded is the control of genetically modified organisms, widely defined to include the products of all forms of genetic engineering other than traditional breeding techniques. Under Part VI of the Environmental Protection Act 1990 and related regulations[84] any person importing, releasing, acquiring or marketing genetically modified organisms must carry out an assessment of the risks to the environment and to human health, and must employ BATNEEC in order to avoid or minimise the risks. The Secretary of State may require notice of the risk assessments and may impose a requirement for consent to be obtained before certain activities are carried out. 1.5.6

Light

Artificial light can be an annoyance to neighbours, change the character of an area, disrupt the behaviour patterns of wildlife and interfere with astronomical observations (whether by professionals or simply by those wishing to see the stars and phenomena such as Comet Hale-Bopp). This is a topic which is beginning to attract official interest, with an increasing number of complaints and even recourse to the courts (*e.g.* an interdict was successfully sought to prevent light from tennis courts interfering with trout fishing on an adjacent river).[85] There can also be significant energy conservation issues to be addressed. Planning controls on the nature and positioning of lights may have a part to play but, beyond possible recourse to the general law of nuisance, there is no clear regulatory framework for 1.5.7

---

[81] Control of Pesticides Regulations 1986 (S.I. 1986 No. 1510) (as amended); see also the Plant Protection Products Regulations 1995 (S.I. 1995 No. 887).

[82] Pesticides (Maximum Residue Levels in Crops, Food and Feeding Stuffs) Regulations 1994 (S.I. 1994 No. 1985).

[83] *e.g.* Control of Pollution (Anti-fouling Paints) Regulations 1987 (S.I. 1987 No. 783).

[84] Genetically Modified Organisms (Contained Use) Regulations 1992 (S.I. 1992 No. 3217); Genetically Modified Organisms (Deliberate Release) Regulations 1992 and 1995 (S.I.s 1992 No. 3280 and 1995 No. 304).

[85] *Stonehaven and District Angling Association v. Stonehaven Recreation Ground Trustees and Stonehaven Tennis Club* (1997) 60 S.P.E.L. 36.

tackling the issues raised by light pollution.[86] It is perhaps significant that the Scottish Office includes light in a recent summary of environmental protection issues and has promised to review this matter further during 1997 prior to giving consideration to whether additional controls are required.[87]

---

[86] Taylor, "'And God Divided the Light from the Darkness' — Has Humanity mixed them up again?" (1997) 9 E.L.M. 32.
[87] *Planning and Environmental Protection* (Planning Advice Note 51, 1997), p. 39.

CHAPTER TWO

AIR

DEVELOPMENT OF THE LEGISLATION RELATING TO AIR

Introduction

The industrial revolution of the late eighteenth and nineteenth centuries 2.1.1
and the urbanisation created by the new industries of that revolution
intensified atmospheric pollution, with its attendant hazards to human health.
Atmospheric pollution resulted both from industrial emissions and smoke
from domestic fires. The Public Health (Scotland) Act 1897 set up some
controls in relation to air pollution, but the main problem of industrial air
pollution caused by smoke and other injurious substances emitted from
factory chimneys was addressed by the first of the Alkali Acts,[1] which were
later consolidated in the Alkali etc. Works Regulation Act 1906.[2] Smoke
from domestic fires and combustion processes was variously dealt with by
a range of enactments which, however, failed to prevent the winter "smogs"
afflicting most large British cities.[3] After a particularly bad smog in London
in December 1952[4] the Beaver Committee was set up by the Government
to examine air pollution, its causes and effects, and the legislation controlling
such pollution.[5] The Beaver Committee's recommendations, in particular
the creation of smoke control areas, were implemented in the Clean Air
Acts of 1956 and 1968.

　　The Health and Safety at Work etc. Act 1974 gave power to the Secretary 2.1.2
of State to make regulations to replace the provisions of and regulations
made under the Alkali etc. Works Regulation Act 1906, to control the

---

[1]　Alkali Act 1863.
[2]　Repealed completely in England and Wales in December 1996 by the Environmental
　　Protection Act 1990 (Commencement No. 18) Order 1996 (S.I. 1996 No. 3056). It is
　　likely that the 1906 Act will be repealed in so far as it still applies in Scotland in the near
　　future.
[3]　See the Smoke Nuisance (Scotland) Acts 1857 and 1865, the Public Health (Scotland) Act
　　1897, s. 16(9) and (10) (all repealed), and various Burgh Police and Local Acts.
[4]　It was estimated that the London smog of 1952 accounted for 4,000 deaths from bronchitis
　　and other respiratory diseases.
[5]　Committee of Air Pollution Interim Report, Cmd. 9011 (1953), and Final Report, Cmd.
　　9322 (1954).

emissions of nauseous or offensive substances to the atmosphere.[6] The Clean Air Acts 1956 and 1968 were concerned with the emission into the air not only of dark smoke from a domestic or industrial chimney or otherwise, but also of grit and dust from combustion processes. The division between the Clean Air Acts and the Alkali Acts was not one between domestic emissions and industrial emissions but a division of responsibility between those bodies with responsibility for controlling emissions. Her Majesty's Industrial Pollution Inspectorate[7] was made responsible for emissions from industrial processes under the Alkali etc. Works Regulation Act 1906, while the district and islands councils had responsibility for the control of smoke, grit and dust from combustion processes under the Public Health (Scotland) Act 1897, s. 12 and the Clean Air Acts.

2.1.3   The Alkali etc. Works Regulation Act 1906 and the Clean Air Acts 1956 and 1968 were U.K. legislation to deal with U.K. pollution of U.K. air. However, it has been increasingly recognised in the latter half of the twentieth century that air pollution is a transboundary or, indeed, global problem requiring regional and often international agreement and co-operation. Since the Stockholm Conference[8] and the Heads of Government of the European Community declaration in 1972[9] U.K. action on air pollution control has been heavily influenced by both international and E.C. measures. The Earth Summit at Rio de Janeiro in 1992 provided further impetus in this regard.[10]

International Measures

2.1.4   At an international level, action has focused on three main concerns. First, it is accepted that acid rain caused by emissions of sulphur dioxide from U.K. power stations is responsible for the damage to forests and surface water bodies in Germany and Scandanavian countries.[11] To combat the

---

[6]   Health and Safety (Emissions into the Atmosphere) Regulations 1983 (S.I. 1983 No. 943) extensively repealed the Alkali etc. Works Regulation Act 1906.

[7]   See paras. 2.2.1–2.

[8]   *Report of the United Nations Conference on the Human Environment*, Stockholm June 15 and 16, 1972 (United Nations, New York: 1973 (A/CONF 48/14 Rev. 1)).

[9]   Communique issued by the Heads of State and of Government of the Enlarged Community at their meeting in Paris on October 19 and 20, 1972, Cmnd. 5109.

[10] The UN Conference on Environment and Development adopted the Rio Declaration on Environment and Development, 1992; Agenda 21 — Action plan for the next century; the Conventions on Biological Diversity and Climate Change, and a Non-Binding Statement of Consensus on Forest Principles. The U.K. was swift to produce the strategies or programmes required by the various instruments: *Sustainable Development: The U.K. Strategy*, Cm. 2426 (1994); *Climate Change: The U.K. Programme*, Cm. 2427 (1994); *Biodiversity: The U.K. Action Plan*, Cm. 2428 (1994), *Sustainable Forestry: The U.K. Programme*, Cm. 2429 (1994).

[11] See, *e.g. This Common Inheritance: Britain's Environmental Strategy*, Cm. 1200 (1990), paras. 11.30–31.

problem of acidification, the UN Economic Commission for Europe's Geneva Convention on Long-Range Transboundary Air Pollution 1979 and subsequent protocols on the reduction of sulphur, nitrogen oxide and volatile organic compounds emissions have been agreed.[12]

Secondly, there is the more profound threat of ozone depletion, which is now firmly believed to be caused by chlorofluorocarbons (CFCs) (used in aerosols, refrigerators and air conditioning units). As ozone depletion increases, higher levels of ultraviolet radiation penetrate the atmosphere thereby increasing the incidence of human skin cancer and damaging the marine food chain. The international legal response to the depletion of the ozone layer, which has been based on the Vienna Convention for the Protection of the Ozone Layer[13] and its better known Montreal Protocol,[14] has been swift and, on present evidence, relatively effective.[15] Despite the initial scientific uncertainty, the threat posed by ozone depletion was so great that precautionary action leading to a complete ban on CFCs and other ozone-depleting substances was considered to be justified. 2.1.5

Finally, it is now widely accepted that climate change, perhaps better known as the "greenhouse effect", is occurring mainly as a result of increasing levels of various anthropogenic substances in the atmosphere, including carbon dioxide caused by the combustion of fossil fuels.[16] This appears to be leading to higher global temperatures, although uncertainties remain and it is not clear what the precise effects might be. However, the potential risks of inaction are so great that the international community has again accepted the need to take precautionary action, with developed countries aiming at returning their greenhouse gas emissions to 1990 levels by the year 2000.[17] 2.1.6

---

[12] Convention on Long-Range Transboundary Air Pollution 1979 (Geneva), UKTS 57, Cmnd. 9034 (1983); (1979) 18 I.L.M. 1442; Protocol on the Reduction of Sulphur Emissions or Their Transboundary Fluxes (Helsinki) 1985; (1988) 27 I.L.M. 707. Protocol Concerning the Control of Emissions of Nitrogen Oxides or Their Transboundary Fluxes (Sofia) 1988, UKTS 1, Cm. 1787 (1992); (1989) 28 I.L.M. 212. Protocol on Further Reduction of Sulphur Emissions (Oslo) 1994; (1994) 33 I.L.M. 1542.

[13] Convention for the Protection of the Ozone Layer (Vienna) 1985, UKTS 1, Cm. 910 (1990); (1987) 26 I.L.M. 1529.

[14] Protocol on Substances that Deplete the Ozone Layer (Montreal) 1987, UKTS 19, Cm. 997 (1990); (1987) 26 I.L.M. 1550.

[15] Further amendments speeding up the phase out of CFCs and other ozone-depleting substances were agreed in London in 1990, UKTS 4, Cm. 2132 (1993); (1991) 30 I.L.M. 541, and Copenhagen in 1994; (1993) 32 I.L.M. 874. The measures are presently implemented throughout the E.C. by Regulation 3093/94 on substances which deplete the ozone layer.

[16] See, *e.g. Intergovernmental Panel on Climate Change First Assessment Report 1990* (1990). It has been accepted by the U.K.: *Climate Change: The U.K. Programme*, Cm. 2427 (1994), para. 1.6.

[17] Framework Convention on Climate Change (New York) 1992, (1992) 31 I.L.M. 848; *Climate Change: The U.K. Programme*, Cm. 2427 (1994), paras. 1.6 and 3.1.

2.1.7   It should also be noted that one of the products of the Earth Summit at Rio, Agenda 21, called on national governments to prepare sustainable development strategies. The U.K.'s strategy acknowledges that good air quality is essential for human health and the well-being of the environment as a whole,[18] and identifies the key issues for sustainability as including limitation of acid emissions, control of photochemical pollution (caused principally by road vehicle emissions) and management of local air quality, "especially in urban areas, and in particular to ensure that all relevant sectors — industry, transport, local authorities and general public — contribute".[19]

E.C. Legislation

2.1.8   The United Kingdom as a member of the European Community must comply with E.C. legislation.[20] The European Community has set up five Environment Action Programmes since 1973 which set out the objectives of E.C. environmental policy. The fifth (1993–2000), *Towards Sustainability*,[21] which adopts a new approach based on shared responsibility and advocates the use of a broader range of instruments to protect the environment, including use of market mechanisms and education to change behaviour over the longer term, acknowledges that progress has been made in reducing emissions of sulphur dioxide and suspended particulates, lead and CFCs, but emphasises that serious air pollution problems, including greenhouse gas emissions and air quality problems, particularly in urban areas, persist or are emerging.[22] The programme goes on to set out long-term objectives in relation to various air related issues:

greenhouse gases:	no exceedance of natural absorbing capacity of planet Earth;
ozone layer depletion:	no emissions of ozone layer depleting substances;
acidification:	no exceedance ever of critical loads and levels;
air quality:	(1) all people should be effectively protected against recognised health risks from air pollution;

---

[18]   *Sustainable Development: The U.K. Strategy*, Cm. 2426 (1994), para. 7.3.

[19]   *ibid.* para. 7.2. A shared responsibility approach to the management of air quality has been adopted by *The U.K. National Air Quality Strategy*, Cm. 3587 (1997) which echoes the final objective set out here. See paras. 2.3.1–9.

[20]   See, generally, Chap. 12.

[21]   Resolution on a Community programme of policy and action in relation to the environment and sustainable development: O.J. [1993] C138/1.

[22]   O.J. [1993] C138/23; see paras. 12.5.10–16.

(2) permitted concentration levels of air pollutants should take into account the protection of the environment;

(3) extension of the list of regulated substances which cause pollution and danger to public health and the environment.[23]

Against this evolving policy background E.C. directives on air pollution   2.1.9
fall broadly into four categories:

(1) *Air quality*. Directives have set limit values for concentrations of sulphur dioxide and smoke,[24] lead,[25] nitrogen dioxide[26] in the air, and air pollution by ozone.[27] The Directive on ambient air quality assessment and management will provide a new framework for air quality standards for 13 pollutants, including those already the subject of the above Directives, which will be replaced.[28]

(2) *Emissions from industrial plants*. Member States are required to ensure that certain industrial[29] and large combustion[30] plants operate only under authorisations which impose pollution controls. Directives have also been adopted to control new and existing municipal waste incinerators.[31] The Directive on integrated pollution prevention and control will progressively replace the existing system of control over emissions from industrial plants provided by Directive 84/360.[32]

(3) *Emissions from motorvehicles*. A number of directives lay down construction requirements for motorvehicles in order to limit the emissions which they produce.[33]

(4) *Product requirements for gas oil and petrol*. The sulphur content of gas oil[34] and the lead content of petrol[35] are controlled.[36]

---

[23] See O.J. [1993] C138/43, 48 and 49. For a definition of critical loads see p. 46, n. 71, below.
[24] Directive 80/779.
[25] Directive 82/884.
[26] Directive 85/203.
[27] Directive 92/72.
[28] Directive 96/62.
[29] Directive 84/360.
[30] Directive 88/609 (as amended by Directive 94/66).
[31] Directives 89/369 and 89/429.
[32] Directive 96/61. See also para. 5.1.5.
[33] See paras. 2.7.4–5.
[34] Directive 93/126.
[35] Directive 85/210 (as amended by Directives 85/581 and 87/416).
[36] See para. 2.7.2.

2.1.10   Other policy instruments which relate indirectly to air pollution include the Environmental Assessment Directive,[37] and market mechanisms which enable people to make decisions in the market-place based on environmental criteria such as the Regulation on eco-labelling,[38] the Regulation on eco-management and audit,[39] and the Directive on freedom of access to environmental information.[40] The European Community is also considering the introduction of fiscal mechanisms to reduce air pollution, particularly a carbon tax.[41]

Recent U.K. developments

2.1.11   The need to implement both international and E.C. obligations, together with growing public awareness and pressure has necessitated the enactment of a considerable amount of legislation. One of the principal pieces of legislation in this regard is the Environmental Protection Act 1990 (EPA 1990) which introduced a system of integrated pollution control (IPC) for the environmental media of air, land and water, together with the system of local air pollution control (LAPC). This integrated approach to pollution control was a radical departure from the previous system of separate controls over emissions to different environmental media. The IPC and the LAPC regimes, which together form the principal means of industrial air pollution control in the United Kingdom, play a significant part in implementing the U.K.'s obligations to reduce greenhouse gas emissions under the Framework Convention on Climate Change[42] and acid gas emission under the Geneva Convention on Long-Range Transboundary Pollution,[43] as well as implementing Directives 84/360 on the combating of air pollution from industrial plants and 88/609 on the limitation of emissions of certain pollutants into the air from large combustion plants. They will also provide the framework for implementing Directive 96/61 on integrated pollution prevention and control. Air quality standards have also been set out in domestic legislation as a result of the various E.C. air quality directives.[44]

2.1.12   Other significant developments have included the consolidation of the Clean Air Acts 1956 and 1968 in the Clean Air Act 1993 (CAA 1993), and the establishment, by virtue of the Environment Act 1995 (EA 1995), of

---

[37]   Directives 85/337 and 97/11.
[38]   Regulation 880/92.
[39]   Regulation 1836/93.
[40]   Directive 90/313.
[41]   See, *e.g.* E.C. Commission Communication, *A Community Strategy to limit carbon dioxide emissions and to improve energy efficiency*, SEC (91) 1744 final, October 14, 1991.
[42]   See n. 17 above.
[43]   See n. 12 above.
[44]   Air Quality Standards Regulations 1989 (S.I. 1989 No. 317). See para. 2.1.9 and nn. 24–26 above for details of E.C. air quality directives.

the Environment Agency in England and Wales and the Scottish Environment Protection Agency (SEPA) in Scotland as the principal pollution control agencies, replacing a variety of predecessor regulators.[45] This institutional integration has been designed, in part, to complement the move towards an integrated approach to pollution control. Continuing concern about air quality issues, especially in urban areas and largely as a result of road vehicle emissions, led to the enactment of Part IV of EA 1995, which provides for a national air quality strategy and for air quality assessment and management by local authorities.[46]

Structure of this chapter

The following discussion considers the regulatory bodies with responsibility for air pollution control (paras. 2.2.1–5); the new overall framework for air quality management introduced by Part IV of EA 1995 (paras. 2.3.1–9); industrial air pollution controls in Part I of EPA 1990 (paras. 2.4.1–2); the application of statutory nuisance controls to air pollution (para. 2.5.1); smoke and related controls under CAA 1993 (paras. 2.6.1–19); controls over vehicle emissions (paras. 2.7.1–7); the various types of standard applied in air pollution control legislation (paras. 2.8.1–12); and concludes with a section on air pollution monitoring and information (paras. 2.9.1–4).[47] The relationship between the IPC and LAPC systems on the one hand, and CAA 1993 and statutory nuisance on the other, is examined in paragraph 2.4.2.

2.1.13

REGULATORY BODIES WITH RESPONSIBILITY FOR AIR POLLUTION CONTROL

Development

The Alkali Act 1863 set up H.M. Alkali Inspectorate and provided for the appointment of an inspector of alkali works with such number of sub-inspectors as was deemed necessary. In December 1971 the name was changed to H.M. Industrial Pollution Inspectorate (HMIPI)[48] which more

2.2.1

---

[45] EA 1995, ss. 1 and 20.

[46] See paras. 2.3.1–9. For an account of the state of air in Scotland and current atmospheric pollution issues at the time of writing, see SEPA, *State of the Environment Report* (1996), pp. 7–21, 45 and 81–84.

[47] Space does not permit a discussion of all air pollution controls in Scotland including, for example, controls over asbestos pollution in the air under the Control of Asbestos in the Air Regulations 1990 (S.I. 1990 No. 556) which, in part, implement Directive 87/217 on the prevention and reduction of environmental pollution by asbestos.

[48] HMIPI did not have the status of a body corporate. Instead, its status and functions were those of the chief inspector or functions delegated to the chief inspector by the Secretary of State.

truly reflected the responsibilities of the inspectorate because, as the years progressed, the alkali aspect of the inspectorate diminished and the "etc." part of the short title of the consolidating Alkali etc. Works Regulation Act 1906 became increasingly important.[49]

2.2.2   When EPA 1990 introduced the system of IPC,[50] HMIPI and the river purification authorities (RPAs)[51] were made responsible for the administration of IPC, with the division of responsibility between them being determined by the environmental media to which releases were made by the process concerned.[52] HMIPI also retained responsibility for air pollution controls under the Alkali etc. Works Regulation Act 1906 over processes not yet subject to IPC. EPA 1990 made district and islands councils responsible for LAPC, and these councils were also responsible for controls under CAA 1993. Subsequently, the establishment of SEPA[53] and the reorganisation of local government in Scotland[54] have brought about significant changes in the institutional arrangements for air pollution control.

SEPA

2.2.3   SEPA is now responsible for both IPC and LAPC, having had the IPC functions of HMIPI and the RPAs[55] and LAPC functions of district and islands councils[56] transferred to it on April 1, 1996. The Government's rationale for the transfer of LAPC functions to SEPA, in contrast to the position in England and Wales where local authorities remain responsible for LAPC, was that processes prescribed for LAPC in Scotland were concentrated in a few local authority areas and there were many areas with very few processes, so that, accordingly, it made more sense to concentrate expertise from local authorities in SEPA rather than leaving a small number of LAPC officers spread thinly across the country.[57] SEPA also inherited HMIPI's residual Alkali Act functions in relation to processes not yet subject to IPC.[58] SEPA has also been given considerable reserve and default powers

---

[49]   In England and Wales these functions were carried out by H.M. Inspectorate of Pollution (HMIP). The status of HMIP, which was attached to the Department of the Environment, was identical to that of HMIPI.

[50]   See Chap. 5 for a detailed discussion, and also paras. 2.4.1–2.

[51]   Rivers (Prevention of Pollution) (Scotland) Act 1951, s. 17(2), as amended.

[52]   Environmental Protection (Determination of Enforcing Authority etc.) (Scotland) Regulations 1992 (S.I. 1992 No. 530).

[53]   EA 1995, s. 20.

[54]   By virtue of the Local Government etc. (Scotland) Act 1994.

[55]   EA 1995, s. 21(1)(a)(iii) and (1)(d).

[56]   *ibid.* s. 21(1)(h).

[57]   See, *e.g.* the Earl of Lindsay, *Hansard*, H.L. Vol. 560, col. 1193.

[58]   EA 1995, s. 21(1)(f). The Environmental Protection Act 1990 (Commencement No. 18) Order 1996 (S.I. 1996 No. 3056) completely repealed the Alkali etc. Works Regulation Act 1906 in England and Wales on December 16, 1996. It is likely that the 1906 Act will be repealed in so far as it still applies in Scotland in the near future.

in relation to the new air quality management regime introduced by Part IV of EA 1995.[59]

Local authorities

When local government reorganisation in Scotland took effect from April 1, 1996, the new councils inherited responsibility for CAA 1993 functions of district and islands councils,[60] but did not inherit responsibility for their LAPC functions (as explained above).[61] However, local authorities have been given an enhanced role in relation to air quality issues by the Environment Act 1995, which requires them to review air quality in their areas and, where appropriate, declare air quality management areas and adopt appropriate measures to restore air quality.[62] In their capacity as weights and measures authorities, local authorities are also responsible for enforcing regulations relating to the content of fuel for motorvehicles, furnaces and engines.[63] Although local authorities are not currently responsible for vehicle emissions testing, the Government has proposed giving them powers to carry out such tests at the roadside.[64]

2.2.4

Secretary of State

The Secretary of State is responsible for ensuring compliance with the standards prescribed by the Air Quality Standards Regulations 1989,[65] in addition to considerable reserve and default powers in relation to other systems mentioned above.[66]

2.2.5

OVERALL AIR QUALITY MANAGEMENT

Introduction

Although air quality problems caused by smoke, grit and dust have almost been overcome by the Clean Air Acts and latterly also Part I of EPA 1990,[67] air quality, particularly in urban areas, continues to be problematic largely

2.3.1

---

[59] EA 1995, s. 85; see also para. 2.3.7.
[60] Local Government etc. (Scotland) Act 1994, s. 180(1), Sched. 13, para. 180.
[61] See para. 2.2.3.
[62] EA 1995, Pt. IV. See paras. 2.3.1–9.
[63] CAA 1993, ss. 30(4) and 31(4).
[64] *The U.K. National Air Quality Strategy* (n. 72 below), para. 6.33.
[65] Air Quality Standards Regulations 1989 (S.I. 1989 No. 317), *e.g.* reg. 2(1).
[66] *e.g.* by virtue of EA 1995, s. 40, the Secretary of State may give SEPA directions in relation to the carrying out of any of its functions.
[67] See paras. 2.6.1–19; see also *The U.K. National Air Quality Strategy* (n. 71 below), *e.g.* paras. 4.40–43.

as a result of increasing vehicle emissions. In recent years a considerable amount of attention has been focused on such air quality problems including, for example, reports of House of Commons Committees[68] and the Royal Commission on Environmental Pollution.[69] Following extensive consultation[70] the Government brought forward the measures which now form Part IV of EA 1995. Part IV, which provides for a national air quality strategy and local air quality management, and its relationship with existing provisions, is considered in more detail in the following paragraphs.

National air quality strategy

2.3.2 Section 80 of EA 1995 imposes a duty on the Secretary of State to produce a national air quality strategy as soon as possible and, before this, to publish a draft strategy. A draft strategy was published in 1996 and the finalised strategy was published in March 1997.[71] The Secretary of State must keep air quality policies under review and may modify the strategy from time to time (EA 1995, s. 80(4)). The strategy indicates that the previous Government's intention was to review the strategy for the first time in 1999 (para. 1.19).[72]

2.3.3   The strategy proposes the adoption of clear, measurable, health-based standards and objectives for eight pollutants: benzene, ozone, 1,3 butadiene, carbon monoxide, sulphur dioxide, particles, lead and nitrogen oxide, with a target date of 2005 for the achievement of the objectives (paras. 3.11 and 3.17).[73] The strategy also outlines the relative contributions made to air pollution by business, industry and transport, and indicates how the existing

---

[68] House of Commons' Transport Committee, *Transport-related Air Pollution in London* (Session 1993–94, Sixth Report, H.C. 506-I and II); House of Commons' Environment Committee, *Volatile Organic Compounds* (Session 1994–95, First Report, H.C. 39-I and II).

[69] Royal Commission on Environmental Pollution, Eighteenth Report, *Transport and the Environment*, Cm. 2674 (1994).

[70] See, *e.g. The Future of Air Quality Monitoring Networks in the U.K.* (1993); *Improving Air Quality* (1994); and *Improving Air Quality: Meeting the Challenge* (1995).

[71] Department of the Environment and Scottish Office, *The U.K. National Air Quality Strategy — Consultation Draft*, (1996); Department of the Environment and Scottish Office, *The U.K. National Air Quality Strategy*, Cm. 3587 (1997). The Labour Government elected in May 1997 has undertaken to implement the strategy in full: Department of the Environment, Transport and the Regions Press Release 288/ENV, July 17, 1997.

[72] The Labour Government elected in May 1997 has indicated that the review will commence immediately with proposals for amendments to the strategy being brought forward in 1998; Press Release, above n. 71.

[73] Standards and objectives will be prescribed by regulations made under s. 87, which are to be based on the recommendations of the Government's Expert Panel on Air Quality Standards (EPAQS). Where EPAQS has made no recommendations, the standards and objectives will be based on the World Health Organisation's air quality guidelines: *The U.K. National Air Quality Strategy, op. cit.*, n. 71, para. 3.13. Draft regulations were issued in late 1996. For a discussion of standards and objectives, see para. 2.8.9.

range of national and local policy instruments can contribute to achieving those targets, together with the new local air quality management provisions of Part IV of EA 1995 and voluntary action by business and the general public. The approach is based on the concept of shared responsibility. The strength of the strategy is that it proposes a co-ordinated and integrated approach to achieving air quality targets at both national and local level, using a variety of instruments.

The strategy will be implemented by a mixture of national and local action 2.3.4 involving the pollution control functions of the Agencies, the smoke control, statutory nuisance, traffic regulation and town and country planning functions of local authorities, together with regulation of motor fuel content and enhanced vehicle emissions compliance testing. The strategy also suggests that voluntary action can play an important part, for example by the development of environmental responsibilities particularly by public service fleet operators and by the public at large, in transport and vehicle use.[74]

At a national level, SEPA must have regard to the strategy in the exercise 2.3.5 of its pollution control functions (EA 1995, s. 81(1)). Although SEPA's IPC and LAPC functions are crucial in this regard, the requirement ensures that the strategy is considered in the exercise of all SEPA's pollution control functions, which demonstrates that the intention is to ensure a co-ordinated approach to air quality issues across the board. To some extent, SEPA is in a better position to secure implementation of the strategy (in so far as it relates to industrial air pollution) than the Environment Agency since it is responsible for both IPC and LAPC whereas the Agency has no responsibility for LAPC. The duty to "have regard to" the strategy means that SEPA need not rigidly adhere to its provisions and may indeed depart from them,[75] but it must not ignore the strategy.[76]

Local air quality management

Local authorities are also given a key role in relation to air quality and the 2.3.6 implementation of the strategy. First, councils are placed under a new duty to conduct reviews, from time to time, of present and likely future air quality in their areas (EA 1995, s. 82(1)). This review must include an assessment of whether prescribed air quality standards and objectives are being attained or are likely to be attained in the area (EA 1995, s. 82(2)). Where quality standards and objectives are not being attained or are not likely to be attained the local authority must identify the parts of its area in which it appears that this is so (EA 1995, s. 82(3)) and must then designate such areas as air quality management areas (AQMAs) (EA 1995, s. 83(1)).

---

[74] See, *e.g. The U.K. National Air Quality Strategy, op. cit.*, n. 71, paras. 6.46–51 and 7.50–58.
[75] *Mazzacherini v. Argyll and Bute D.C.*, 1987 S.C.L.R. 475.
[76] *Kelly v. Monklands D.C.*, 1986 S.L.T. 169.

2.3.7   Where an AQMA is designated, the local authority must, for the purpose
of supplementing its information on the AQMA, assess the existing and
likely air quality in the area and the respects in which it appears that the air
quality standards and objectives are not being attained or are not likely to
be attained within the area (EA 1995, s. 84(1)). The local authority must
also, within 12 months from the coming into operation of the designation
order, prepare a report of the results of the above assessment and prepare
an action plan to indicate how it will ensure attainment of the applicable
standards and objectives (EA 1995, s. 84(2)). The action plan may be
achieved by any powers exercisable by the authority (EA 1995, s. 84(2)(b)).
This is a very important provision as it enables the authority to co-ordinate
the exercise of, for example, its statutory nuisance functions, smoke control
functions under CAA 1993, planning functions under the Town and Country
Planning (Scotland) Act 1997,[77] road traffic regulation functions,[78] and any
functions under regulations made in relation to air quality under section 87
of EA 1995 which may include, for example, powers to carry out roadside
tests to check compliance with vehicle emission standards and road pricing
powers.[79] The action plan, which may be revised from time to time (EA
1995, s. 84(4)), must include a timescale for implementation of the measures
included in the plan (EA 1995, s. 84(3)). Although local authorities are not
placed under any duty to implement their action plans, SEPA has extensive
reserve powers in the event of default or non-implementation by a local

---

[77] For example, by integrating air quality issues into development plan preparation (see, *e.g.*
DoE, *Environmental Appraisal of Development Plans* (1993)), including promotion of the
use of public transport by strategic transport planning (see, *e.g.* PPG13 and the SDD's
draft NPPG on Transport and Planning (May 1996)) and into development control decisions,
e.g. by permitting retail developments which are easily accessible by public transport and,
hence, reduce the volume of emissions from private cars (NPPG 8, Retailing (1996)). As
regards England and Wales, the Department of the Environment and Welsh Office issued a
consultation document, *Air Quality and Land Use Planning*, in December 1996. See also
Scottish Office, *Keeping Scotland Moving: A Scottish Transport Green Paper*, Cm. 3565
(1997), p. 34.

[78] Formerly, the provisions in the Road Traffic Regulation Act 1984 enabling the closure of
roads could not be exercised for the purposes of reducing air pollution: *R. v. Greenwich
L.B.C., ex p. Williams* [1997] Env. L.R. 190. However, EA 1995 amends the Road Traffic
Regulation Act 1984 so that, in exercising their functions under the 1984 Act, local authorities
must do so with regard to the strategy. The closure of roads to vehicles other than buses
and taxis, as illustrated by the example of Princes Street in Edinburgh, may be one method
of using road traffic regulation powers to achieve both safety and air quality goals. It is
questionable, however, whether, in general, the exercise of road closure powers would do
anything other than displace air pollution problems to other areas. Use of various traffic
management measures, including road-pricing mechanisms, is likely to be one method of
trying to reduce overall emissions in urban areas: *The U.K. National Air Quality Strategy*,
op. cit., n. 71, paras. 7.43–46. As regards England and Wales, the Department of the
Environment and Welsh Office issued a *Consultative Local Authority Circular on Air Quality
and Traffic Management* in December 1996.

[79] See, *e.g. The U.K. National Air Quality Strategy*, *op. cit.*, n. 71, *e.g.* paras. 7.44–46.

authority (EA 1995, s. 85).[80] Given budgetary constraints it is unlikely that SEPA will exercise these powers. However, their existence may in itself act as an encouragement to local authorities. An individual might also conceivably seek judicial review of a local authority's failure to fulfil one of its duties.[81]

Regulations and the Secretary of State's role

Under EA 1995, s. 87 the Secretary of State has extensive powers to make regulations for: (a) the implementation of the strategy; (b) the implementation of E.C. or international obligations relating to air quality; or (c) otherwise with regard to the assessment or management of air quality. For example, regulations may prescribe air quality standards or objectives.[82] In this regard the existence of the Air Quality Standards Regulations 1989,[83] which were made to implement various E.C. air quality directives, should be noted. Section 87 also enables the Secretary of State to make regulations with respect to: air quality reviews; assessments; orders designating air quality management areas or action plans (EA 1995, s. 87(2)(h)). More particularly, regulations may provide for matters such as: the scope or form of a review, assessment or action plan; the methods to be employed in carrying out reviews or assessments or in monitoring the effectiveness of action plans; the factors to be taken into account in preparing action plans; the treatment of representations; and publication arrangements in relation to reviews, assessments, orders or action plans (EA 1995, s. 87(3)). 2.3.8

The Secretary of State has an extensive role in the context of Part IV of EA 1995 besides his regulation making powers under section 87. He is also responsible for preparing the national air quality strategy and for issuing guidance to local authorities under section 88 on their functions under Part IV.[84] Furthermore, his role, for example in developing national planning policy which local authorities must have regard to in discharging their 2.3.9

---

[80] In England and Wales it is the Secretary of State who exercises these powers: s. 85(1)(a).
[81] For an example of such a challenge in the context of statutory nuisance duties, see *R. v. Carrick D.C., ex p. Shelley* [1996] Env. L.R. 273.
[82] Draft Air Quality Regulations 1997 setting standards and objectives were issued in late 1996. The Labour Government elected in May 1997 has indicated that finalised regulations will be in place by the end of 1997; Press Release, above n. 71.
[83] S.I. 1989 No. 317.
[84] The Department of the Environment, Scottish Office and Welsh Office have issued the following draft guidance for consultation: *General Principles of Reviewing and Assessing Air Quality* (November 1996); and *Developing Local Authority Strategies* (January 1997). In addition, as regards England and Wales only, the Department of the Environment and Welsh Office have issued the following draft guidance for consultation: *Air Quality and Land Use Planning* (December 1996); and *Consultative Local Authority Circular on Air Quality and Traffic Management* (December 1996).

planning functions, is no less important since, in the longer term, it may have a significant impact on air quality.[85]

CONTROL OF INDUSTRIAL AIR POLLUTION: IPC AND LAPC

2.4.1   The principal industrial air pollution control legislation in Scotland is now contained in Part I of EPA 1990, which provides for the systems of integrated pollution control (IPC) and local air pollution control (LAPC). SEPA is responsible for the administration and enforcement of IPC and LAPC (EPA 1990, s. 4(3)). Although a full discussion of these systems is provided in Chapter 5, it may be noted briefly here that processes are prescribed for control by IPC or LAPC by regulations made by the Secretary of State (EPA 1990, s. 2).[86] The present regulations divide processes into Part A processes, which are designated for IPC covering the release of substances to all three media, and Part B processes, which are designated for LAPC under which only their releases into the air are regulated under Part I of EPA 1990. An authorisation is required from SEPA for the operation of any prescribed process (EPA 1990, s. 6). The authorisation may contain conditions, for example imposing limits on emissions to air (EPA 1990, s. 7). The operators are also under a continuing obligation to employ the best available techniques not entailing excessive cost (BATNEEC) to prevent, reduce or render harmless emissions (EPA 1990, s. 7(4)). SEPA must review authorisations every four years, which gives it an opportunity to tighten standards progressively (EPA 1990, s. 6(6)). In exercising its IPC and LAPC functions SEPA must have regard to the provisions of the national air quality strategy.[87] This is to ensure that the IPC and LAPC systems play their part in securing the targets set out in the strategy and related air quality standards regulations.

2.4.2   Where a process is prescribed for IPC or LAPC, the CAA 1993 controls on the emission of dark smoke, smoke, grit, dust and fumes and provisions on smoke control areas do not apply to it.[88] Similarly, local authorities may not, without the approval of the Secretary of State, initiate statutory nuisance proceedings under Part III of EPA 1990 with respect to statutory nuisances consisting of smoke, dust, steam, smell or other effluvia, any accumulation or deposit, noise emitted from premises or noise emitted from vehicles, machinery or equipment in a road so as to be prejudicial to health or a

---

[85] See paras. 7.3.1–6 and, *e.g.* NPPG 8, Retailing (April 1996); draft NPPG on Transport and Planning (May 1996).

[86] Environmental Protection (Prescribed Processes and Substances) Regulations 1991 (S.I. 1991 No. 472), as amended.

[87] EA 1995, s. 81(1); see para. 2.3.5.

[88] CAA 1993, s. 41.

nuisance in relation to processes prescribed for IPC or LAPC.[89] However, it should be noted that a local authority's right of action is preserved in relation to certain statutory nuisances, including the emission of fumes or gases from premises, and that the right of individuals to apply to a sheriff by way of summary application[90] under Part III of EPA 1990 remains unaffected.

CONTROL OF AIR POLLUTION: STATUTORY NUISANCES

Part III of EPA 1990 (which replaced the former statutory nuisances provisions in the Public Health (Scotland) Act 1897 from April 1, 1996) provides for certain statutory nuisances,[91] that is, various defined circumstances which are "prejudicial to health or a nuisance". Section 79 of EPA 1990, which defines statutory nuisances, includes not only smoke emitted from premises so as to be prejudicial to health or a nuisance, but also fumes or gases emitted from premises and any dust, steam, smell or other effluvia arising on industrial, trade or business premises which are prejudicial to health or a nuisance (EPA 1990, s. 79(1)(b)–(d)). If a local authority receives a complaint from a member of the public regarding a possible statutory nuisance, its duty to investigate its area for such nuisances is triggered and it has no discretion. If it is satisfied after carrying out such an investigation that a statutory nuisance exists it again has no discretion, and must serve an abatement notice on the person responsible for the nuisance (EPA 1990, s. 80(1)–(2)).[92] Aggrieved individuals may also enforce statutory nuisance legislation by way of summary application to the sheriff (EA 1990, s. 82). For discussion of the relationship between Parts I and III of EPA 1990, see paragraph 2.4.2. The statutory nuisance regime is discussed in more detail in paragraphs 8.3.2–13 and 9.4.1–5. 2.5.1

CONTROL OF SMOKE POLLUTION: THE CLEAN AIR ACT 1993

Control of Smoke Pollution of Air

As stated above, air pollution control in Scotland is divided between those emissions which are controlled by SEPA and those emissions which are subject to local authority control. While the Environment Act 1995 2.6.1

---

[89] EPA 1990, s. 79(10).
[90] *ibid.* s. 82.
[91] EPA 1990, Pt. III, was extended to Scotland by s. 107 of and Sched. 17 to EA 1995. The statutory nuisance provisions of the Public Health (Scotland) Act 1897 were repealed by s. 120(3) of and Sched. 24 to EA 1995.
[92] *R. v. Carrick D.C., ex p. Shelley* [1996] Env. L.R. 273.

transferred LAPC functions under EPA 1990 from local authorities to SEPA, it did not affect local authority controls under CAA 1993.[93] The Act is concerned with "smoke", which includes soot, ash, grit and gritty particles emitted in smoke (CAA 1993, s. 64(1)) and includes visible non-carbonaceous vapours such as water and solid particles. The Secretary of State is also empowered to make regulations applying the legislation to fumes and prescribed gases, although this power has not been exercised (CAA 1993, s. 47).

2.6.2   The great London "smog" of December 1952, which lasted an impenetrable five days, alerted the Government to the fact that much of the atmospheric pollution at that time came not only from industry but also from the burning of coal in domestic grates. The Clean Air Act 1956 introduced a system of smoke control which, together with smoke-control areas and the change to other means of domestic heating, reduced significantly the emission of smoke into the air. Local authorities have the responsibility for control of "dark smoke".[94] Smoke which is not dark smoke is controlled either by a smoke control order[95] or by the statutory nuisance provisions of EPA 1990.

Control of dark smoke

2.6.3   Local authorities have power to control the emission of "dark smoke" which is smoke that is "as dark or darker than shade 2 on the [Ringlemann] chart" (CAA 1993, s. 3(1)).[96] Section 1 of CAA 1993 prohibits the emissions of dark smoke from a chimney[97] of any building on any day[98] and from railway engines[99] and vessels within territorial waters[1] and from chimneys serving furnaces of boilers in industrial plants on land.[2] The prohibition includes the emission of dark smoke from industrial or trade premises whether or not the emission is from a chimney (CAA 1993, s. 2(1)).[3] The purpose for

---

[93]   The relationship of Pt. I of EPA 1990 to CAA 1993 is governed by s. 41 of the 1993 Act, and is discussed in para. 2.4.2.

[94]   CAA 1993, s. 55(1).

[95]   See paras. 2.6.13–16.

[96]   Named after Professor Ringlemann, who devised the chart.

[97]   "'Chimney' includes structures and openings of any kind from or through which smoke, grit, dust or fumes may be emitted and, in particular, includes flues, and references to a chimney of a building include references to a chimney which serves the whole or part of a building but is structurally separate from the building" (CAA 1993, s. 64(1).)

[98]   "Day" means a 24-hour period beginning at midnight (CAA 1993, s. 64(1)).

[99]   CAA 1993, s. 43(1); however, the 1993 Act does not apply to smoke, dust or grit from such engines: s. 43(5).

[1]   *ibid.* s. 44(1).

[2]   *ibid.* s. 1(2).

[3]   This section does not affect any emission of dark smoke to which CAA 1993, s. 1 applies (s. 2(2)). This extension to the prohibition was brought about by the Clean Air Act 1968, s. 1(1) and (1A), as amended by the Control of Smoke Pollution Act 1989, s. 2.

which premises are used is the crucial factor in determining whether they are, in fact, industrial or trade premises.[4] Industrial premises have been held to include a demolition site,[5] and it has been accepted that trade premises include farm land.[6] The emission of dark smoke from such premises includes a movement of smoke above the ground within the boundaries of the premises in question, since the purpose of the legislation is the abatement of air pollution in itself, regardless of ownership boundaries.[7] Where material is burned on industrial or trade premises, and the circumstances are such that there is likely to be an emission of dark smoke, it will be presumed that there has been an emission of dark smoke unless the occupier or person in charge of the burning can show that no dark smoke was emitted (CAA 1993, s. 2(3)). Where an emission of dark smoke occurs, the occupier of the building or premises is guilty of an offence (CAA 1993, ss. 1(1) and 2(1)). Similarly, if the owner of a railway engine fails to use any practicable means to minimise the emission of smoke from the engine he is also guilty of an offence (CAA 1993, s. 43(3)).[8] However, there are certain statutory defences to a charge under CAA 1993.

Statutory defences to a charge for emitting dark smoke

Where the offence is one of emitting dark smoke from a chimney, the 2.6.4 occupier of the building containing the emitting grate has certain statutory defences which he must prove to escape liability under CAA 1993 (CAA 1993, s. 1(4)). The occupier must prove:

(a) that the contravention was due solely to lighting up a cold furnace and that all practicable steps had been taken to prevent or minimise the emission;

(b) that it was solely due to the failure of some furnace or apparatus used with the furnace and that the failure could not reasonably have been foreseen or, if foreseen, could not have been reasonably provided against or prevented or action taken until after the failure occurred;

(c) if it was due solely to the use of unsuitable fuel, that this was because suitable fuel was unobtainable and that the least unsuitable fuel available was used and, again, that all practicable steps had been taken to prevent or minimise the emission; or

---

4 *Thames Water Authority v. Blue and White Launderettes* [1980] 1 W.L.R. 700 (C.A.).
5 *Sheffield C.C. v. ADH Demolition* (1984) 82 L.G.R. 177.
6 *O'Fee v. Copeland B.C.* [1996] Env. L.R. 66.
7 *ibid.*
8 See also CAA 1993, s. 44(2) in relation to vessels.

(d) that the emission was caused by a combination of two or more of the causes specified in (a) to (c) above that the requisite preventive or mitigating action was taken.

Regulations provide for periods during which it is permissible to emit dark smoke from domestic chimneys.[9] "Practicable" is defined as being practicable having regard to local conditions and circumstances, financial implications and the current state of technical knowledge (CAA 1993, s. 64(1)).

2.6.5   The owner of a locomotive engine has the defence that he used any practicable means available for minimising the emission of smoke from his engine's chimney (CAA 1993, s. 43(3)).

2.6.6   Where the occupier of industrial or trade premises has been charged with emitting dark smoke, it is a statutory defence that the emission was inadvertent and that all practicable steps had been taken to prevent or minimise the emission (CAA 1993, s. 2(4)).[10]

Furnaces

Smoke from furnaces

2.6.7   Any new furnace to be installed must have prior consent from the local authority (CAA 1993, s. 4(1)). Building regulations consent is not sufficient, and consent to the installation does not imply consent to the emission of dark smoke. Furthermore, any new furnace installed either in a building or in a boiler or industrial plant attached to a building must be capable of being operated continuously without emitting smoke, otherwise an offence is committed by the person installing the furnace (CAA 1993, s. 4(2)). Contravention of the requirements of section 4(1) or 4(2) is an offence (under section 4(4)).

Grit and dust from furnaces

2.6.8   Power is given under section 5(2) of CAA 1993 for regulations to be made prescribing limits for the emission of grit and dust from non-domestic furnaces.[11] The occupier of a building which has a furnace burning solid,

---

[9]   Dark Smoke (Permitted Periods) (Scotland) Regulations 1958 (S.I. 1958 No. 1933).

[10]   There are also certain exemptions prescribed in regulations made under s. 1(3) of the Clean Air Act 1968, the predecessor section of s. 2(2)(b) of CAA 1993, for the emission of dark smoke and the burning of certain materials: Clean Air (Emission of Dark Smoke) (Exemption) (Scotland) Regulations 1969 (S.I. 1969 No. 1389).

[11]   Domestic furnaces are those designed solely or mainly for domestic purposes and used for heating a boiler with a maximum heating capacity of less than 16.12 kilowatts (CAA 1993, s. 64(1)). No regulations have been made under this provision, but see the Clean Air Act (Emission of Grit and Dust from Furnaces) (Scotland) Regulations 1971 (S.I. 1971 No. 625), which were made under s. 2(1) of the Clean Air Act 1968, the predecessor section of CAA 1993, s. 5(2) and have effect as if made thereunder.

liquid or gaseous matter and whose chimney is emitting grit and dust in excess of prescribed limits is guilty of an offence (CAA 1993, s. 5(3)). The occupier, to avoid a charge under this provision, must prove that he used the "best practicable means" to minimise the emission (CAA 1993, s. 5(4)). Where no limits have been prescribed for a particular type of chimney or furnace the onus is on the local authority to prove that the occupier failed to avail himself of any practicable means (CAA 1993, s. 5(5)). Note the different standards between the two offences, and the more stringent standard for prescribed limits. Occupiers may be required to measure emissions of grit, dust and fumes (CAA 1993, s. 10).[12]

Arrestment equipment on furnaces

Section 6 of CAA 1993 requires all new furnaces which burn pulverised fuel or which burn solid fuel at the rate of 45.4 kilograms per hour or more, or non-domestic furnaces burning solid, liquid or gaseous matters at a rate equivalent to 366.4 kilowatts or more to be fitted with approved equipment for arresting grit and dust. Approval of equipment is by the local authority (CAA 1993, s. 6(1)). Reasons for refusing approval must be given in writing, and an appeal from an adverse decision lies to the Secretary of State within 28 days of notification of the decision (CAA 1993, s. 9(1) and (2)). Any occupier using a non-domestic furnace not equipped with approved arresting equipment is guilty of an offence (CAA 1993, s. 6(5)). The Secretary of State is empowered to make regulations exempting prescribed furnaces from the requirement to have arrestment equipment fitted to new furnaces (CAA 1993, s. 7(1)). Regulations exempt mobile furnaces for purposes relating to construction, research or agriculture, or certain furnaces used for the incineration of refuse. Furnaces may also be exempted if a local authority is satisfied that any emission of grit and dust is not prejudicial to health or a nuisance (CAA 1993, s. 7(2)). Appeal against refusal to allow an exemption may be made to the Secretary of State (CAA 1993, s. 7(4) and (5)). It is an offence to use for another purpose a furnace exempted from the need to have arresting equipment for one purpose (CAA 1993, s. 7(6)). 2.6.9

Control of chimney heights

The dispersal of pollutants away from the area of production by means of high chimneys has served Britain well, but not her neighbours. Prevailing winds carry the pollutants away from Britain. With increasing international concern, for example regarding sulphur dioxide emissions, more attention 2.6.10

---

[12] See also the Clean Air (Measurement of Grit and Dust from Furnaces) (Scotland) Regulations 1971 (S.I. 1971 No. 626).

is now being paid to diminishing the emissions rather than simply dispersing them. However, the provisions of CAA 1993 on the approval control of chimney heights by local authorities discussed in the following paragraphs may still play a significant role in the achievement of air quality standards and objectives as part of the new air quality management regime provided for by Part IV of EA 1995.[13]

2.6.11   It is an offence for the occupier of a building knowingly to cause or permit a furnace to be used in the building to burn: (a) pulverised fuel; (b) any other solid matter at a rate of 45.4 kilograms per hour; or (c) any liquid or gaseous matter at a rate equivalent to 366.4 kilowatts without prior approval of the furnace's chimney height or in contravention of any conditions imposed in the approval (CAA 1993, s. 14(2)). It is also an offence for a person having possession of any fixed boiler or industrial plant,[14] knowingly to cause or permit the furnace of such a boiler or plant (besides exempted boilers or plant) to be used without prior approval of the furnace's chimney height or in contravention of any conditions imposed in the approval (CAA 1993, s. 14(4)). The Secretary of State is empowered to exempt boilers and plant from the requirements of section 14(4) (CAA 1993, s. 14(7)).[15] Applications for approval of furnace chimney heights must be made to the local authority (CAA 1993, ss. 14(7) and 15). A local authority must not grant approval unless it is satisfied that the chimney height will be sufficient to prevent, so far as practicable, the smoke, grit, dust, gases or fumes from the chimney from becoming prejudicial to health or a nuisance having regard to: (a) the chimney's purpose; (b) the position and descriptions of neighbouring buildings; (c) the levels of neighbouring land; and (d) any other relevant matters (CAA 1993, s. 15(2)). Such matters may include air quality standards and/or objectives for substances laid down by E.C. or U.K. legislation.[16] Approval may be granted unconditionally or subject to conditions in relation to the rate and/or quality of emission from the chimney (CAA 1993, s. 15(3)). In the event of non-determination by the local authority within four weeks of the application, the approval is treated as being granted unconditionally (CAA 1993, s. 15(4)). Where the local authority refuses to grant approval, it must notify the applicant in writing giving the reasons for its decision and specifying the lowest height of chimney it would be prepared to approve (CAA 1993, s. 15(5)). The applicant may appeal to the Secretary of State within 28 days of receiving notification under section 15(5) (CAA 1993, s. 15(6)).

---

[13] See paras. 2.3.1–9.

[14] "Fixed boiler or industrial plant" means any boiler or industrial plant which is attached to a building or is for the time being fixed to or installed on any land (CAA 1993, s. 64(1)).

[15] Clean Air (Height of Chimneys) (Exemption) (Scotland) Regulations 1969 (S.I. 1969 No. 465).

[16] See, *e.g.* paras. 2.3.8 and 2.8.6–11.

In addition to their role in approving the height of furnace chimneys, local authorities also have a role in approving chimneys which do not serve furnaces. Where a local authority has submitted to it in accordance with building regulations,[17] plans for a new building or an extension to an existing building, other than a shop, office or residence, and the buildings show a proposed chimney to carry smoke, grit, dust or gases from the building, the authority must refuse a building warrant[18] if the height of the chimney is insufficient to prevent, so far as practicable, the emission of smoke, grit, dust or gases (but not fumes) which would be prejudicial to health or a nuisance having regard to the same factors as in the case of furnace chimneys (see para. 2.6.11) (CAA 1993, s. 16(2)). Appeal against refusal of a building warrant lies to the sheriff within 21 days of the refusal.[19] 2.6.12

Smoke control orders and smoke control areas

The introduction of smoke control areas or smokeless zones by the Clean Air Act 1956 was the biggest factor in clearing the air in British cities. While a certain diminution of pollution could have been expected from the change to central heating, the 1956 Act[20] certainly accelerated the process. A local authority may make an order declaring the whole or part of its district to be a smoke control area (CAA 1993, s. 18(1)), where it is an offence for smoke (not only dark smoke) to be emitted from a chimney of a building (CAA 1993, s. 20(1)). The occupier of a building has a defence that the emission was not caused by the use of an unauthorised fuel (CAA 1993, s. 20(4)).[21] Different provisions for different parts of the control area may limit the operation of section 20 to specified classes of buildings in the area or may exempt specified buildings, or specified fireplaces can be contained in the smoke control order (CAA 1993, s. 18(2)).[22] The Secretary of State may exempt certain fireplaces from the control order and has exercised this power on frequent occasions (CAA 1993, s. 21).[23] SEPA has taken over the Secretary of State's default powers 2.6.13

---

[17] Building Standards (Scotland) Regulations 1990 (S.I. 1990 No. 2179).
[18] Under the Building (Scotland) Act 1959, s. 6.
[19] *ibid.* s. 16.
[20] Now consolidated in CAA 1993.
[21] "Authorised fuel" is a fuel authorised under regulations for the purposes of this Part of the Act (s. 20(6)); Smoke Control Areas (Authorised Fuels) Regulations 1991 (S.I. 1991 No. 1282) with effect from July 1, 1991 (further amended by S.I. 1992 No. 72, S.I. 1992 No. 3148 and S.I. 1993 No. 2499). Fuel manufactured before that date which was authorised by the earlier regulations may be used, notwithstanding their revocation.
[22] "Fireplace" includes any furnace, grate or stove whether open or closed (CAA 1993, s. 64(1)).
[23] Smoke Control Areas (Exempted Fireplaces) (Scotland) Order 1982 (S.I. 1982 No. 448), which has been much amended.

to require an authority to submit proposals for a smoke control order (CAA 1993, s. 19).[24]

2.6.14   Prior to making a smoke control order a local authority must publish a notice in the *Edinburgh Gazette* and for at least two successive weeks in a newspaper which circulates in the area to be affected by the order (CAA 1993, s. 18(4) and Sched. 1). Objections to the order must be in writing and must be considered by the local authority (CAA 1993, Sched. 1, paras. 1(c) and 3). An order should come into force six months after it is made (CAA 1993, Sched. 1, para. 4).

2.6.15   It is an offence not only to burn solid fuel other than smokeless fuel in a smoke control area but also to acquire or sell solid fuel other than an authorised fuel for use in a fireplace in a building or for use in a boiler or industrial plant or for delivery to premises where there is a boiler or industrial plant (CAA 1993, s. 23(1)). The retailer charged with selling an unauthorised fuel has a defence if he can show that he believed and had reasonable grounds for believing that the fuel would be used within the limits of an exemption from control (CAA 1993, s. 23(5)).

2.6.16   Local authorities have the power by notice in writing served on owners or occupiers of private dwellings to require the adaptation of fireplaces within smoke control areas to prevent smoke emissions (CAA 1993, s. 24(1)). Grants of 70 per cent may be made by the local authority towards the cost of adapting fireplaces in private houses and, in cases of hardship, it can increase the amount to up to 100 per cent (CAA 1993, s. 25(1) and Sched. 2). Grants may also be made towards the adaptation of fireplaces in churches, chapels, church hall or premises used by charitable organisations (CAA 1993, s. 26).

Miscellaneous smoke controls

Straw and stubble burning

2.6.17   A problem which has given rise to considerable public concern in recent years is the burning of stubble or other crop residues by farmers after the harvesting of their crops. The smoke produced by stubble burning has been considered by the public at large as a nuisance and as a potential hazard to traffic when the smoke crosses motorways and other roads.[25] Control of straw and stubble burning was originally by voluntary codes and local authority byelaws. However, it was considered that these methods were unable to control the problem, and legislation was introduced in EPA 1990

---

[24] This function was transferred to SEPA by s. 21(2)(c) of EA 1995.
[25] In *MacPhail v. Clark*, 1983 S.L.T. (Sh.Ct.) 37 a farmer who set fire to stubble in a field near a road and omitted to take any precautions to stop the fire from spreading was convicted of recklessly endangering the lieges since the fire spread to the roadside and resulted in a road accident involving injuries.

whereby the Secretary of State has power to make regulations to prohibit or restrict the burning of straw stubble or any other crop residue on agricultural land, and may provide exemptions which will apply in all or only specified areas, to specified crop residues or in specified circumstances.[26] Regulations have been made for England and Wales but not for Scotland.[27] They impose a general ban on burning cereal straw and stubble and the residues of oil-seed rape, field beans harvested dry and peas harvested dry subject to specific limited exceptions.[28] Breach of the regulations is an offence.

Cable burning

Section 33 of CAA 1993 makes it an offence for a person to burn insulation   2.6.18
from a cable in order to recover metal from the cable unless the burning is carried out as part of a process prescribed for IPC or LAPC by EPA 1990. Local authorities are responsible for enforcing this provision.[29]

Colliery bings

Section 42 of CAA 1993 addresses the problem of burning colliery bings,   2.6.19
which is of less importance today with the virtual demise of the deep mining industry and the landscaping of many disused bings. The owner of a coal or shale mine or quarry must use all practicable means to prevent combustion of refuse from the mine or quarry and to prevent or minimise the emission of smoke and fumes from such refuse (CAA 1993, s. 42(1) and (2)). It is an offence for the owner to fail to do so, and cumulative penalties may apply (CAA 1993, s. 42(3)). Both the smoke control provisions of CAA 1993 and the statutory nuisance provisions of Part III of EPA 1990 are disapplied in the case of burning bings (CAA 1993, s. 42(5)). Once again, the local authority is responsible for enforcement.[30]

CONTROL OF VEHICLE EMISSIONS

Introduction

In 1991, 35 years after the passing of the Clean Air Act 1956, London again   2.7.1
suffered a "smog" due to a climatic condition of freezing air holding

---

[26] EPA 1990, s. 152; "Agricultural land" has the same meaning as in the Agriculture (Scotland) Act 1948.
[27] Crop Residues (Burning) Regulations 1993 (S.I. 1993 No. 1366), which revoke and replace the Crop Residues (Restriction of Burning) (No. 2) Regulations 1991 (S.I. 1991 No. 1590).
[28] Exceptions are applicable in the case of education or research, disease control and the disposal of straw stack remains or broken bales (reg. 4).
[29] CAA 1993, s. 55(1).
[30] *ibid.*

pollution in the atmosphere, due not on this occasion to smoke from domestic fires, but to nitrates and oxides, carbon monoxides, hydrocarbons and particulates which contain lead — all emissions coming from motorvehicles. Such emissions are now widely acknowledged as the major source of outdoor exposure to air pollution.[31] Road transport is one of the key areas addressed by the national air quality strategy.[32] Improvement in fuel and vehicle technology is one of the principal means by which air pollution from vehicles is to be addressed.[33] U.K. legislation in this field is designed mainly to implement legislation from the European Community which has been active for some considerable time in trying to reduce air pollution from vehicle emissions. Legislative measures essentially relate to two areas: (1) fuel composition; and (2) approval, construction and use of vehicles, although economic instruments have also played a significant role in reducing emissions from vehicles.

Fuel content

2.7.2 The European Community has, for some time, set limits on the sulphur and lead content of various types of fuel, which have been progressively reduced over time.[34] The Secretary of State has the power under section 2(2) of the European Communities Act 1972 to make regulations implementing such directives, together with a power under CAA 1993 to make regulations setting down requirements for the composition and content of any motor fuel after consultation with representatives of the oil fuel industry, users, and experts in pollution.[35] The current regulations set out the maximum permissible sulphur and lead content of petrol and diesel fuel,[36] which are

---

[31] See, *e.g.* Royal Commission on Environmental Pollution, *Transport and the Environment*, Eighteenth Report (1994); and Scottish Office, *Keeping Scotland Moving, A Scottish Transport Green Paper*, Cm. 3565 (1997), p. 35.

[32] *The U.K. National Air Quality Strategy, op. cit.*, n. 71, Chap. 6.

[33] Longer-term measures include changes in planning and transport policies to reduce the need to travel and reliance on cars.

[34] Directive 93/12 relating to the sulphur content of certain liquid fuels, which replaced Directive 75/716 on the approximation of the laws of Member States relating to the sulphur content of certain liquid fuels from October 1, 1994; and Directive 85/210 (as amended by Directives 85/581 and 87/416) on the approximation of the laws of Member States concerning the lead content of petrol, replacing Directive 78/611 from December 31, 1985.

[35] CAA 1993, s. 30 (which replaced s. 75 of the Control of Pollution Act 1974). S. 31 of CAA 1993 enables the Secretary of State to make regulations relating to the sulphur content of oil fuel for furnaces and engines.

[36] Motor Fuel (Composition and Content) Regulations 1994 (S.I. 1994 No. 2295), which revoked and replaced the Motor Fuel (Sulphur Content of Gas Oil) Regulations 1976 (S.I. 1976 No. 1989), as amended; and the Motor Fuel (Lead Content of Petrol) Regulations 1981 (S.I. 1981 No. 1523), as amended. The sulphur content of gas oil, apart from gas oil used in motorvehicles, is regulated by the Marketing of Gas Oil (Sulphur Content) Regulations 1994 (S.I. 1994 No. 2249), which implement, in part, Directive 93/12 and which revoked and replaced the Oil Fuel (Sulphur Content of Gas Oil) Regulations 1990 (S.I. 1990 No. 1096).

enforced by the trading standards departments of local authorities acting in their capacity as weights and measures authorities.[37] Regulations made in 1979 permitted the sale from January 1, 1986 of unleaded petrol.[38]

In *Budden v. BP Oil & Shell Oil; Albery-Speyer v. BP Oil & Shell Oil*[39] 2.7.3 it was held by the Court of Appeal that compliance with the then current statutory regulations on lead content in fuel by petrol companies was a defence to a claim in negligence based on the alleged adverse impact of vehicle emissions containing organo-lead additives on children's health. The court took the view that the Secretary of State must be presumed to have acted in the public interest in setting the standards in the regulations, that Parliament had impliedly approved those standards and that the court could not usurp the authority of Parliament by laying down a different permissible limit. It is not clear, however, that this decision is correct since neither the statute under which those regulations were made, the Control of Pollution Act 1974, nor its successor, CAA 1993, indicates that Parliament wanted compliance with the standards in the regulations to provide a statutory defence to the common law liabilities of polluters. In this regard it should be noted that compliance with standards set out in an environmental licence is not necessarily a defence to a common law action.[40] Nevertheless, in *Budden* Megaw L.J. did say that: "[T]his is not to say that the courts are bound to hold, where a limit has been prescribed in the interests of safety by statute or statutory regulations, that one who keeps within these limits cannot be guilty of negligence at common law." It has been suggested that since local authorities are encouraged to promote guide values for various substances in the air within prescribed E.C. limits, an enforceable duty of care to observe stricter emission limits than those specified in legislation may arise.[41]

Type approval, construction and use of motorvehicles

The European Community has also been concerned to ensure that new 2.7.4 motorvehicles comply with increasingly stringent emission limits. Directive

---

[37] CAA 1993, s. 30(4).
[38] Motor Fuel (Lead Content of Petrol) Regulations 1979 (S.I. 1979 No. 1), consolidated in the Motor Fuel (Lead Content of Petrol) Regulations 1981 (S.I. 1981 No. 1523), and revoked by the Motor Fuel (Composition and Content) Regulations 1994 (S.I. 1994 No. 2295).
[39] [1980] J.P.L. 586.
[40] This appears to be the implication of *R. v. Carrick D.C., ex p. Shelley* [1996] Env. L.R. 273, albeit in the context of statutory nuisance, where there seemed to be no question that the existence of a discharge consent would necessarily provide a defence to statutory nuisance proceedings. Also of relevance is *Wheeler v. JJ Saunders Ltd* [1995] Env. L.R. 286, which established that a grant of planning permission would not necessarily act as a defence to a nuisance action at common law.
[41] Hawke, *Clean Air Act 1993* (Current Law Statutes), pp. 11–32; and Leeson, *Environmental Law* (1995), p. 237.

70/220, the principal legislation in this regard, which has been much amended as noted below, set limits for the emissions of carbon monoxide and unburnt hydrocarbons from petrol engine vehicles, with the exception of agricultural tractors and public works vehicles. It has subsequently been amended by Directive 74/290, which further reduced the limits, and Directive 77/102, which added limits for nitrogen oxides. The limits for all three pollutants were further reduced by Directives 78/665, 83/851 and 88/76. Directive 88/76 also changed the categories for deciding on emissions from vehicle weight to the engine capacity, and required that new vehicles must run on unleaded petrol. Subsequently, limit values for particulate emissions from diesel engines were introduced by Directive 88/436; more stringent standards for gaseous emissions for cars with an engine capacity of less than 1400 cm^3 were introduced by Directive 89/458; and those emissions standards were extended to all cars regardless of engine capacity by Directive 91/441, which also introduced more stringent particulate emission standards for cars with diesel engines. The emissions standards for cars designed to carry more than six passengers, light commercial vehicles and off-road vehicles which had been subject to less stringent standards were made subject to the same standards as cars by virtue of Directive 93/59. More recently, Directive 94/12 has introduced more stringent emissions limits for diesel and petrol engined cars.[42]

2.7.5   These measures are implemented by regulations made under the Road Traffic Act 1988. First, the Secretary of State is empowered to make type approval regulations to ensure that vehicles comply with the relevant requirements before they are brought into production and that adequate arrangements have been made to ensure that other vehicles of that type will conform with the relevant requirements.[43] Secondly, the Secretary of State may prescribe standards of construction and use applicable to the operation of road vehicles[44] and, in particular, regulations may be made governing the emission or consumption of smoke, fumes or vapour and the emission of sparks, ashes and grit.[45] Vehicles must be constructed and maintained so

---

[42] Limits for emissions of carbon monoxide, unburnt hydrocarbons and nitrogen oxides from heavy goods vehicle diesel engines are set by Directive 88/77, as amended by Directive 91/542.

[43] Road Traffic Act 1988, s. 54. Separate regulations have been made for private and goods vehicles. The principal regulations for private vehicles are the Motor Vehicles (Type Approval) (G.B.) Regulations 1984 (S.I. 1984 No. 981), as amended. Type approval of goods vehicles is governed by the Motor Vehicles (Type Approval for Goods Vehicles) (G.B.) Regulations 1982 (S.I. 1982 No. 1271), as amended.

[44] Road Traffic Act 1988, s. 41(1). The s. 54 power (see n. 43 above) exists without prejudice to the s. 41 power.

[45] *ibid.* s. 41(2)(b). The present regulations are the now much amended Road Vehicles (Construction and Use) Regulations 1986 (S.I. 1986 No. 1078), which replaced all earlier regulations. Amendments have been made to introduce more stringent limits on emissions required by E.C. directives, *e.g.* by S.I. 1988 No. 1524; S.I. 1990 No. 1131; and S.I. 1991 No. 1526.

as not to emit any avoidable smoke or visible vapour.[46] Vehicles with petrol engines first used on or after April 1, 1991 must be designed and constructed to run on unleaded petrol.[47] If such a vehicle is altered or adjusted to run on leaded petrol and is incapable of running on unleaded petrol, this is an offence. These provisions are enforced through the Motor Vehicle (Tests) Regulations 1981.[48] In this regard a high-profile series of roadside vehicle emissions compliance tests has been staged by the Department of Transport's Vehicle Inspectorate as one measure designed to help implement *The U.K. National Air Quality Strategy*.[49] The Government is also proposing to empower local authorities to carry out roadside emissions tests with the assistance of the police to ensure better compliance with emissions standards.[50]

Economic instruments

The most significant economic instrument which has resulted in reducing vehicle emissions has been the tax differential introduced by the March 1987 Budget in favour of unleaded petrol.[51] The price of unleaded petrol has been reduced in relation to the price of leaded petrol in successive years. Although lead levels in the air resulting from vehicle emissions have been very substantially reduced by this measure[52] concerns regarding the impact of unleaded petrol on human health have surfaced.[53] 2.7.6

Other economic instruments include increases of at least 5 per cent per year above the rate of inflation in vehicle fuel excise duty which the previous Government expected to result in savings of 2.5 million tonnes of carbon as part of its Climate Change Programme,[54] although the effect of these rises has been offset by very low fuel prices.[55] The previous Government recognised that there are good grounds for increasing prices for road use on the basis that they do not reflect wider social and environmental costs.[56] Hence, the previous Government was considering the introduction of a range 2.7.7

---

[46] Road Vehicles (Construction and Use) Regulations 1986 (S.I. 1986 No. 1078), reg. 61(1).

[47] S.I. 1988 No. 1524.

[48] S.I. 1981 No. 1694, as amended.

[49] *The U.K. National Air Quality Strategy, op. cit.*, n. 71 above, para. 6.33.

[50] *ibid.*

[51] Finance Act 1987, s. 1, adding s. 13A to the Hydrocarbon Oil Duties Act 1979.

[52] See, *e.g. This Common Inheritance*, Cm. 1200 (1990), paras. 11.53–54; *The U.K. National Air Quality Strategy, op. cit.*, n. 71 above, para. 6.29. The latter indicates that levels of air-borne lead in urban areas have dropped by up to 70 per cent.

[53] See, *e.g.* (1994) 234 *ENDS Report* 28–29.

[54] *Climate Change: The U.K. Programme*, Cm. 2427 (1994), para. 3.66.

[55] *Sustainable Development: The U.K. Strategy*, Cm. 2426 (1994), para. 26.22.

[56] *ibid.* para. 26.19.

of measures, including electronic tolling on motorways, a tax on non-residential parking, and congestion charging.[57] It appears that the Labour Government elected in May 1997 has adopted these policies in full although it intends to bring forward a review of the national air quality strategy (see para. 2.3.2).

STANDARDS APPLIED IN AIR POLLUTION CONTROL LEGISLATION

2.8.1   Various standards are employed in air pollution legislation. These include (1) process standards, (2) emission standards, (3) quality standards and (4) product standards.[58] The following paragraphs discuss the different types of standard employed and their interrelationship.

Process standards

2.8.2   Since the nineteenth century until recently control of pollution was based upon the flexible process standard "best practicable means" (BPM), rather than by a system of fixed emission or quality standards contained in statutes. The disadvantage of the latter system is that as techniques and technical knowledge advance such standards quickly become obsolete. The owner of a works registered for control under the Alkali etc. Works Regulation Act 1906 had to use the BPM to prevent the escape of nauseous or offensive gases into the atmosphere.[59] "Best practicable means" was defined in the 1906 Act and had reference, under section 27, not only to the provision and efficient maintenance of appliances for preventing an escape, but also the manner in which appliances are used and to the proper supervision by the owner of any operation where such appliances are involved. The financial implications of using particular means were taken into account. The use of BPM was linked to emission standards, but these were non-binding and, moreover, there were no clearly defined, binding air quality standards which the use of BPM was aimed at achieving. However, the progressive replacement of the Alkali etc. Works Regulation Act 1906 by EPA 1990 has meant that BPM no longer has a role in relation to processes prescribed

---

[57] *Sustainable Development: The U.K. Strategy, op. cit.,* n. 55, paras. 26.34–35; *Climate Change: The U.K. Programme, op. cit.,* n. 54, *The U.K. National Air Quality Strategy, op. cit.* n. 71 above, para. 7.44. However, the Government does not consider that a move towards charging motorists directly for the costs of road provision by surcharge on fuel would be likely to be successful: *Transport — The Way Forward: The Government's response to the Transport Debate,* Cm. 3234 (1996), p. 53; Scottish Office, *Keeping Scotland Moving, A Scottish Transport Green Paper* (1997), p. 42.

[58] Other standards, such as the phasing out and prohibition of CFCs by virtue of Regulation 3093/94 on substances that deplete the ozone layer, are also employed.

[59] Alkali etc. Works Regulation Act 1906, s. 2(1) (now repealed).

for IPC or LAPC, although the standard is still relevant under CAA 1993.[60]

The impact of E.C. legislation has necessitated a move away from flexible 2.8.3 process standards towards tighter process standards which are linked to binding emissions standards and overall environmental quality standards. For example, the Directive on the combating of air pollution from industrial plants requires that authorisations for such plants should not be granted unless the "best available technology" not entailing excessive costs, is applied to prevent air pollution.[61] This requirement is implemented by Part I of EPA 1990, which provides that best available techniques not entailing excessive cost (BATNEEC) must be used for preventing the release of substances into the air, and, where that is not practicable by such means, for reducing the release of such substances to a minimum and for rendering harmless any such substances which are so released and to render harmless any other substances which might cause harm if released into the air.[62] The BATNEEC standard appears to be more stringent than the BPM requirement, since only *excessive* costs will be taken into account. The continuing requirement to use BATNEEC is designed to ensure that, over time, cleaner technology is employed and operated efficiently so that pollution will be reduced. In practice, the general requirement to use BATNEEC is not applied in isolation, but is translated into authorisation conditions which set binding emission standards for various substances.

Emission standards

An emission standard focuses on the source of pollution and may, for 2.8.4 example, impose a limit on the amount or concentration of a particular substance which may be emitted from a chimney over a specific period. Such standards would be applied, for example, through conditions imposed in IPC or LAPC authorisations under EPA 1990.[63] Although such standards are also applied in the legislation relating to emissions from vehicle exhausts,[64] this discussion focuses on emission standards as applied to industrial plants, particularly combustion plants. At E.C. level the large combustion plants Directive[65] has adopted a dual approach to the imposition

---

[60] See, *e.g.* paras. 2.6.4 and 2.6.8.
[61] Directive 84/360, Art. 4(1). Directive 96/61 on integrated pollution prevention and control (which will progressively replace Directive 84/360) requires the use of best available techniques in this regard, which are, again, defined by reference to take into consideration costs.
[62] EPA 1990, s. 7. See discussion on the meaning of BATNEEC and the relationship of BATNEEC and BPEO in paras. 5.4.11–20.
[63] See also para. 2.8.3.
[64] See para. 2.7.4.
[65] Directive 88/609 on the limitation of emissions of certain pollutants into the air from large combustion plants (as amended by Directive 94/66).

of emission standards. First, it has stipulated uniform limits on emissions of sulphur dioxide, nitrogen oxide and particulate matter from large new combustion plants.[66] These are applied through conditions imposed in IPC authorisations. More stringent limits may be applied by Member States, which enable standards to be tailored to the sensitivity of the receiving environment.[67] Secondly, Member States are required to draw up a programme for the progressive reduction of the total annual emissions of sulphur dioxide and nitrogen oxide from existing plants in accordance with stipulated limits.[68] This requirement is implemented in part by means of section 3 of EPA 1990, which empowers the Secretary of State *inter alia* to make plans for establishing limits for the total amount of any substance which may be released into the environment in any period within the U.K., or any part of the U.K. Quotas may be allocated to persons carrying on processes producing substances in respect of which any such limit is established.[69] The Secretary of State adopted a U.K. Programme and National Plan for Reducing Emissions of Sulphur Dioxide and Nitrogen Oxide from power stations, refineries and other industry, on December 20, 1990.[70] Maximum annual emission quotas have been allocated to the various companies and, within these overall quotas, individual quotas have been allocated to specific plants. However, these quotas are not legally binding. Binding emission limits are laid down in the IPC authorisations for the plants in question. In most cases the binding limits were initially set at significantly higher levels than the National Plan quota levels. This enables companies to trade emissions allocations between their own plants, although they must keep within their overall quota and must not exceed the binding IPC authorisation conditions for each plant. Where a plant's emissions are likely to cause exceedances of critical loads[71] for acid deposition in sensitive areas the limits set in the authorisation are likely to be set at the same level or a lower level than those set in the plant's National Plan allocation in order to constrain the

---

[66]   Directive 88/609, Art. 4(1), Annexes III–VII.

[67]   *ibid.* Art. 4(3).

[68]   *ibid.* Art. 3(1)–(2); Annexes I and II.

[69]   EPA 1990, s. 3(5). Notice must be given in the *Edinburgh Gazette* of such plans: EPA 1990, s. 3(7).

[70]   The National Plan was substantially amended in 1994 and, again, in 1995. It should be noted that the Plan is also designed to ensure the fulfilment of the U.K.'s obligations under the Geneva Convention on Long-Range Transboundary Pollution 1979, and its sulphur and nitrogen oxide protocols.

[71]   Defined as "a quantitative estimate of exposure to one or more pollutants below which significant harmful effects on sensitive elements of the environment do not occur, according to present knowledge" (Protocol on Further Reduction of Sulphur Dioxide Emissions 1994).

company's freedom to operate that plant intensively and, hence, cause environmental damage.[72]

An alternative method of achieving annual emissions limits is by 2.8.5 establishing a system of tradeable emission permits. Section 3(5) of EPA 1990 is broad enough to permit the establishment of a system of tradeable emission permits. By progressively restricting available permits, prices are forced up and an incentive is created to reduce emissions. Where a company reduces its emissions any surplus permits may be sold. Such a system already exists in the United States.[73]

Quality standards

A quality standard is one which relates not to the source of pollution but to 2.8.6 the effect of the pollutant on the receiving environment. It will usually be set by reference to the level of a particular pollutant in the air. Increasingly, process and emission standards are linked to the achievement of quality standards. For example, SEPA is now required to have regard to the provisions of the national air quality strategy, which will contain air quality standards for eight pollutants, in exercising pollution control functions such as IPC and LAPC.[74] In one sense, this is actually necessary, since, without any clear goals as to acceptable levels of pollutants in the air in terms of human health or environmental impact, the setting of emission or process standards appears futile.

Once again, as a result of E.C. legislation[75] the Government has been 2.8.7 obliged to lay down air quality standards for sulphur dioxide, suspended particulates, nitrogen oxides and lead under the Air Quality Standards Regulations 1989.[76] These Regulations oblige the Secretary of State to take any necessary measures to ensure that the concentrations of the above pollutants do not exceed certain levels — known as limit values.[77] Time-limits, which have all now expired, were set for bringing areas not complying

---

[72] It is known that in England and Wales HMIP used critical load (see n. 70 above) calculations in setting emission limits in IPC authorisation conditions. However, it did not disclose the methodology employed, apparently fearing a challenge from the English power generators. See, *e.g.* Allott, *Integrated Pollution Control: The First Three Years* (1994), p. 86.

[73] U.S. Clean Air Act 42 U.S.C.A., paras. 7651a to 7651o, introduced by the Clean Air Act Amendments 1990.

[74] EA 1995, s. 81(1). See also para. 2.3.5.

[75] Directives 80/779; 82/884; and 85/203.

[76] S.I. 1989 No. 317. The Secretary of State is also empowered by s. 3 of EPA 1990 to make regulations to establish standards, objectives or requirements in relation to particular prescribed processes or substances. No regulations have yet been made under this section.

[77] S.I. 1989 No. 317, regs. 2(1), 4(1) and 6.

with the limit values into compliance.[78] In relation to sulphur dioxide and suspended particulates in zones where limit values are being or are likely to be exceeded as a result of development, values must be fixed at a lower level than the limit values, taking more stringent limits (known as guide values) as a reference point.[79] Member States are also obliged to endeavour to achieve the more stringent guide values for sulphur dioxide and suspended particulates wherever measured concentrations are higher than the guide values, in order to protect human health.[80]

2.8.8   The Directive on ambient air quality assessment and management[81] adopts a different approach, requiring the E.C. Commission to submit proposals for the establishment of limit values[82] and alert thresholds[83] for 13 pollutants,[84] including those which are already the subject of existing air quality directives, which will be replaced.[85] In the case of ozone, given its formation mechanisms, target values[86] are set in addition to or as an alternative to limit values.

2.8.9   This Directive will be implemented principally by means of Part IV of EA 1995,[87] which empowers the Secretary of State to prescribe air quality standards and objectives.[88] Air quality standards, which reflect or are more stringent than E.C. limit values, are to be set by reference to concentrations of particular pollutants in the atmosphere, and are based on an assessment of the effects of each pollutant on health.[89] The Government's primary

---

[78]   Directive 80/779, Art. 3(2); Directive 82/884, Art. 3(2) and (3); and Directive 85/203, Art. 3(2).

[79]   Directive 80/779, Art. 4(1). A discretionary power to the same effect is provided for in Directive 85/203, Art. 4(1).

[80]   Directive 80/779, Art. 5.

[81]   Directive 96/62.

[82]   Levels set by reference to a scientific effects-based approach which must not be exceeded, although exceedance by a margin of tolerance is permitted in certain conditions: Directive 96/62, Art. 2.

[83]   Levels beyond which there is a health risk from brief exposure and which necessitate immediate action to restore limit value levels: Directive 96/62, Art. 2.

[84]   Sulphur dioxide, nitrogen dioxide, fine particulate matter, suspended particulate matter, lead, ozone, benzene, carbon monoxide, poly-aromatic hydrocarbons, cadmium, arsenic, nickel and mercury: Directive 96/62, Annex I.

[85]   Directive 96/62, Art. 4(1).

[86]   Levels fixed with the aim of avoiding more long-term harmful effects on human health and/or the environment to be attained where possible over a given period: Directive 96/62, Art. 2.

[87]   See paras. 2.3.1–9.

[88]   *The U.K. National Air Quality Strategy*, Cm. 3587 (1997) proposes standards and objectives for 8 pollutants (see para. 2.3.3 above); legislative standards and objectives have been proposed in draft regulations made in late 1996. The Labour Government elected in May 1997 has indicated that finalised regulations will be in place by the end of 1997; Press Release, p. 26 n. 71 above.

[89]   *The U.K. National Air Quality Strategy, op. cit.* n. 88 above, paras. 3.8–13.

objective is to ensure that all citizens have access to public places without risk to their health or quality of life, where this is economically and technically feasible. More specifically, objectives are quantified assessments of air quality representing the targets which the Government presently believes are generally achievable by the year 2005, having regard to available evidence on costs and benefits.[90]

It appears that limit values in E.C. air quality legislation may be directly 2.8.10 effective.[91] In *E.C. Commission v. Federal Republic of Germany*[92] the European Court of Justice held that by implementing the limit values set out in Directive 80/779 by means of an administrative circular rather than by means of a general mandatory rule, Germany had failed to fulfil its obligations under E.C. law. One of the principal reasons for this decision was that since the requirement on Member States to prescribe limit values was imposed by the Directive for the protection of human health in particular, that implied that "the persons concerned must be in a position to rely on mandatory rules *in order to assert their rights.* Furthermore, the fixing of limit values in a provision whose binding nature is undeniable is also necessary in order that all those whose activities are liable to give rise to nuisances may ascertain precisely the obligations to which they are subject".[93] However, while it might be possible for an individual to obtain a declarator that the relevant limit values are not being attained, in practice it would be very difficult to require the Secretary of State to undertake specific measures to implement the standards.[94]

The widespread adoption of air quality standards has necessitated the 2.8.11 establishment of extensive systematic air quality monitoring to ensure that quality standards are being achieved. The issue of monitoring is considered more fully in paragraphs 2.9.1–4.

Product standards

Considerable use has also been made of product standards as a means of 2.8.12 controlling air pollution. For example, the maximum sulphur and lead content of fuel has been prescribed.[95]

---

[90] *The U.K. National Air Quality Strategy, op. cit.,* paras. 3.15–21.
[91] See paras. 12.4.6–8.
[92] Case C–361/88 [1991] E.C.R. I–2567.
[93] *ibid.* para. 16 (emphasis added).
[94] See *R. v. Secretary of State for the Environment, ex p. Friends of the Earth* [1996] Env. L.R. 198. It is understood that an individual complaint was made to the E.C. Commission regarding sulphur dioxide and particulate levels in Sunderland, and that this led to the initiation of Art. 169 enforcement proceedings against the U.K.: *The Surveyor,* January 23, 1992.
[95] See para. 2.7.2.

AIR QUALITY MONITORING AND INFORMATION

2.9.1   The purpose of this section is principally to outline the air quality monitoring arrangements in Scotland, and to indicate how information is disseminated to the public. However, it should be noted that a variety of information is also available to the public on emission standards monitoring. For example, an IPC or LAPC authorisation under EPA 1990 may require monitoring of emissions on a continuous or regular interval basis to ensure compliance with emissions limits imposed in the authorisation. Data from such monitoring should normally be placed on the relevant public register.[96] The public registers are open during SEPA's normal working hours and may be inspected without charge, although a charge will be levied for any copies from the registers.[97] It should be noted that concerns have been voiced about the quality of data supplied where self-monitoring of emissions is carried out.[98] More general information on air pollution held by public bodies and certain other bodies may also be available to the public by virtue of the Environmental Information Regulations 1992.[99]

2.9.2   The need for air quality monitoring in the light of the adoption of air quality standards was outlined in paragraph 2.8.11. At the time of writing, air quality standards were prescribed for sulphur dioxide, suspended particulates (*i.e.* smoke), lead and nitrogen dioxide by the Air Quality Standards Regulations 1989[1] which also require the Secretary of State to establish monitoring sites to measure concentrations of these substances in the air in places where pollution is considered to be highest.[2] In addition, monitoring for ozone (a pollutant at ground level) is also required by the Ozone Monitoring and Information Regulations 1994,[3] which implement Directive 92/72 on air pollution by ozone. Monitoring for other substances such as carbon monoxide is carried out, although it is not yet a legislative requirement. However, the forthcoming adoption of air quality standards for eight pollutants (including the five mentioned above) in regulations to be made under Part IV of EA 1995[4] will necessitate further monitoring to provide systematic and accurate information on whether or not prescribed

---

[96]   EPA 1990, s. 20; Environmental Protection (Applications, Appeals and Registers) Regulations 1991 (S.I. 1991 No. 507), as amended, reg. 15(n).

[97]   EPA 1990, s. 20(7). Any member of the public may inspect such registers free of charge, regardless of his motive for doing so: *Stirrat Park Hogg v. Dumbarton D.C.*, 1996 S.L.T. 1131.

[98]   See, *e.g.* "HMIPI's secret prosecutions" (1995) 247 *ENDS Report* 43; "Unilever firm's IPC fine for 1,000 unreported breaches" (1995) 250 *ENDS Report* 44.

[99]   S.I. 1992 No. 3240, implementing Directive 90/313 on freedom of access to environmental information.

[1]   S.I. 1989 No. 317.

[2]   Air Quality Standards Regulations 1989 (S.I. 1989 No. 317), regs. 3, 5 and 7.

[3]   S.I. 1994 No. 440.

[4]   EA 1995, s. 87; and see para. 2.3.8.

standards are being met. The E.C.'s air ambient air quality assessment and management Directive will require monitoring for additional pollutants.[5]

An extensive network of automatic and sampler monitoring sites exists in both rural and urban areas for various pollutants.[6] Although criticism has been levelled at the Government in the past for not locating monitoring sites in areas of the highest pollution and for not having sufficient monitoring sites, particularly in the case of nitrogen oxide, the introduction of the Enhanced Urban Network (EUN) of monitoring sites has helped to allay such criticism to an extent.[7] The EUN presently consists of 23 urban sites across the U.K., to measure ozone, nitrogen dioxide, sulphur dioxide, carbon monoxide and particulates. In order that achievement of the air quality targets in the national air quality strategy are measured, the Government is seeking to enhance the network of monitoring sites and to integrate national and local government monitoring networks.[8]   2.9.3

The dissemination of information gathered by monitoring networks to the public is vital. This is partly to keep the public informed as to whether standards are being attained, but also to enable members of the public to take precautionary measures where excessive levels of a pollutant are present. For example, when excessive levels of ozone are in the atmosphere the public must be warned as soon as possible to enable precautionary measures to be taken.[9] More generally, information is distributed via the publication of reports,[10] the Department of the Environment, Transport and the Regions' Internet site[11] and telephone services, and by way of Meteorological Office weather bulletins.   2.9.4

---

[5] Directive 96/62. See also paras. 2.8.8–9.

[6] See, *e.g. The U.K. National Air Quality Strategy, op. cit.*, n. 88, paras. II.1.5–II.1–13. Brief details of current monitoring arrangements in Scotland may be found in SEPA, *State of the Environment Report* (1996), pp. 8–12.

[7] See, *e.g.* Ball and Bell, *Environmental Law* (3rd ed., 1995), p. 330.

[8] See *e.g. The U.K. National Quality Strategy, op. cit.*, n. 88, para. II.1.6 and *The Future of Air Quality Monitoring Networks in the U.K.* (DoE, 1993).

[9] Ozone Monitoring and Information Regulations 1994 (S.I. 1994 No. 440) which implement Directive 92/72 on air pollution by ozone.

[10] See, *e.g.* SEPA, *State of the Environment Report* (1996).

[11] At http://www.open.gov.uk/doe/doehome.htm which contains current and archive air quality information for a range of pollutants from automatic monitoring sites around the U.K.

Chapter Three

WATER POLLUTION

INTRODUCTION

3.1.1 Water is of fundamental importance to life. The problems of its use and equitable regulation have, therefore, accumulated a considerable body of law.[1] In former centuries the common law was the principal mode through which water was dealt with. The Victorians recognised that the public interest required a more general approach to such questions. Statutory bodies, controls and procedures began to be introduced. The present statutory system is traceable in its major principles to previous decades, although the administrative structure has undergone major alteration and the implementation of E.C. requirements has required the introduction of objective, scientific water quality standards.

COMMON LAW

3.2.1 Since water is so important, it is not surprising that a considerable body of common law is involved in this area. In particular, the developing law of nuisance contains many "water" cases. Of these, an important statement of general principle remains that of Lord Justice-Clerk Inglis in his charge to the jury in *Duke of Buccleuch v. Alexander Cowan and Sons*,[2] which can be summarised as: (1) the separate proprietors of a watercourse may use a stream as they choose, but must send the water down to lower proprietors undiminished in quantity and unimpaired in quality; (2) since streams have (variable) self-cleansing properties, there can be no absolute standard of quality at common law, so that minor impairment of quality by use of the stream for such natural purposes as washing, drinking or watering of cattle, is not actionable. However, (3) the addition of unnecessary and artificial pollutants to a water system is actionable. In such an action (4) a complainer must show that a defender has polluted a stream so as to be a nuisance to

---

[1] Ferguson, *The Law of Water and Water Rights in Scotland* (W. Green and Son, 1907); Murray, Keith and Thomson, "Water And Water Rights", and Keith "Water Supply" in *Encyclopaedia of the Laws of Scotland* (1933), Vol. 15; Lyall, "Water", and Bain, "Water Supply" in *The Laws of Scotland: Stair Memorial Encyclopaedia* (1988), Vol. 25.

[2] (1866) 5 M. 214 at 215–220.

him according to the normal concepts of nuisance. Later cases on nuisance establish that by acquiescence an individual may lose the right to complain about a given level of pollution, although not to object to an increased level.[3] A polluter cannot acquire an unfettered "right" to pollute by prescription.

Other common law rules regarding landownership and the ownership and use of streams, lochs and stagna can play a role in questions of pollution, notably relating to the alteration of a watercourse. Particular difficulties arise when an artificial watercourse is involved, either one which is completely artificial, or where a natural watercourse has been substantially altered in the past. Here much depends upon the law relating to servitudes, and in some cases to statutory provisions as to land drainage (see para. 3.7.9). **3.2.2**

Although it is still competent to proceed by action of nuisance in appropriate cases, the common law is not an entirely satisfactory method of dealing with questions of water pollution. An action will normally be raised only after the pollution has occurred. Pre-emptive action is occasionally competent, but is rare. There is no duty imposed on anyone to raise a common law action. In effect, only riparians have the right to take action. Proof can be difficult. To bring a case is expensive and the outcome is often uncertain. Someone with the necessary standing to bring an action is unlikely to qualify for legal aid, since standing, in most instances, will be based on the ownership of property. For all these reasons, to bring an action would be worrying as well as time and energy-consuming. In some instances there may be conflict of interest. Thus, in Victorian times many streams and rivers were grossly polluted, but landowners were not willing to take action because they were shareholders or the proprietors of the manufacturing industries causing the pollution. In water cases the "public interest" had only a small part to play in private law remedies. The result was that the use of nuisance was patchy and irregular. Other solutions were (and are) required. **3.2.3**

INTERNATIONAL AND E.C. LAW[4]

Before the statutory arrangements dealing with water pollution are considered, the impact of international obligations,[5] E.C. directives[6] and **3.3.1**

---

[3] *M'Gavin v. M'Intyre Bros* (1890) 17 R. 818; aff'd (1893) 20 R. (H.L.) 49.

[4] See generally Chap. 12, especially paras. 12.5.3–9.

[5] See Birnie and Boyle, *International Law and the Environment* (1992); *Basic Documents on International Law and the Environment* (1995).

[6] Important relevant directives are: the Dangerous Substances Directive (76/464); the Groundwater Directive (80/68); the Surface Water Directive (75/440); the Bathing Water Directive (76/160); the Drinking Water Directive (80/778); and the Urban Waste Water Directive (91/271). Some of these have been amended, and some have spawned daughter directives. Not all have been fully implemented in the U.K.

other legislation must be acknowledged. The statutory provisions are adapted to implement international obligations, not only those from the European Community, and contain powers to modify regulations, orders, consents, permissions and authorisations to reflect any changes in these obligations.

3.3.2   One particular matter must, however, be specially noted. A problem or restriction of both common and statutory law in the past has been the question of standing — whether an individual (or pressure group) had the technical legal interest (as opposed to altruistic concern) to intervene in an environmental matter. Some of the langauge of E.C. directives may avoid that problem. Depending on its terms, a directive may make it possible for citizens to take action to require statutory authorities to implement their obligations under the directive without the citizens having to show a legal interest in the previous technical sense.[7]

STATUTORY ARRANGEMENTS: AGENCIES

3.4.1 Statutory measures dealing with water pollution fall into four major divisions: river purification (including parts of the territorial sea); sewerage; questions of water supply; and a general category of miscellaneous provisions.

3.4.2   The raising of a common law action is optional. Although a person may have a good case on the facts there is no requirement on him to go to court. Therefore, an essential step in the statutory arrangements was the placing of a duty on local authorities to take matters up. Following the Second World War this duty was laid on the Secretary of State for Scotland, who is required by section 1 of the Rivers (Prevention of Pollution) (Scotland) Act 1951 to promote the cleanliness of the rivers and other inland waters and the tidal waters of Scotland. Other duties in respect of water quality and resource management have been added to governmental responsibilities.[8]

3.4.3   In 1996 a major reorganisation of local government and environmental responsibilities occurred. Not all the statutory provisions have yet come into force, but, as this will not be long delayed, what follows assumes that the major Acts, etc., have been brought into effect.

3.4.4   A variety of agencies with interlocking duties and powers discharge environmental responsibilities. The main agencies are outlined where appropriate below, but, to summarise, in Scotland there is now a Scottish Environment Protection Agency (SEPA), three water authorities which also deal with sewerage, a Water and Sewerage Customers Council, and, of course, local government bodies, which still retain some environmental

---

[7]   See paras. 12.4.6–8.
[8]   See, *e.g.* the Water (Scotland) Act 1980, s. 1, as substituted by the Local Government etc. (Scotland) Act 1994, s. 65(1); EA 1995, ss. 33 and 34.

duties. Former public utilities, now privatised, also bear environmental responsibilities.

Before these matters are considered, however, a complaint must be made 3.4.5 in respect of the tattered state of the relevant legislation. Repeals, amendments and insertions have left the material very difficult to work with. I have done my best, but it is unsatisfactory that one cannot be wholly confident of having coped with the debris our legislature has chosen to produce. A consolidating re-enactment would be useful.

WATER POLLUTION

Agencies

The main agency dealing with water pollution matters in Scotland is 3.5.1 now SEPA, established under section 20 and Chapter II of Part I of the Environment Act 1995 (EA 1995). SEPA is the dominant body in many environmental matters in Scotland, with broad duties in respect of pollution control under EA 1995, s. 33 and in respect of water matters under section 34. SEPA operates through three area boards (north, east and west), and a main board. The new water authorities, combining the functions of water supply and the provision of sewerage services, established by section 62 of the Local Government etc. (Scotland) Act 1994 impact on pollution questions. Other agencies, including local government, still have some responsibilities which either directly or indirectly affect water. Planning procedures must take pollution, sewerage and water supply questions into account. Waste disposal authorities must have regard to the effect of their activities on water, as must other authorities with licensing and authorising powers in environmental matters (see para. 3.5.10).

In respect of water, SEPA's powers and responsibilities are to administer 3.5.2 and enforce a considerable body of law. The main statutory water pollution provisions are contained in Part II of the Control of Pollution Act 1974 (COPA 1974), but readers are warned not to rely on the 1974 text alone. *Inter alia*, Schedule 23 to the Water Act 1989 substituted new sections 30A–E, 31,[9] 33 to 42, 46 to 51 and 53 to 56 in Part II of the 1974 Act, and section 106 of, and Schedule 16 to EA 1995 inserted new sections 30F to J.[10]

---

[9] A new s. 31D and s. 32, both inserted by the 1989 Act, were repealed by Sched. 24 to EA 1995.
[10] An unofficial consolidation of this legislation is printed as Appendix 4 of Tromans (with Nash and Poustie), *The Environment Acts 1990–1995* (1996).

Controlled waters

3.5.3   Virtually all waters within Scotland, as well as parts of the sea off the Scottish coast, are subject to pollution controls. The intention is that water systems are considered as units, the totality of the aqueous environment of a water catchment area being dealt with on a "source to sea" basis. From 1951 this was the responsibility of river purification authorities, whose role was extended over the years. In 1996 the functions of river purification authorities were transferred to SEPA by section 21(1)(a) of EA 1995.

3.5.4   Waters which are under statutory control are defined by section 30A of COPA 1974 to consist of all naturally occurring inland waters (*i.e.* landward of the territorial sea) which form any sort of watercourse, and include underground waters, lochs and ponds,[11] and certain reservoirs which are treated as lochs or ponds,[12] together with, in appropriate cases, freshwater coastal waters, the territorial sea up to three nautical miles from its baselines, and areas of the territorial sea beyond that limit if added by order of the Secretary of State.[13]

Water quality of streams, etc.[14]

3.5.5   Under section 30B of the Control of Pollution Act 1974, the Secretary of State has power to prescribe a system for the classification of waters in Scotland generally as to their purpose, and, specifically, as to the substances and their concentrations to be present or absent in designated waters, as well as to other characteristics. Regulations have been issued as to the classification of waters for supply after treatment as drinking water by water supply authorities, and as to the presence of certain dangerous substances.[15] Under section 30C the Secretary of State may serve a notice specifying the quality objectives for any waters. Such a notice may be reviewed after five

---

[11]   Lochs and ponds which do not drain are excluded, but may be added by order: COPA 1974, s. 30A(5)(b).

[12]   Controlled Waters (Lochs and Ponds) (Scotland) Order 1990 (S.I. 1990 No. 120).

[13]   The breadth of the territorial sea is 12 nautical miles, one nautical mile being 1.852 metres or 2,025 yards (1.15 statute miles) (Territorial Sea Act 1987, s. 1(1)(a); COPA 1974, s. 30A(4)), the baselines for its measurement being established by that Act and by the Territorial Waters Order in Council of 1964 (printed at the end of the statutory instrument volumes for that year) and the Territorial Sea (Amendment) Order 1996 (S.I. 1996 No. 1628), made under the 1987 Act.

[14]   The quality of water supplied for public use is dealt with separately below at paras. 3.6.8–10.

[15]   Surface Water (Classification) (Scotland) Regulations 1990 (S.I. 1990 No. 121); Surface Waters (Dangerous Substances) (Classification) (Scotland) Regulations 1990 (S.I. 1990 No. 126). The latter has a schedule of dangerous substances and concentrations. See also the Bathing Waters (Classification) (Scotland) Regulations 1991 (S.I. 1991 No. 1609) and the Surface Waters (Dangerous Substances) (Classification) (Scotland) Regulations 1992 (S.I. 1992 No. 574).

years, or earlier. Under section 30D it is the duty of the Secretary of State and SEPA to ensure that the water quality objectives are met. SEPA maintains a register of quality objectives for each area, and this is open to the public (COPA 1974, s. 41(1)(a)).

Under section 34(1) of EA 1995, specify duties are placed on SEPA to 3.5.6 promote the cleanliness of waters, and to conserve, as far as practicable, the water resources of Scotland. The promotion of the conservation and enhancement of water-related natural beauty and amenities, and of fauna and flora dependent on the aquatic environment, is also a duty of SEPA "to such an extent as it considers desirable" (EA 1995, s. 34(2)).

Under section 40 of EA 1995 the Secretary of State may give general or 3.5.7 specific directions to SEPA as to the carrying out of its functions. In particular, these directions may be used to implement international and E.C. obligations (s. 40(2)). Similar powers are given in respect of Part I (Integrated Pollution Control) of EPA 1990 by section 156 of that Act. Powers therefore exist to conform to the changing requirements of the E.C. and international environmental agreements in force for the U.K.

Mechanisms for attaining water quality

The major controlling mechanism on water pollution is a general prohibition 3.5.8 on the entry of matter or pollutants into a water system except with the consent of SEPA (see below). Breach of that prohibition invites a criminal sanction. A second mechanism is SEPA's power to issue prohibition notices under section 30G of COPA 1974. A prohibition notice may be specific in relation to a person, or generally applicable to particular substances or processes. A third mechanism is that water supply authorities have statutory powers to secure that their water sources are kept free from pollution. A fourth mechanism empowers the Secretary of State to prohibit or restrict the carrying on of prescribed activities within a designated area without SEPA's consent so that water pollution may be lessened (COPA 1974, s. 31(4)).

An offence is committed where a person is found guilty of causing or 3.5.9 knowingly permitting the unlawful entry into controlled waters of solid matter, or of poisonous, noxious or polluting matter, or of trade and sewage effluent (COPA 1974, s. 30F(1)–(4)). In the past, construing similar language, "causing" has been interpreted in a simple, common sense way: had something been done the result of which was the entry of matter or pollution? Knowledge or intention is not, therefore, required to establish causation.[16]

---

[16] *Lockhart v. National Coal Board,* 1981 S.C.C.R. 9, 1981 S.L.T. 161; *cf. Alphacell Ltd v. Woodward* [1972] A.C. 824. Note, however, *National Rivers Authority v. Yorkshire Water Services Ltd* [1995] 1 A.C. 444 for the case of sewerage, where the operator did not know of an unauthorised discharge into its system.

Lawful entry of matter and of pollutants

3.5.10 Fundamentally, what is not unlawful is lawful. The entry of noxious, poisonous or polluting matter (including effluent)[17] or any solid waste matter into controlled waters is now dealt with under sections 30F–J of COPA 1974.[18] Such an entry is unlawful (COPA 1974, s. 30F) and, in serious cases, the offence may be dealt with on indictment (COPA 1974, s. 30F(6)). In addition, section 30G empowers SEPA by notice to prohibit the discharging of matter or other effluent by a person, and such a notice can be used to prohibit the entry of a prescribed substance, or of matter from a prescribed process.[19] The prohibition notice may contain conditions under which the discharge is lawful (COPA 1974, s. 30G(1)(b)). Contravention of a prohibition notice may be an element of an offence (COPA 1974, s. 30F(2) and (4)). The intention of such procedure is to provide a simpler process in appropriate instances where a general or a particular notice is a more efficient way to regulate water matters.

3.5.11   The base position, therefore, is that under section 30F a discharge or entry of poisonous, noxious or polluting matter or solid waste matter, or any matter whatever (see para. 3.5.16) into controlled waters is unlawful. Lawful entry occurs when the terms of a statutory defence is available (see paras. 3.5.19–21). Alternatively, certain discharges are exempt under regulations issued by the Secretary of State.[20]

Trade and sewage effluent

3.5.12 Particular provision is made on the entry of trade and sewage effluent into controlled waters. The sewerage system as such will be dealt with separately below (see paras. 3.6.3–7).

3.5.13   By section 56 of COPA 1974, "effluent" means any liquid, including particles of matter and other substances in suspension in the liquid. By section 105 "trade effluent" includes any liquid (with or without particles of matter in suspension) discharged from premises used for any trade or

---

[17] As noted below, effluent is defined by s. 56 of COPA 1974 as meaning "any liquid, including particles of matter and other substances in suspension in the liquid". Trade and sewage effluents are additionally defined with regard to their origins.

[18] Inserted by s. 106 of, and Sched. 16 to EA 1995. Sched. 24 to that Act repeals the formerly relevant provisions of s. 31, which were inserted by s. 169 of, and Sched. 23 to the Water Act 1989.

[19] "Prescribed substance" is defined in ss. 1(13) and 2(7) of the Environmental Protection Act 1990, "prescribed process" being defined by s. 1(5) of that Act; see Chap. 5.

[20] See the Control of Pollution (Exemption of Certain Discharges from Control) (Scotland) Order 1983 (S.I. 1983 No. 1182), as modified by the Control of Pollution (Exemption of Certain Discharges from Control) (Scotland) (Variation) Orders 1986 (S.I. 1986 No. 1623), 1987 (S.I. 1987 No. 1782) and 1993 (S.I. 1993 No. 1154).

industry, other than surface water and domestic sewage. Agricultural and horticultural premises, as well as premises used for scientific research or experiment, are included. Whether or not the activities within premises are carried on for profit or otherwise, is not relevant for their classification. "Sewage effluent" includes effluent from a sewage disposal plant or sewage works of a sewerage authority (see paras. 3.6.3–7).

Except in enumerated instances, it is an offence to cause or knowingly 3.5.14 to permit the discharge of trade or sewage effluent into controlled waters, or by a pipe from land in Scotland into the sea outside controlled waters or from any building or plant onto or into any land or into any waters which are not inland waters (COPA 1974, s. 30F(2)–(4)).

Such a discharge is not unlawful if it is authorised by a consent from 3.5.15 SEPA (see para. 3.5.21), nor where the discharge takes place in an emergency to avoid danger to life or health, as long as the Agency is notified as soon as possible. A licence granted under Part II of the Food and Environment Protection Act 1985 or an authorisation under Part I of EPA 1990 for a prescribed process subject to central control will also make the discharge of trade or sewage effluent lawful.[21] In addition, the Secretary of State can, by statutory instrument, exempt discharges of a type or within a specified area from control by the consent system.[22]

Matter

An offence is committed where matter is allowed to enter inland waters 3.5.16 which, by impeding the flow of the waters, may tend substantially to aggravate pollution (COPA 1974, s. 30F(5)).

Unless with the consent of SEPA, it is an offence to disturb a deposit 3.5.17 accumulated by a dam, weir or sluice with the result that the material is carried in suspension downstream. It is also an offence without such consent to allow any substantial amount of vegetation cut or uprooted in a stream, or falling into it, to remain in the stream. In both cases, SEPA's consent must not be unreasonably refused (COPA 1974, s. 49).

The entry of matter into a watercourse consequent upon good agricultural 3.5.18 practice is not unlawful (COPA 1974, s. 31(4) and (9)). Under section 51 of COPA 1974, after consulting SEPA, the Secretary of State can, by regulation, approve a code of good agricultural practice, whether issued by himself or by others.[23] Contravention of such a code does not, of itself, ground civil or criminal liability, but SEPA may take such a contravention into account when deciding on the use of any of its powers. (See also para. 3.7.2.)

---

[21] COPA 1974, s. 32(4), as amended by Sched. 15, para. 16 to the Environmental Protection Act 1990.
[22] See n. 20 above.
[23] See n. 37 below.

Defences

3.5.19 Various defences to a charge under section 30F of COPA 1974 are available. Under section 30I an entry of polluting matter, etc., is not unlawful if it has been authorised by another appropriate authority. This, most obviously, includes a consent by SEPA, which is discussed below (at para. 3.5.21). It also includes: an authorisation under the Environmental Protection Act 1990 (notably the terms of an authorisation under Part I (integrated pollution control) or a waste management licence under Part II (waste on land); a water authority making a temporary discharge for the purpose of construction works under section 33 of the Water (Scotland) Act 1980; a discharge licensed under Part II of the Food and Environment Protection Act 1985; or a discharge sanctioned by a local Act or statutory order conferring power to discharge effluent.

3.5.20   Under section 30J other defences are available. An entry is permitted in an emergency to avoid danger to life or health provided the person making it takes all reasonably practicable steps to minimise the entry and its effects, and notifies SEPA as soon as possible (COPA 1974, s. 30J(1)). The discharge of trade or sewage effluent from a vessel is not covered by section 30F (COPA 1974, s. 30J(2)); nor is the entry of liquid pollutants from a mine unlawful unless the mine is abandoned after December 31, 1999 (COPA 1974, s. 30J(3)–(6)).[24] Pollution of water originating from a deposit of solid refuse from a mine or quarry is not unlawful if the deposit was made with the consent of SEPA, no other site is reasonably practicable, and reasonably practicable steps have been taken to avoid the entry of the polluting matter (COPA 1974, s. 30J(7)). A roads authority may keep open a drain for its purposes unless in contravention of a prohibition notice under section 30G (COPA 1974, s. 30J(8)).

Consent to entry

3.5.21 Other than in the instances indicated above, a discharge or entry of matter or of poisonous, noxious or polluting matter into controlled waters requires the consent of SEPA. A consent is not personal to the applicant, but attaches to the site concerned (COPA 1974, s. 37(7)). In the absence of an appropriate consent, or where an entry of matter or a discharge does not comply with the terms of a consent, a person causing or knowingly permitting the event commits an offence under section 30F of COPA 1974. As indicated above (see para. 3.5.9) causation is to be interpreted simply, without necessarily

---

[24] As to the abandonment of mines in Scotland and notices to be given to SEPA, see ss. 30Y and 30Z of COPA 1974, inserted by s. 59 of the Environment Act 1995 (curiously, just ahead of ss. 30A to J of COPA 1974).

requiring proof of knowledge or intention.[25] Summary conviction will lead to a fine of up to £20,000 or three months in prison, or both, while conviction on indictment may be followed by prison for up to two years, or to an unlimited fine, or both (COPA, 1974, s. 30F(6)).

Procedure

An application for the appropriate consent to the entry of matter or of a liquid discharge is made to SEPA. The receipt of an application is publicly advertised in a local newspaper, and copies sent to the appropriate local authority (COPA 1974, s. 36).[26] The information that must accompany an application is determined by SEPA (COPA 1974, s. 34(1)). This usually includes the site of the proposed discharge, the nature and composition of the discharge, the maximum to be discharged in any one day, and the highest rate of discharge. Falsification of data or recklessness as to its accuracy is an offence (COPA 1974, s. 34(5)). Where an unlawful discharge has taken place, SEPA may require a consent application to be filed where it is likely that there will be future occurrences. Consent given under these circumstances, however, does not eliminate the unlawful quality of the earlier occurrence. 3.5.22

It is the duty of SEPA to deal with the matter within three months or such longer period as it may agree with an applicant. The Secretary of State has power to call in particular applications (with or without representations having been made to him), or applications of a prescribed type (COPA 1974, s. 35), in which case the three-month limit does not apply. Applicants, SEPA and interested parties are given the opportunity to make representations whether the matter is dealt with by the Secretary or the Agency. 3.5.23

An application may be granted, refused, or granted subject to conditions. Conditions listed in section 34(4) of COPA 1974 as being reasonable for the Agency to impose include: the place of discharge; the construction and maintenance of the outlet; the composition and temperature of the discharge, and its chemical composition, volume and rate of discharge. Other conditions can include the provision and operation of measuring apparatus, record-keeping, and the forwarding of information to the Agency. Most importantly, steps to be taken to minimise the effects of pollution by the discharge can be required. Finally, conditions can be varied as to time, and different conditions set for different periods. 3.5.24

---

[25] See n. 16 above.
[26] By s. 36 (2A) and (2B) of COPA 1974, inserted by s. 120 of, and Sched. 22 to EA 1995, publication and circulation of information may be barred by the issue of a certificate by the Secretary of State that in the given instance either national security, or, to an unreasonable degree, the commercial interests of any person, would be affected.

3.5.25   A consent may not be unreasonably refused, and an appeal lies to the Secretary of State on the grant, refusal or conditions of a consent (COPA 1974, s. 39), although the matter may, in fact, be referred to a person appointed for the purpose (EA 1995, s. 114). Under section 41 of COPA, SEPA maintains a register of applications and consents issued together with considerable detail as to their conditions, and other data including enforcement notices (see para. 3.5.30), convictions and directions given by the Secretary of State.[27] The register is open to public inspection.

Failure to comply with consent

3.5.26 Where a consent is in force, a failure to comply with its terms, including any conditions, removes the protection the consent provides from prosecution for allowing an entry into the water system.

Review of consents

3.5.27 Consents state the period for which they are valid, and are not subject to review for a minimum of two years from the date on which they take effect without the agreement of the person making the discharge, unless SEPA considers it reasonable (COPA, 1974, s. 38). This could apply where there is a significant change of circumstances. In addition, the Secretary of State may intervene to require the terms of a consent to be altered, or even cancelled, in order to protect public health or the aquatic environment, following upon representations made to him, or to give effect to an international obligation (COPA 1974, s. 37(2)). Under section 38A the Secretary of State may order a general review of consents issued by SEPA.

3.5.28   The holder of a consent may ask for a review to be undertaken. In any event, it is the duty of SEPA from time to time to review consents it has issued, and their conditions. As a result of any such review the Agency may revoke a consent, alter its conditions or attach conditions to a previously unconditional consent (COPA 1974, s. 37).

Information

3.5.29 In order to carry out its functions as to consents, SEPA has considerable powers to gain information through access, inspection and requiring the giving of information. Under section 113 of EA 1995 SEPA is restricted as to the further disclosure of information it obtains. Further, as indicated above, SEPA keeps a public record of applications for

---

[27]   The detail of what is required to be held is contained in the Control of Pollution (Registers) (Scotland) Regulations 1993 (S.I. 1993 No. 1155).

consents, and a register open to public inspection of the consents that it has issued, and of their terms. Under sections 42A and 42B of COPA 1974 the detail of an application and the terms of a consent may be exempt from disclosure either on grounds of national security or on the ground that disclosure would reveal trade secrets to an unreasonable extent.

Enforcement: precaution and works

Of course, the criminal sanctions contained in the legislation offer one mode of enforcement of the environmental requirements. In addition, under sections 49A and 49B of COPA 1974 (added by Schedule 22 to EA 1995) an enforcement notice may be served requiring action where a discharge is unlawful — failure to comply with the notice being a criminal offence. However, on occasion it may be sensible to anticipate the consequences of pollution, and SEPA may require operations to be carried out where there is a threat of pollution because of a person's actions (actions which are not, of themselves, yet unlawful), or to remedy pollution which has occurred (COPA 1974, s. 46). Under sections 46A to 46D (also added by Schedule 22 to EA 1995) procedure is available for the giving of notice requiring appropriate works. 3.5.30

SEWERAGE AND WATER SUPPLY

Agencies

When the reorganisation of local government was debated in the early 1990s there was a possibility that privatisation of water and sewerage on the English model might be adopted. This, however, was strongly resisted, and Scotland has a different system. 3.6.1

With the coming into force in 1996 of the Local Government etc. (Scotland) Act 1994, water supply and sewerage, formerly the responsibilities of local government, were transferred to new authorities. These are, respectively, the East of Scotland, the West of Scotland, and the North of Scotland Water Authorities. Under Schedule 7 to the Act these authorities are bodies corporate, with members appointed by the Secretary of State. They now perform the functions of their predecessors for their areas. However, it is possible for an authority to involve private capital under the "build, own, operate" schemes, under which private sector companies can provide services for payment.[28] In addition, to provide for 3.6.2

---

[28] The provisions making this possible are scattered within Pt. II of the Local Government etc. (Scotland) Act 1994.

consumers' interests to be represented under the new system, a Scottish
Water and Sewerage Customers Council was established as a body corporate
under sections 67 to 71 of, and Schedule 9 to the 1994 Act.

Sewerage

3.6.3   Apart from the various discharges of trade effluent into the water system,
the major single pollutant of the waters of Scotland is the outpourings
of the sewerage system. This system is subject to separate regulation down
to the point at which sewage effluent is discharged into controlled waters
supervised by SEPA, at which point the matter comes under the pollution
mechanisms outlined earlier in this chapter. As such, sewerage largely falls
outside the scope of this chapter, but a brief sketch is necessary in order to
understand the whole picture of the control of water pollution.[29]

3.6.4   As indicated above, sewerage is now the responsibility of the appropriate
water authority for the area. The detail of sewerage law is dealt with largely
by the Sewerage (Scotland) Act 1968, as amended.[30] The duty of the
sewerage authority is to provide and maintain the public sewers necessary
for domestic sewage, surface water and trade effluent, and the necessary
sewage treatment works, etc. (see para. 3.7.1). In the performance of its
functions the sewerage authority must have due regard to other
environmental considerations.[31]

3.6.5   The authority must lead a public sewer to a point where the owners of
premises may, at reasonable cost, connect their drains or private sewers to
the public system. The duty, however, is limited to providing what is
necessary at reasonable cost. Owners connecting their buildings must give
notice before connecting their systems, and receive permission to do so.
By a new section 10, substituted into the 1968 Act by section 102 of the
Local Government etc. (Scotland) Act 1994, there is now a duty on sewerage
authorities to empty septic tanks where this is reasonably practicable, and
charge for the service. Trade effluent disposal is not a duty under section
10, but may be contracted for by the authority; otherwise, it will be for the
trade or business to deal with this itself, probably through the normal consent
processes involving SEPA (dealt with above).

3.6.6   The use of the sewerage system mirrors, to a degree, the regulation of
the use of controlled waters. It is a general offence to put into the sewerage

---

[29] Note that the administrative arrangements for sewerage were changed in 1996 with the
reorganisation of local government. On the previous system, and the detail of powers, etc.,
now exercised by the new authorities, see Lyall, "Water and Water Rights" in *The Laws of
Scotland: Stair Memorial Encyclopaedia, op. cit.*, n. 1, Vol. 25, section 14, paras. 429–
500, "Sewerage", and the updating annotations for that section.

[30] On detail, see Lyall, *op. cit.*, n. 29. Some changes are indicated below.

[31] See ss. 65(2) and 73 of the Local Government etc. (Scotland) Act 1994.

system anything which will damage it. Trade effluent is separately handled, requiring the consent of the sewerage authority. This consent may be subject to conditions. Only trade effluent discharges which existed prior to May 16, 1973 (the date when the 1968 Act was brought into force) and which have not been altered subsequently are exempt from the requirement of consent. A sewerage authority may agree with the owner or occupier of trade premises as to the building of treatment works on the site of the premises.

The treatment and disposal of the contents of the sewer system is a matter 3.6.7 for the sewerage authority. At the final stage this may involve discharge into the water system, at which point the consent of SEPA is required, and conditions may have to be complied with, as noted above. Section 30H of COPA 1974[32] restricts the circumstances under which the sewerage authority is liable to a criminal charge in respect of a discharge from the sewerage system.

Water supply

Providers of the public water supply are the other major actors with powers 3.6.8 and responsibilities affecting water pollution in Scotland. As indicated above, the supply of water in an area is the responsibility of the appropriate water authority. The water authorities operate under water supply legislation which is largely codified by the Water (Scotland) Act 1980, as amended.[33]

It is the duty of a water authority to supply wholesome water to the 3.6.9 public. This duty has been refined by sections 76A to 76L of the 1980 Act, which were added by Schedule 22 to the Water Act 1989. These new sections, and the regulations made under them, impose and provide mechanisms to secure implementation of the E.C. water directives regarding fitness of water for human consumption. Water for food production must meet similar standards under the Food Safety Act 1990, and regulations made thereunder.

In order to fulfil these duties and requirements the water authorities have 3.6.10 extensive powers to construct reservoirs and pipelines, as well as to seek and secure supplies of wholesome water. In supplying wholesome water an authority has powers under sections 70 to 76 of the Water (Scotland) Act 1980 to prevent the contamination or pollution of water which may contribute to its water supply, and to require the owner or occupier of land to take steps for that purpose. In addition, the water authority may itself enter into agreements as to land drainage, or, in the last resort, impose such

---

[32] Added by EA 1995, s. 106 and Sched. 16, para. 2.
[33] See Bain, "Water Supply" in *The Laws of Scotland: Stair Memorial Encyclopaedia, op. cit.*, Vol. 25 and annotations in the *Service* volume.

an agreement in order that the purity of its water supplies is not prejudiced by the intermixture of foul water (see also para. 3.7.1).

MISCELLANEOUS

Urban waste water

3.7.1 The Urban Waste Water (Treatment) (Scotland) Regulations 1994,[34] implementing E.C. Directive 91/271, require the introduction of treatment mechanisms for urban waste water immediately in "sensitive" areas — areas of Scotland where the environment is especially sensitive to water pollution. In addition, the Regulations require that all areas with population equivalents of over 15,000 shall have such treatment processes by December 31, 2000, and that, by 2005, similar provision will have been made for areas of population equivalents between 2,000 and 15,000.

Agriculture and horticulture[35]

3.7.2 As noted above, the entry of matter into controlled waters consequent upon good agricultural practice is not unlawful. The Secretary of State has power to approve a code of good agricultural practice, but breach of the code will not ground a civil or criminal action.[36] Other restrictions apply in the field of agriculture and horticulture which are, in part at least, intended to minimise and lessen the occasions on which water pollution is caused by agricultural operations and requirements. The major elements are as follows.

Silage, slurry and oil

3.7.3 A growing number of pollution control regulations deal with specific matters germane to the conduct of agriculture. In particular, section 31A of COPA 1974 permits the Secretary of State to make regulations on the custody, storage and use of potentially polluting material.[37] While most of the regulations relate to other uses and abuses of these substances, one element is designed to secure that as little water pollution as possible is caused by the escape of polluting material into the water system.

---

[34] S.I. 1994 No. 2842.
[35] See also paras. 3.7.5–8.
[36] This power was exercised by the Water (Prevention of Pollution) (Code of Practice) (Scotland) Order 1992 (S.I. 1992 No. 395). The Code is available from the Scottish Office.
[37] See, *e.g.* the Control of Pollution (Silage, Slurry and Agricultural Fuel) (Scotland) Regulations 1991 (S.I. 1991 No. 346).

Nitrates

The Protection of Water against Nitrate Pollution (Scotland) Regulations 3.7.4
1996[38] put into effect the requirements of Directive 91/676, and gave SEPA
a duty to monitor nitrate concentrations in water in Scotland. Section 31B
of COPA 1974 allows the Secretary of State to designate an area as a "nitrate
sensitive area". He may then agree with owners of land in the area as to its
management, or, where necessary, impose on them an order for its
management, including provisions as to prohibitions or restrictions on how
the land is to be worked. Compensation may be paid for such restrictions.
Under section 31C the agreement is registered in the Land Register of
Scotland or the appropriate division of the Sasine Register, and is enforceable
by the Secretary of State against successors of the person entering into the
agreement, and anyone (*e.g.* a tenant) deriving title from him. Termination
of the agreement may be agreed by the Secretary of State and the other
party to an agreement or his successor. The making and modification of a
nitrate sensitive area order is governed by Schedule 1A to COPA 1974.[39]

Irrigation

Modern agriculture and horticulture frequently require irrigation. Water 3.7.5
pollution can be increased if the flow of a river or stream is reduced below
a critical point. The use of the stream for irrigation can have such an effect.
Such matters are now dealt with under sections 15 to 19 of the Natural
Heritage (Scotland) Act 1991, and by the making of appropriate control
orders, which is governed by Schedule 5 to the 1991 Act. On the request of
SEPA, the Secretary of State may, by statutory instrument, control the
amount of water taken for any purpose, including irrigation, from controlled
waters within a designated area. If SEPA is not minded to make an
application in a suitable case, the Secretary of State, as he is under a duty to
secure the conservation of water and the cleanliness of rivers, may require
SEPA to apply for an order. When a control order is in place, it is an offence
to abstract water for irrigation purposes, except in terms of a licence issued
by the Agency. The licence may be limited or suspended when there is
either drought or an abundance of water.

Drought

Although water pollution may be significantly increased by a lack of water 3.7.6
in a watercourse, the maintenance of water supplies to the public can be

---

[38] S.I. 1996 No. 1564.
[39] Added by the Water Act 1989, Sched. 23, para. 8.

given an overriding importance. In the case of drought, powers exist to take water from various sources for supply purposes, as well as otherwise to control what is done with a water system, whether a river, stream or loch.

3.7.7   In times of drought a water authority may now apply to the Secretary of State to act under Part III of the Natural Heritage (Scotland) Act 1991. By section 20 of the Act where, by reason of an exceptional lack of rain, there is a serious deficiency of supplies of water in any place, the Secretary of State may make an "ordinary drought order" or an "emergency drought order". These may be made only on the application of a water authority.

3.7.7   Ordinary orders authorise an authority to take water from any specified source to meet its needs, or to discharge to any specified place. Ordinary orders may allow the authority to prohibit or limit the use of water for specified purposes, although the Secretary of State can direct the authority on the use it makes of that power. The order may also authorise the applicant to prohibit anyone from taking water from a source, and allow it to vary any arrangement it has entered into as to the taking, discharge or filtration and supply of water. Emergency orders can allow the applicant to prohibit or limit the use of water for such purposes as it thinks fit, and to supply by tankers, stand-pipes, etc. In the case of an emergency order, the Secretary of State can direct the applicant on the use of the powers it has been given.

3.7.8   An offence against a drought order is a criminal offence punishable by fine.

Land drainage

3.7.9   Statutory provisions allow for the drainage of land in order to facilitate enterprises which they authorise or encourage. The construction and maintenance of roads, railways or water transport systems such as canals, the safety of mines and the operation of mineral workings and hydroelectric schemes all are helped by the availability of statutory powers allowing for drainage. In addition, water supply authorities have specific powers to construct or require the construction of drainage works to ensure that foul waters are kept separate from clean sources of supply they require.

3.7.10   Apart from these measures, statutory schemes have existed since the nineteenth century under which owners and occupiers of land can establish, by official authority in the absence of agreement, drainage schemes to improve their land.[40] If this were not the case, the artificial increase or alteration of the drainage of surface and other waters would constitute a nuisance, to which neighbouring proprietors may object. A variety of statutes

---

[40] See Lyall, "Water and Water Rights" in *The Laws of Scotland: Stair Memorial Encyclopaedia, op. cit.*, n. 1, Vol. 25 section 10, paras. 363–374 and updating annotations.

now govern such matters. SEPA may be a party to a land drainage scheme, and may be obliged to involve itself if there is any question of altering the flow of a stream, or adding polluting material to it.

Readers are also referred to the regulations on the treatment of urban waste water (see para. 3.7.1). 3.7.11

Fishing offences

Under various provisions it is an offence to put any noxious or poisonous substances in or near water in order to take or destroy fish.[41] 3.7.12

Vessels

Pollution from vessels, particularly pleasure vehicles on rivers and lochs, is an increasing problem. SEPA has been given power to make byelaws applicable to any inland waters (*i.e.* inland of the baselines of the territorial sea, and including lochs and rivers) to prohibit or otherwise regulate the keeping or using of vessels fitted with sanitary appliances (COPA 1974, s. 33). "Sanitary appliances" includes appliances designed to permit polluting material to pass into the water (but not sinks, baths or showers). It is an offence punishable by a fine to contravene such a byelaw. As a corollary of these powers, SEPA has a duty to arrange for the collection and disposal of waste from vessels, to arrange facilities for the washing out of prescribed appliances, and to provide sanitary facilities onshore (COPA 1974, s. 47, as substituted by Schedule 23 to the Water Act 1989).[42] These duties may be discharged on behalf of SEPA by a port local authority constituted under the Public Health (Scotland) Act 1897. 3.7.13

A further power to cope with the pollution of controlled waters from vessels is provided by section 48 of COPA 1974, under which SEPA may, under bye-law, require that vessels in controlled waters be registered by it or be exempt from such registration (*i.e.* a particular type of boat could be so exempt). A reasonable registration charge may be imposed, in which case no charge can be made on persons from registered vessels for the use of those onshore facilities listed at paragraph 3.7.13 (COPA 1974, s. 48). 3.7.14

Waste[43]

The entry of matter into a water system is not unlawful if it conforms to the terms of a waste management licence issued under Part II of EPA 1990. 3.7.15

---

[41] See also paras. 10.2.17–18.
[42] See para. 11.2.8.
[43] See also Chap. 4 on Waste.

However, other questions could arise. In the past consultation arrangements were required between the waste regulation and river purification authorities, but now that SEPA is responsible for both functions these are unnecessary. The Waste Management Licensing Regulations 1994,[44] however, impose special obligations in relation to the licensing of any site from which certain materials may enter groundwater.

Entry and enforcement

3.7.16   Finally, it should be noted that in virtually every case discussed above, the appropriate authority or the Secretary of State has powers to enter on land or property, inspect, take samples and conduct other investigations to determine whether a licence, permission or other authority should be issued, whether such is being complied with, or whether an order or control or other enforcement procedure should be initiated. In some instances a duty is imposed on the owners or occupiers of land and property to supply that information, where necessary establishing a monitoring system to provide the required information.

---

[44]   S.I. 1994 No. 1056, reg. 15, implementing Directive 80/68; see para. 4.3.18.

CHAPTER FOUR

WASTE*

INTRODUCTION

Part II of the Environmental Protection Act 1990 (EPA 1990) imposed new, 4.1.1
more stringent controls on waste production, management, and disposal. It
extended the liability of those involved in the waste cycle by the introduction
of a cradle-to-grave duty of care in respect of waste production, carriage,
storage and disposal, and increased the powers of the regulatory authorities
to regulate waste management by the use of licensing powers. These new
measures have come into force in the years since 1990, the duty of care for
waste from April 1992 and the waste licensing scheme from May 1994
when the Waste Management Regulations 1994[1] took effect, but the
provisions in Part II of EPA 1990 have been amended by the Environment
Act 1995 (EA 1995).

Two main changes have been made. The first change reflects the broader 4.1.2
reorganisation of regulatory responsibilities, with the Scottish Environment
Protection Agency (SEPA) taking over the role of waste regulation authority
from local authorities. The second change is the introduction of a new
definition of "waste" in order to comply with the requirements of E.C. law.
The need to ensure that the Waste Framework Directive[2] is properly
implemented lies behind this change and a number of other features of the
new regime, and further measures, *e.g.* the Packaging Waste Directive (see
paras. 4.6.1–3) and proposals, *e.g.* the proposed landfill directive,[3] at E.C.
level have had and are likely to have a major impact on the law and practice
of waste disposal in this country.

---

* This chapter is based on the version provided for the previous edition by Paul Watchman of
  Freshfields, whose contribution is gratefully acknowledged. Sincere thanks also go to Mark
  Poustie for his very prompt and helpful comments on a draft of this chapter.
[1] S.I. 1994 No. 1056, amended by S.I.s 1995 Nos. 288 and 1950, and S.I. 1996 No. 1279;
  see also the Waste Management Regulations 1996 (S.I. 1996 No. 634), the Waste
  Management Licensing (Scotland) Regulations 1996 (S.I. 1996 No. 916), and the Waste
  Management (Miscellaneous Provisions) Regulations 1997 (S.I. 1997 No. 351).
[2] Directive 75/442, as amended by Directive 91/156.
[3] See (1997) 265 *ENDS Report* 40.

WASTE AND WASTE AUTHORITIES

Waste

4.2.1 The definition of waste originally given in section 75 of EPA 1990 has been replaced in order to comply with E.C. law. Initially, this was achieved through the Waste Management Regulations 1994, reg. 1(3) introducing the concept of "Directive waste", but now section 75 itself has been amended (EA 1995, Sched. 22, para. 88). Waste is now defined as "any substance or object in the categories set out in Schedule 2B to this Act which the holder discards or intends or is required to discard". As the categories in Schedule 2B[4] begin with "production or consumption residues not otherwise specified below" (paragraph 1) and end with "any materials, substances or products which are not contained in the above categories" (paragraph 16), the Schedule serves more to provide examples of waste than to assist in setting the limits of the definition.

4.2.2   The definition of waste is broad, and the fact that the material involved has some intrinsic value does not remove it from the category of being waste. The emphasis is firmly on considering the issue from the viewpoint of the person discarding or disposing of the material and not from that of the person acquiring it.[5] This is very clear from the European case law[6] and was the approach taken in the case law in the U.K. even before the new definition was introduced. For example, in *HL Friel & Son Ltd v. Inverclyde District Council*[7] it was held that ash and building rubble constituted waste even though they were said to be valuable resources for which customers were willing to pay an economic price.[8] Further guidance is given in Annex 2 to the Scottish Office Environment Department Circular 10/94,[9] where one general test (under para. 2.14) is that material should be regarded as waste once it "fall[s] out of the commercial cycle or chain of utility". The transfer of worn but functioning objects which are still usable (albeit after repair) for their original purpose is unlikely to constitute a discard of waste, whereas if a substance can only be put to

---

[4]   Added by EA 1995, Sched. 22, para. 95, following the E.C. measures above.

[5]   *cf.* the definition in the Finance Act 1996, s. 64.

[6]   Cases C–206/88 and C–207/88, *Vessoso and Zanetti* [1990] 1461 E.C.R. I–1461.

[7]   1995 S.L.T. 1310; the definition involved here was that under COPA 1974, s. 30, which included "any unwanted surplus substance arising from the application of any process".

[8]   See also *Kent C.C. v. Queensborough Rolling Mill Co.* (1990) 2 L.M.E.R. 28 where material from the demolition site of a former pottery was waste notwithstanding its subsequent use as infill material; *R. v. Rotherham M.B.C., ex p. Rankin* [1990] J.P.L. 503 where contaminated solvents were considered waste notwithstanding that after the removal of contaminants the solvents could be reused; *Meston Technical Services Ltd and Wright v. Warwickshire C.C.* [1995] Env. L.R. 380.

[9]   Department of the Environment Circular 11/94.

use after being subject to specialised waste recovery operations, then it is likely to be waste (under para. 2.33).

Controlled waste

Controlled waste is defined by section 75(4) of EPA 1990 as "household, 4.2.3 industrial and commercial waste or any such waste". Controlled waste is, therefore, a narrower term than "waste" itself, or "Directive waste".[10] Section 75(4) also differentiates between "household", "commercial" and "industrial" waste and "special" waste. Special waste is subject to stricter controls and the definition and controls are set out in the Special Waste Regulations 1996.[11]

Waste authorities

The structure of waste regulation in Scotland is very different from that 4.2.4 which operates in England and Wales. In Scotland, the functions of waste regulation authorities, waste disposal authorities and waste collection authorities were generally combined in the islands and district councils, but, following the Local Government etc. (Scotland) Act 1994 and EA 1995, the regulatory function now rests with SEPA and the other functions with the new unitary councils. Unlike England and Wales the statutory obligation to create local authority waste disposal companies does not apply to Scotland (EPA 1990, s. 32(12)).

National waste strategy

In addition to its direct regulatory function, SEPA is also responsible for 4.2.5 the production of a national waste strategy for Scotland, setting out its policies on the recovery and disposal of waste in Scotland (EPA 1990, s. 44B).[12] In particular, this strategy must include a statement of how SEPA intends to attain the objectives specified in Schedule 2A to EPA 1990,[13] which include ensuring that waste is recovered and disposed of without risk to water, air, soil, plants or animals, and without causing nuisance or adversely affecting the countryside. A further objective is the establishment of an integrated and adequate network of waste disposal installations, taking into account the best available technology not involving excessive costs and enabling waste to be disposed of in one of the nearest appropriate sites.

---

[10] See Tromans, *The Environment Acts 1990–1995* (1996), pp. 182–192.
[11] S.I. 1996 No. 972, as amended; the definition follows that adopted in E.C. law (Decision 94/904, following Directive 91/689, as amended by Directive 94/31).
[12] Added by EA 1995, s. 92.
[13] Added by EA 1995, Sched. 12.

Also listed as an objective is encouraging both the reduction of waste production and the recovery of waste by recycling, reuse, reclamation or use as an energy source. A draft strategy was issued by SEPA in March 1997,[14] setting out policies and objectives, but the targets included are indicative and voluntary, as opposed to the fixed targets in the White Paper for England and Wales.[15]

WASTE MANAGEMENT LICENCES

4.3.1 Waste disposal licences under COPA 1974 have been replaced by waste management licences (EPA 1990, s. 35). Similarities exist between waste management licensing and liquor and betting and gaming licensing, particularly in respect of the offences, *e.g.* knowingly permitting, and in respect of licensing criteria, such as a "fit and proper person".[16]

4.3.2 It is necessary under section 35 of EPA 1990 to obtain a waste management licence from SEPA to authorise the following:

(1) the treatment, keeping or disposal of any specified description of controlled waste in or on specified land ("site licence");

(2) the treatment or disposal of any specified description of controlled waste by means of specified mobile plant ("mobile plant licence").

Exempt activities

4.3.3 In view of the breadth of the definition of terms such as "waste" and "treatment" the basic provisions noted above could have the effect of requiring a waste management licence for many activities involving used materials which are not likely to give rise to environmental problems of the nature best dealt with by a full licensing scheme. Accordingly, Schedule 3 to the Waste Management Regulations 1994 lists almost 50 categories of "exempt activities", although, under regulation 18, in most cases there is a requirement for these activities to be registered. Subject to particular limits and conditions in each case, the activities listed include the temporary storage of waste where it is produced, some operations for recovering, reusing or recycling wastes, the burning of waste oils and even the burial of dead domestic pets. The terms of a site licence do not apply to activities relating to exempt materials.[17]

---

[14] *Draft National Waste Strategy: Scotland — A Blueprint for Progress 1997–2001* (1997).
[15] *Making Waste Work: A Strategy for Sustainable Waste Management in England and Wales,* Cm. 3040 (1995).
[16] See paras. 4.3.21–23.
[17] *London Waste Regulation Authority v. Drinkwater Sabey Ltd* [1997] Env. L.R. 137.

Waste management licence offences

Under section 33(1) of EPA 1990, it is an offence for any person to deposit 4.3.4
controlled waste, or knowingly to cause or permit controlled waste to be
deposited in or on any land unless a waste management licence authorising
the deposit is in force and the deposit is in accordance with the licence.
Similarly, it is an offence for any person to treat, keep, or dispose of
controlled waste or knowingly to cause or permit controlled waste to be
treated, kept or disposed of, in or on any land or by means of any mobile
plant except under or in accordance with a waste management licence. It is
also an offence to treat, keep or dispose of controlled waste in a manner
likely to cause pollution of the environment or harm to human health. This
last offence applies even in relation to exempt activities for which no licence
is required.

It will be apparent that in relation to the first limbs of the first two offences 4.3.5
the mere act of deposit, treatment, keeping or disposal is sufficient to attract
criminal liability. However, in relation to the second limbs of these offences
a test of knowledge must also be satisfied. In the case of the second limb of
the first offence where controlled waste is carried in and deposited from a
motorvehicle, constructive knowledge is attributed to the person who
controls the motorvehicle or is in a position to control the vehicle. In this
case that person is treated as knowingly causing the waste to be deposited
whether or not he gave instructions for that to be done. This, in effect,
reverses the onus of proof. However, it should be noted that apart from this,
and although the knowledge of an employee has, in some circumstances,
been imputed to the employer,[18] in Scots law in general the knowledge of
an employee who has sole charge of operations will not normally be imputed
to the employer.[19]

Knowledge relates to knowledge of fact not law. If there is a bona fide 4.3.6
belief that there was an appropriate waste management licence in force it is
likely that the courts would hold that an accused did not knowingly cause
or permit the deposit, etc., of controlled waste to take place at an unlicensed
site or an inappropriately licensed site. However, knowledge may be imputed
from wilful ignorance.[20] The onus rests on the prosecution to establish
"knowledge". In *Ashcroft v. Cambro Waste Products Ltd*[21] (which concerned
the offence of "knowingly permitting the deposit of controlled waste in
contravention of a waste disposal licence" under section 3 of COPA 1974)
it was held that the prosecution only had to prove that the company

---

[18] *Hawker v. Robinson* [1973] Q.B. 178.
[19] *Noble v. Heatley*, 1967 S.L.T. 26.
[20] *Smith of Maddiston Ltd v. McNab*, 1975 S.L.T. 86; *MacPhail v. Allan and Dey Ltd*, 1980
S.L.T. (Sh. Ct.) 136, *Knox v. Boyd*, 1941 J.C. 82.
[21] [1981] 1 W.L.R. 1349.

knowingly permitted the deposit of the controlled waste. It was unnecessary for the prosecution also to prove that the company knowingly permitted the alleged breach of the licence conditions.[22]

4.3.7   To "cause" means to give an express or positive order.[23] However, if the accused does something which sets off a natural chain of events this will be sufficient.[24] To "permit" means to give a general or particular licence or authorisation, but permission may be inferred from conduct.[25]

4.3.8   Although previously it had been held that a deposit is made when waste has reached its final resting place,[26] recent case law has made it clear that a broader definition of "deposit" applies, which can extend to the situation where waste will be moved at a later stage. This was the conclusion in *R. v. Metropolitan Stipendiary Magistrate, ex p. London Waste Regulation Authority,*[27] where the court concluded that there was no reason for limiting the term "deposit" to the placing of waste in its final resting place.[28] The temporary storage of waste in some circumstances will, however, be an exempt activity under the 1994 Regulations (see para. 4.3.3).

Penalties

4.3.9   The penalties for the above offences are:

(1)   summary conviction: the maximum is six months' imprisonment or a £20,000 fine, or both;

(2)   conviction on indictment: the maximum is two years' imprisonment (five years' imprisonment in respect of special waste) or an unlimited fine, or both.

The law does, therefore, provide for serious penalties, and directors, officers and senior employees can be held personally liable and fined or imprisoned (EPA 1990, s. 157). Although, in many cases, the penalties actually imposed are low, there are several instances of offenders being imprisoned.[29] Moreover, to the direct penalty must be added the possibility of licences

---

[22] See also *Shanks & McEwan (Teesside) Ltd v. Environment Agency, The Times,* January 28, 1997.

[23] *Price v. Cromack* [1975] 1 W.L.R. 988.

[24] *Lockhart v. N.C.B.,* 1981 S.L.T. 161; *Alphacell Ltd v. Woodward* [1972] A.C. 824. See also *National Rivers Authority v. Yorkshire Water Services Ltd* [1995] 1 A.C. 444.

[25] *Smith of Maddiston Ltd v. Macnab,* 1975 S.L.T. 86.

[26] *Leigh Land Reclamation Ltd v. Walsall M.B.C.* [1991] Crim. L.R. 298.

[27] [1993] 3 All E.R. 113.

[28] See also *Thames Waste Management Ltd v. Surrey C.C.* [1997] 2 C.L. 275, following *Scott v. Westminster Council* [1996] 2 C.L. 645 where the word "deposit" was construed in a different context.

[29] *e.g. H.M. Advocate v. McBride,* 1995 G.W.D. 25–1340; *London Waste Regulation Authority v. Gray* (1995) 241 *ENDS Report* 43.

being revoked if the person in question is not regarded as a fit and proper person following conviction,[30] and the effects of adverse publicity which may follow conviction and even prosecution.

Defences

If it is established that there has been a prima facie breach of section 33, three defences under section 33(7) are available to the accused to avoid criminal liability: 4.3.10

(1) that all reasonable precautions were taken and all due diligence was exercised to avoid the commission of the offence; or
(2) that the acts were done under instruction from an employer and the accused did not know, and had no reason to suppose, that the acts done constituted a section 33(1) offence; or
(3) that the acts were done in an emergency in order to avoid danger to the public and that as soon as reasonably practicable particulars of the acts were reported to SEPA.

The most contentious defence is the question whether the person charged with a section 33 offence took all reasonable precautions and exercised all due diligence to avoid the commission of the offence. It has been said that "all reasonable precautions" means setting up a system to ensure that things will not go wrong, whereas "all due diligence" means seeing that the system works properly. This is a question of fact, but it has been held that the larger the enterprise the higher the standard of care.[31]   4.3.11

In order to use the first defence the accused must show that he made all relevant investigations to ascertain whether a waste management licence was in force and whether the deposit was in accordance with the licence, and that he ascertained the exact nature of the waste to be deposited. The defence will also include ensuring that detailed written instructions were given to employees and contractors as to the deposit, treatment, storage and disposal of waste. This test cannot be satisfied by documentation alone.   4.3.12

The exercise of due diligence to avoid a section 33(1) offence being committed places a positive duty on the person to ensure that, in practice, an offence is not committed. This will involve the appropriate systems for monitoring, sampling and checking. It will also be insufficient simply to rely on paper documentation to establish this defence.   4.3.13

It has been held that a company took all reasonable precautions and exercised all due diligence when it had set up a careful and elaborate system of supervision,[32] but spot checks have been held to be insufficient to amount   4.3.14

---

[30] See paras. 4.3.22–23.
[31] *Garrett v. Boots Chemists Ltd* (unreported) July 16, 1980.
[32] *Tesco Supermarkets Ltd v. Nattrass* [1972] A.C. 153.

to all reasonable precautions and due diligence.[33] It is not enough to satisfy these tests either to provide in a document that the other party will comply with statutory requirements[34] or to carry out sampling which is inadequate.[35] In *Byrne v. Tudhope*[36] it was held that a publican had not exercised due diligence when she failed to draw an employee's attention to his duties under the Licensing (Scotland) Act 1976.

Civil liability for waste

4.3.15   Section 73(6) of EPA 1990 imposes civil liability on any person who deposits, treats or keeps waste in such a way as to commit an offence under section 33(1) or 63(2), which respectively relate to controlled and non-controlled waste. It is a defence, however, if the damage was due wholly to the fault of the person who suffered it or the damage was suffered by a person who voluntarily accepted the risk of the damage being caused. The defences noted at paragraph 4.3.10 in relation to the section 33 offences also apply. Liability under this provision does not prejudice any liability arising otherwise.

Clean-up powers of SEPA

4.3.16   SEPA can require the clean-up of a site where controlled waste has been unlawfully deposited (EPA 1990, s. 59). SEPA must give a minimum of 21 days' notice and must specify the steps to be taken to clean up the site. There is a right of appeal to the sheriff by way of summary application within the notification period. The sheriff may quash the notice if the appellant did not deposit or knowingly cause or knowingly permit the waste to be deposited, or modify the requirement or dismiss the appeal. If an appeal is lodged the SEPA action is suspended. A person who fails to comply with an effective clean-up order is liable on summary conviction to a fine not exceeding level 5 on the standard scale (currently £5,000), plus a daily fine of £500 for each day of continuing failure. SEPA may also clean up the site itself and recover expenses from the person who was required to do so. There is also provision for SEPA to take immediate action where it is necessary to do so to avoid pollution or to protect human life.

---

[33]   *Simmons v. Potter* [1975] R.T.R. 347.
[34]   *Riley v. Webb* [1987] Crim. L.R. 477; *Garrett v. Boots Chemists Ltd* (unreported) July 16, 1980; *Taylor v. Lawrence Fraser (Bristol) Ltd* (1977) 121 S.J. 157.
[35]   *Rotherham M.B.C. v. Raysun (U.K.)*, *The Times*, April 27, 1988.
[36]   1983 S.C.C.R. 337.

Application for licences

There are two types of waste management licences: site licences and mobile 4.3.17
plant licences. A site licence is granted to the occupier of the land, whereas
a mobile plant licence is granted to the operator of the plant. A mobile plant
licence is not site specific but allows the licensee to operate the specified
plant on any site.

In general, SEPA has four months in which to determine the application, 4.3.18
after which the application is deemed to have been rejected and the applicant
may appeal to the Secretary of State (EPA 1990, ss. 36(9), 43(1)). Details
of what must be contained in an application are prescribed in the Waste
Management Licensing Regulations 1994, regulation 2 and Schedule 1.
Consultations must be held with other regulatory bodies (the Health and
Safety Executive, and Scottish Natural Heritage if a site of special scientific
interest (SSSI) is likely to be affected) and with others with an interest in
the land (EPA 1990, ss. 36(4), (7), 36A) and particular investigations must
be carried out if the licence is likely to lead to certain discharges to
groundwater.[37]

Grounds for refusal of a licence

A waste management licence is not to be issued for land for which planning 4.3.19
permission is required unless there is an extant planning permission or an
established use certificate for that use of the land (EPA 1990, s. 36(2)). In
the case where only an established use certificate is available, SEPA may
refuse to grant a waste management licence if it is necessary to do so to
prevent "serious detriment to the amenities of the locality" (EPA 1990,
s. 36(3)(c)). When EPA 1990 came into force, existing waste disposal
licences under COPA 1974 became site licences subject to the increased
regulatory powers in the new Act.

Apart from the question of the existence of a planning permission or an 4.3.20
established use certificate, which is a question of fact, the grounds on which
SEPA may refuse a waste management licence may be grouped into two
categories: suitability of the applicant; and environmental risk. These
grounds call for an evaluation of suitability or environmental risk by SEPA
and are likely to be the subject of dispute.

Suitability of the applicant

Section 36(3) of EPA 1990 states that SEPA "shall not reject the application 4.3.21
if it is satisfied that the applicant is a fit and proper person". The concept of

---

[37] Waste Management Licensing Regulations 1994, reg. 15, giving effect to Directive 80/68.

a "fit and proper person" appears in several licensing systems, but in this context it is given a particular meaning.

4.3.22   Section 74 of EPA 1990 provides that a person is to be treated as not being a fit and proper person if it appears to SEPA that any of the following apply:

> (1) the applicant or another relevant person has been convicted of a relevant offence;
> (2) the management of the activities which are or are to be authorised by the licence is not or will not be in the hands of a technically competent person; or
> (3) the applicant has not made or has no intention of making or is in no position to make adequate financial provision to discharge the obligations imposed by the licence.

SEPA has discretion to treat an applicant as being a fit and proper person notwithstanding conviction for a relevant offence. The Waste Management Licensing Regulations 1994, as amended, provide a definition of "relevant offences" (reg. 3), and specify "technical competence" in terms of certification by the Waste Management Industry Training and Advisory Board, subject to transitional provisions for those with appropriate experience when the new rules took effect (regs. 4 and 5).

4.3.23   "Relevant persons" are defined by section 74(7) as persons who, at the time of commission of the relevant offence, fell into one of the following categories:

> (1) employee, or
> (2) partner of the applicant or licence holder, or
> (3) body corporate of which the applicant or licensee was director, secretary of similar officer,

who either has been convicted of the relevant offence, or was the director, secretary, or similar officer of another body corporate when a relevant offence for which that body corporate was convicted was committed.

Environmental risk

4.3.24 Where there is planning permission or an established use certificate in respect of the use of the land for waste management, and the applicant satisfies the eligibility test of being a fit and proper person, a presumption is raised in favour of the granting of a waste management licence. Section 36(3) of EPA 1990 states that in these circumstances SEPA must not reject the application unless it is satisfied that the prevention of environmental damage makes it necessary so to do.

4.3.25   The environmental risk tests differ depending on whether or not planning permission for the use has been granted or there is only an established use certificate: if the former, only the first two tests are applicable; if the latter, all three tests are applicable. The tests are based on the necessity to prevent pollution of the environment, harm to human health, and serious detriment to the amenities of the locality. The first two tests are based on the tests in the previous legislation, but pollution to the environment is wider than pollution to water, and harm to human health is more specific than danger to human health.

Licence conditions

SEPA is empowered to grant waste management licences "on such terms 4.3.26
and conditions as appear to SEPA to be appropriate" (EPA 1990, s. 35(3)). It is a criminal offence to fail to comply with a licence condition (EPA 1990, s. 33(6)). It is specifically provided that such conditions may relate to the activities authorised by the licence, the precautions to be taken, and the works to be carried out in connection with or in consequence of those activities. In addition, it is provided that conditions may encompass pre-development and post-development activities, matters beyond the immediate control of the applicant and, in respect of special waste, the treatment, keeping or disposal of that waste (EPA 1990, s. 35(4) and (5)).

The discretion of SEPA to impose conditions, is not unlimited. Section 4.3.27
35(6) of EPA 1990 empowers the Secretary of State to prescribe or proscribe waste management licence conditions by regulation.[38] The terms of all licences must cover the types and quantities of waste, technical requirements, security precautions, and the treatment method.[39] In *Guthrie v. SEPA*[40] a licence was held to be invalid because it did not state the quantities of waste to be deposited. Conditions may also be struck down by the courts as being *ultra vires*. In *Attorney-General's Reference (No. 2 of 1988)*[41] a condition requiring that an industrial incinerator used for the purpose of the disposal of hazardous waste "at all times be managed and operated so as to avoid creating a nuisance to the inhabitants of the neighbourhood" was struck down as being too wide in scope. Although the environmental risk tests have been widened by the Environmental Protection Act it is considered that this remains a correct statement of the law.

Variation of licence conditions

SEPA may, on its own initiative or on application, modify waste management 4.3.28
licence conditions (EPA 1990, s. 37(1)). However, if SEPA takes the

---

[38] *e.g.* no condition can be imposed solely to secure the health of persons at work and certain conditions are specified for any waste oil regeneration: 1994 Regulations, regs. 13–14.

[39] 1994 Regulations, reg. 19 and Sched. 4, para. 6, giving effect to the Waste Framework Directive 74/442 (see n. 2 above).

[40] 1997 G.W.D. 6–244.

[41] [1990] 1 Q.B. 77.

initiative its discretion is limited by the need to satisfy itself that the modification is desirable and is unlikely to require unreasonable expense on the part of the licence holder. Consultation requirements apply to variations in waste management licences and their conditions (EPA 1990, ss. 37(5), 37A).

4.3.29   SEPA may only consider a variation of management licence conditions to the extent which it considers is required for the purpose of ensuring that the activities authorised by the licence do not cause pollution of the environment or harm to human health or become seriously detrimental to the amenities of the locality (EPA 1990, s. 37(2)); and to the extent required by regulations (EPA 1990, s. 35(6)). The Waste Management Licensing Regulations 1994 include a requirement to review at least every four years every licence under which groundwater may be affected by certain substances (under regulation 15(9)).[42]

Supervision of licensed activities

4.3.30 SEPA is under a duty to supervise the activities authorised by the licence (EPA 1990, s. 42(1)). Its duty includes an obligation to take such steps as are necessary to ensure compliance with licence conditions, and that the activities authorised by the licence do not cause pollution of the environment or harm to human health, and do not become seriously detrimental to the amenities of the locality.

4.3.31   SEPA is empowered to authorise its officers in writing in the case of emergency to carry out necessary work (EPA 1990, s. 42(3)). The cost of such work is recoverable from the licence holder or from the former holder of a surrendered licence unless the licence holder or former licence holder can establish there was no emergency requiring such work or the expenditure was unnecessary (EPA 1990, s. 42(4)).

Revocation and suspension of a licence

4.3.32 SEPA may partially or fully revoke a licence if it appears to it that the holder of the licence has ceased to be a fit and proper person by reason of his having been convicted of a relevant offence, or that the continuation of the activities authorised by the licence would cause pollution of the environment of harm to human health or would be seriously detrimental to the amenities of the locality affected, and the pollution, harm or detriment cannot be avoided by modifying the conditions of the licence (EPA 1990, s. 38(1)).

---

[42] The requirement to hold such a review is not triggered by the proposed variation of a licence; see *Guthrie v. SEPA*, 1997 G.W.D. 6–244, where the absence of a clear time-scale in reg. 15 is noted.

Where SEPA considers that the holder of the licence has ceased to be a 4.3.33
fit and proper person by reason of the management of the activities having
ceased to be in the hands of a technically competent person, it may revoke
the licence in so far as it authorises the carrying out of the activities specified
in the licence or such of them as the authority specifies in revoking the
licence (EPA 1990, s. 38(2)).

SEPA may suspend a waste management licence if it appears that either 4.3.34
the licence holder has ceased to be a fit and proper person by reason of the
management of the activities authorised by the licence having ceased to be
in the hands of a technically competent person, or that serious pollution of
the environment or serious harm to human health has resulted, or is about
to be caused, by the activities to which the licence relates or the happening
or threatened happening of an event affecting those activities, and that
continuing to carry on those activities (or any of those activities) in the
circumstances will continue or, as the case may be, cause serious pollution
of the environment or serious harm to human health (EPA 1990, s. 38(6)).

There is clearly an overlap between the grounds for revocation and 4.3.35
suspension of a licence. However, it is clear from the greater stringency of
the environmental detriment tests that the object of suspension differs from
the object of revocation of a waste management licence. The option of
suspension is considered to be appropriate only in cases of utmost gravity,
emergencies, and circumstances of more than a temporary nature.

When a waste management licence is fully or partially revoked, the 4.3.36
activities covered by the licence, completely or to the extent specified by
the revocation, are no longer authorised, and any unauthorised waste
operations will be a criminal offence (see para. 4.3.4). However, SEPA can
specify that certain of the requirements imposed by the licence continue to
bind the licence holder (EPA 1990, s. 38(5)).

Where a waste management licence is suspended, the licence for the 4.3.37
specified activities ceases to have effect. During suspension, however, the
licence holder is bound to comply with the conditions of the licence, and
SEPA may require the licence holder to take such measures to deal with the
pollution or the harm as it considers necessary (EPA 1990, s. 38(8) and
(9)). Subject to consultation requirements, these measures can include
operations which the licence holder is not entitled to carry out, but there is
an obligation on the person whose consent is required to grant that consent
(EPA 1990, s. 38(9A)). In the absence of a reasonable excuse, failure to
carry out such required measures is an offence, and a court order requiring
compliance can be sought if SEPA is of the opinion that criminal proceedings
are likely to be an ineffectual remedy (EPA 1990, s. 38(13)).

Transfer of licences

A licence may be transferred to another person, and SEPA is obliged to 4.3.38
transfer a waste management licence if it is satisfied that the transferee is a

fit and proper person (EPA 1990, s. 40(4)). The procedure for transfer of a licence requires a joint application for transfer to be made in the prescribed form[43] to SEPA by the licence holder and the proposed transferee, accompanied by the licence itself, and the specified fee (EPA 1990, s. 40).

Surrender of licences.

4.3.39   EPA 1990 imposes stricter controls than the Control of Pollution Act 1974 in respect of the surrender of waste management licences. Whereas under the 1974 Act it was possible to surrender a waste disposal licence at any time to the authority, under the 1990 Act a site licence may be surrendered to SEPA only if it accepts the surrender (EPA 1990, s. 39(1)). SEPA will accept the surrender of a site licence only if it is satisfied that the condition of the land arising from the treatment, keeping or disposal of waste is unlikely to cause pollution or harm to human health (EPA 1990, s. 39(6)).[44]

The procedure for licence surrender

4.3.40   Application for the surrender of a licence must be made by the licence holder, who must provide the prescribed information and evidence.[45] On receiving an application for surrender of a site licence, SEPA must inspect the land (EPA 1990, s. 39(4)). SEPA has discretion to require the licence holder to provide further information or evidence (EPA 1990, s. 39(4)). SEPA must determine whether the condition of the land is likely or unlikely, in consequence of the treatment, keeping or disposal of waste, to cause pollution of the environment or harm to human health. If SEPA proposes to accept the surrender, it must refer the proposal to the planning authority and consider any representations which it makes. An application is deemed to be rejected if not determined within three months.

Certificate of completion

4.3.41   If the surrender of the licence is accepted by SEPA, it is obliged to issue a certificate of completion stating that it is satisfied that the condition of the land is unlikely to cause pollution of the environment or harm to human health. On the issue of the certificate of completion, the site licence ceases to have effect (EPA 1990, s. 39(9)).

4.3.42   It should be noted that the issue of a certificate of completion will not release waste disposal companies or purchasers of reinstated land from civil

---

[43]   1994 Regulations, reg. 2 and Sched. 1.
[44]   See *Waste Management Paper No. 26A: Landfill Completion* (DOE, 1993).
[45]   1994 Regulations, reg. 2 and Sched. 1.

liability under the common law of nuisance or negligence, or from liability for criminal offences or clean-up costs under other environmental legislation, such as the new provisions on contaminated land (see Chapter 6).

Licence fees

In accordance with the polluter pays principle, there is a scheme for licence fees and charges in connection with waste licence applications. SEPA is to draw up a scheme of charges, subject to the Secretary of State's approval, and, in giving approval, the Secretary of State is to have regard to the desirability of ensuring that the charges will be sufficient to enable SEPA to recover the full costs of regulation (EA 1995, ss. 41–42). 4.3.43

Appeals

Given the powers of SEPA to regulate the granting of waste management licences and its power to vary, revoke or suspend licences, it is important that there are rights of appeal against the decisions of SEPA to an independent body. Section 43 of EPA 1990 provides for appeal to the Secretary of State by licence holders, applicants for licences and proposed transferees. Appeal may be made against the rejection or deemed rejection of an application for a licence or for a modification of the conditions of a licence, against the imposition of licence conditions, the modification of licence conditions, the suspension or revocation of a licence, and the rejection or deemed rejection of an application for the transfer of a licence. 4.3.44

The Secretary of State may appoint a person to hear any matter on the appeal but retain the power of final decision, or may delegate the decision to a person appointed by him (EPA 1990, s. 43(2A), applying EA 1995, s. 114 and Sched. 20). In England and Wales appeals have been delegated to the Planning Inspectorate, but no such move has been made in Scotland. The appeal may be made by written representation, or may, and must if a party so requests, take the form of a hearing which may be held, wholly or partly, in private (EPA 1990, s. 43(2)). SEPA is bound by the decisions of the Secretary of State or the person empowered by the Secretary of State to determine the appeal (EPA 1990, s. 43(3)). The Waste Management Licensing Regulations 1994 specify the form and time-limits for appeals (regs. 6–9). 4.3.45

The effect of appealing to the Secretary of State against the decision of SEPA varies depending on the circumstance of appeal. In general, where the appeal is against the modification of licence conditions or the revocation of a licence, the decision of SEPA is ineffective until the appeal is either dismissed or withdrawn. However, lodging an appeal has no effect on the decision where the notice effecting the modification or revocation states that, in SEPA's opinion, it is necessary, for the purpose of preventing or minimising pollution of the environment or harm to human health, that the appeal should not suspend the effect of the appeal pending determination. 4.3.46

Where the appeal is against the suspension of a licence, making an appeal similarly has no effect on the decision of SEPA.

4.3.47   There is provision for compensation where SEPA has acted unreasonably in suspending the licence or in excluding the operation of the general principle that its decision is to have no effect while the appeal is being considered, and there is provision for arbitration in the event of dispute, whether as to entitlement to compensation or to the amount of compensation (EPA 1990, s. 43(7)).

Licence application offences

4.3.48   It is an offence in connection with applying for a licence, for modification of licence conditions, for the surrender of a licence, or for the transfer of a licence for a person knowingly to make a statement which is false in any material particular or recklessly to make any statement which is false in any material particular (EPA 1990, s. 44).[46]

PUBLIC REGISTERS RELATING TO WASTE

4.4.1   It is the duty of SEPA under section 64 of the Environmental Protection Act 1990 to maintain a public register containing prescribed information giving particulars of or relating to licences granted, applications for licences, applications for licence modifications, notifications of licence modifications, notices of revocation or suspension of licences, notices imposing requirements on licence holders, appeals relating to decisions, certificates of completion, conviction of licence holders, discharge of SEPA's functions in respect of supervision of licensed operators, directions given to SEPA by the Secretary of State, and such other matters relating to the treatment, keeping or disposal of waste or pollution of the environment as may be prescribed, and a statement of exclusion of confidential information under section 66. The relevant prescriptions are made in regulations 10 and 11 of the Waste Management Regulations 1994.

4.4.2   There are two categories of excluded information: information affecting national security (EPA 1990, s. 65) and commercially confidential information (EPA 1990, s. 66). The exclusion of commercially confidential information is limited by the ability of the Secretary of State to override commercial confidentiality in the public interest (EPA 1990, s. 66(7)). There is a right of appeal to the Secretary of State against the refusal of SEPA to treat information as being commercially confidential (EPA 1990, s. 66(1)).

---

[46]   As substituted by EA 1995, Sched. 19, para. 4.

If, on an application for information to be treated as being commercially 4.4.3
confidential and, hence, excluded from the register, SEPA does not make a
determination within 14 days, the information is deemed to be commercially
confidential (under section 66(3)). It should be noted that the protection against
the entry of information in the public register lasts for only four years unless
the person who provided the information applies for the exclusion to continue
to operate and SEPA determines that the information remains commercially
confidential (EPA 1990, s. 66(8)). Information is only commercially
confidential if, in relation to any individual or person, that information, if
contained in the register, would prejudice to an unreasonable degree the
commercial interests of that individual or person (EPA 1990, s. 66(11)).

DUTY OF CARE FOR WASTE

The most important innovation in Part II of EPA 1990 is the duty of 4.5.1
care for waste contained in section 34. The intention is that this duty
should ensure that everyone within the waste chain has to take some
responsibility for what others are doing, so that the law becomes, in a
sense, self-policing.

Who is liable?

The duty of care applies to each stage of the waste chain, from production 4.5.2
to final disposal, or "from cradle to grave". The categories of persons liable
under the duty are any person involved in the import, production, carriage,
keeping, treatment, disposal or brokerage, provided the broker has control
of the waste. Households are exempt from the duty of care in respect of
their own household waste (EPA 1990, s. 34(2)).

What is the duty?

The duty of care relates to controlled waste, and the obligation on those 4.5.3
liable under this duty is to take all such measures in their particular capacities
as are reasonable in the circumstances:

(1) to prevent anyone else committing an offence under section 33
    of the Act (the deposit, treatment or keeping of waste without a
    licence or in breach of the conditions in a licence);
(2) to prevent the escape of waste from his control or that of any
    other person; and
(3) to ensure that, on transfer, waste is transferred to an authorised
    person and that the waste is accompanied by a written descrip-
    tion of the waste sufficient to enable other persons to avoid con-
    travention of section 33 and to comply with the duty of care in
    respect of the escape of waste.

Regulations specify the details of the documentation to be provided and kept,[47] but this requirement is simplified by an amendment to the Act to enable the transfer of waste in stages or a series of transfers to be treated as a single transaction (EPA 1990, s. 34(4A)[48]).

4.5.4   Breach of the duty of care is a criminal offence (EPA 1990, s. 34(6)).

Code of practice

4.5.5   The Secretary of State is obliged, after consultation with representative bodies, to prepare and issue a code of practice, which must be laid before Parliament. The current code was issued in March 1996. The purpose of the code of practice is to provide practical guidance on how to discharge the duty of care, and it is admissible in evidence (EPA 1990, s. 34(7)–(11)). Breach of the code is not, in itself, a criminal offence, but the court must take account of the code in determining any question arising in proceedings where it appears to the court that the code is relevant to that question (EPA 1990, s. 34(10)).

4.5.6   The code of practice gives step-by-step advice on the identification and description of waste, management of waste, transfer of waste to an authorised person, receiving and holding waste, and monitoring compliance. Waste producers are expected to do more than merely rely on assurances from those carrying and disposing of their waste that it will be dealt with in an authorised and safe manner. The code also provides a useful checklist, guidance on how to obtain expert help and advice, and a model waste-transfer note.

4.5.7   It is important to emphasise that compliance with the guidance provided by the code may not be sufficient to discharge the duty to take all reasonable measures in the circumstances, as particular circumstances may dictate that more onerous or less onerous steps should be taken to comply with the duty. Therefore, it may be possible for the prosecution to establish that although the accused complied with the code in all respects he did not comply with the duty of care.[49]

4.5.8   The duty of care applies to waste producers, etc., in their own capacity, and its precise requirements will depend on the circumstances. If it is fully observed, then, at each stage in the waste production/disposal chain, adequate measures should be taken to ensure that waste is properly described, consigned and handled until it reaches an appropriate final disposal. Research suggests, however, that the duty is widely ignored.[50]

---

[47]   Environmental Protection (Duty of Care) Regulations 1991 (S.I. 1991 No. 2839).

[48]   Added by the Deregulation and Contracting Out Act 1994, s. 33.

[49]   See "Dicing with Death at the Landfill Face" (1996) 258 *ENDS Report* 21, discussing a series of successful prosecutions for waste offences in which it is arguable that the convicted carrier had followed the code (p. 23).

[50]   See Poustie, "A Load of Rubbish? The Duty of Care for Waste Revisited" (1997) 60 S.P.E.L. 28.

PACKAGING WASTE

The problems arising from the disposal of waste can be reduced if the volume 4.6.1
of waste to be disposed of is itself reduced. In application of this basic idea,
the European Community has taken an initiative aimed at reducing the
volume of waste, turning its attention to packaging waste. Directive 94/62
on packaging and packaging waste calls on Member States to take measures
to prevent the formation of packaging waste (under Article 4) but, more
specifically, to ensure that a large proportion of such waste is recovered,
reused or recycled (under Article 6). Targets are set for the overall percentage
of such waste, which must be recovered within five years (between 50 per
cent and 65 per cent by weight), with further targets for the proportion
within that which must be recycled.

Wide powers to introduce schemes to promote or secure an increase in 4.6.2
the reuse, recovery or recycling of products and materials are contained in
EA 1995, ss. 93 to 95, and have led to the Producer Responsibility
Obligations (Packaging Waste) Regulations 1997.[51] These complex
Regulations impose obligations on producers of more than the specified
weight of packaging (50 tonnes per year) to register with SEPA and to meet
their recovery targets, determined by formulae according to their capacity
(manufacturer, convertor, packer/filler, importer, wholesaler or seller) and
the nature of their supply. A certificate of compliance must be produced to
demonstrate that the obligations have been met. However, producers are
exempt from individual registration if they are members of a registered
scheme which undertakes to meet the recovery obligations of all its members.
It is expected that most producers will satisfy their obligations through
membership of such schemes, which will be subject to scrutiny on
competition grounds. Non-compliance with the requirements imposed by
the Regulations can lead to fines and the cancellation of the registration of
individuals or schemes.

The Regulations came into force in March 1997, and the producers' 4.6.3
recovery obligations take effect in 1998 in most cases, but in 2000 for
wholesalers. Charities are exempt from these obligations.

LANDFILL TAX

A further way of discouraging the production of waste is to use economic 4.7.1
mechanisms. The more strict regulation of waste management by itself has
led to significant increases in the cost of disposing of waste, but a more
direct financial approach has been taken by the introduction of the landfill
tax. It is the operator of the landfill site who is liable to pay landfill tax on

---

[51] S.I. 1997 No. 648.

the waste disposed of at the site, but obviously this cost is passed on to the producers of the waste, encouraging them to consider ways to prevent the production of the waste, of recovering it in some way or of disposing of it by other means.

4.7.2 The Finance Act 1996 introduced the landfill tax as from October 1996. The tax is administered by the Customs and Excise and is payable at two rates (under section 42): £7 per tonne and £2 per tonne for "qualifying material" — inactive or inert material as defined in the Landfill Tax (Qualifying Materials) Order 1996.[52] Under a detailed scheme, tax credits are available to operators which make contributions to bodies the objects of which include environmental protection and which use the funds for any of the specified purposes.[53]

4.7.3 Certain materials are exempt from the tax under sections 43 to 45, including certain dredgings and materials produced by mining and quarrying operations; pet cemeteries are also exempt. A broader exemption under sections 43A and 43B,[54] applies to the disposal of materials as part of the remediation of contaminated land where the work has been certified for this purpose. The precise extent of this final exemption has been the subject of dispute between the construction industry and Customs and Excise, particularly in relation to when the (exempt) clearance of a site ends and the (non-exempt) construction work begins.[55]

CARRIAGE OF WASTE

4.8.1 Subject to specified exceptions, any person who transports controlled waste to or from any place in Great Britain in the course of any business of his or otherwise with a view to a profit must be registered to do so.[56]

4.8.2 Section 1 of the Control of Pollution (Amendment) Act 1989 makes it an offence to transport controlled waste without being registered. It is not an offence, however, to transport controlled waste between different places within the same premises. The import or export of waste is separately regulated.[57] Under the Controlled Waste (Regulation of Carriers and Seizure of Vehicles) Regulations 1991[58] SEPA is required to establish and maintain a register of waste carriers and to set out the basis on which the registration system operates, provide guidance on the seizure of vehicles used for fly-

---

[52] S.I. 1996 No. 1528.
[53] Finance Act 1996, s. 53; Landfill Tax Regulations 1996 (S.I. 1996 No. 1527), regs. 30–36.
[54] Added by the Landfill Tax (Contaminated Land) Order 1996 (S.I. 1996 No. 1529).
[55] (1997) 265 *ENDS Report* 9, 266 *ENDS Report* 16, 268 *ENDS Report* 38.
[56] Registration applies to the carrier, not to the vehicles used: *Cosmick Transport Services v. Bedfordshire C.C.* [1996] Env. L.R. 78.
[57] Transfrontier Shipment of Waste Regulations 1994 (S.I. 1994 No. 1137).
[58] S.I. 1991 No. 1624; see also Scottish Office Environment Department Circular 18/1991.

tipping and on the enforcement of registration of waste carriers and the seizure of vehicles.

The duty of care requires that if controlled waste is transferred it must 4.8.3 be transferred only to an authorised person. "Authorised person" includes any person registered with SEPA or the Environment Agency as a carrier of controlled waste, and any person who is exempt by virtue of regulations made under section 1(3) of the Control of Pollution (Amendment) Act 1989. Regulation 2 of the 1991 Regulations sets out persons exempt for the purposes of section 1(3): these include charities and voluntary organisations, waste collection authorities, some rail and ferry operators and the producers of the waste, except in the case of building and demolition waste.

CLOSED LANDFILLS

One aspect of contaminated land which attracted particular concern during 4.9.1 the 1980s was the hazards posed by old landfill sites. In response to this, EPA 1990, under section 61, contained provisions imposing on local authorities a duty to inspect their land for dangers to the environment or human health created by such sites. If such hazards were found, the authority was to take remedial action and recover the costs of this from the current owner of the land (unless the surrender of the waste management licence for the site had been formally accepted). It has been accepted, however, that such sites should be treated in the same ways as other forms of contaminated land, and the Environment Act 1995 repealed the relevant provisions without their ever coming into force. Closed landfills will, therefore, be treated in the same way as other contaminated land once the measures in the 1995 Act come into force (see Chapter 6).

CHAPTER FIVE

INTEGRATED POLLUTION CONTROL

INTRODUCTION

5.1.1 The need for a broad approach to the problems of pollution affecting several environmental media at once has been recognised for some time as requiring an "holistic" approach to regulation of human polluting activity. The Environmental Protection Act 1990 (EPA 1990), as amended by the Environment Act 1995 (EA 1995), contains in its provisions on integrated pollution control (IPC) the most significant British legislative effort so far to achieve a comprehensive and all-embracing system of control over all (or at least most) aspects of certain potentially polluting processes. The EPA 1990 is substantially prompted by E.C. law, such as the Air Framework Directive[1] and allows future E.C. rules and international agreements to be carried into effect in the United Kingdom (EPA 1990, s. 156), for example by prescribing emission standards which must then be complied with by operators and adopted by enforcing authorities (EPA 1990, s. 3).

5.1.2 IPC is introduced by Part I of EPA 1990 and, in general terms, deals with processes in which the discharges affecting all environmental media are regulated. Both fixed and mobile plant can fall under IPC. Part I also brings in new provisions for air pollution control, which is dealt with more fully in Chapter 2. Many of the rules apply to both, and in this chapter, while the provisions of the Act described also relate to air pollution control in many cases, air pollution control is not considered in detail.

5.1.3 IPC deals with some of the situations formerly regulated under the Control of Pollution Act 1974 (COPA 1974). Areas covered by IPC were, in the past, also regulated in some cases by other statutes such as the Alkali etc. Act 1906. Following the expiry of the transitional periods during which the operators of existing processes had to apply for IPC authorisation, the IPC system now covers all processes intended to be within its ambit, other than a few which (in 1997) were still in the course of receiving their first IPC authorisation. IPC does not, however, affect the final disposal of controlled waste by deposit on land. Such disposal is covered by EPA 1990, Pt. II (see Chapter 4).

---

[1] Directive 84/360.

IPC in Practice

In Scotland, there are approximately 200 processes covered by IPC. This 5.1.4
system of IPC has now been established for five years, and is increasingly
well understood within industries to which it applies. The change to the
regulatory arrangements brought in by the establishment of the Scottish
Environment Protection Agency (SEPA) should result in a consistent
application of the system, and by bringing all the former authorities together,
should produce a more coherent organisation for the regulated industries to
deal with. The fact that SEPA, unlike the Environment Agency in England
and Wales, also regulates Part B processes under EPA 1990, as well as the
more complex Part A processes (see para. 5.3.2) has made the overall system
of regulation easier. SEPA officers are generally prepared to discuss
processes which may require regulation under EPA 1990, Part I in advance
of their coming into operation, and can produce drafts of authorisations. At
present, the fees charged by SEPA do not cover the cost of regulation. Most
variations (see paras. 5.5.1–11) have, in practice, taken place through the
voluntary mechanism (EPA 1990, s. 11) after discussion with SEPA. There
have been relatively few appeals and notices served in Scotland.

Integrated pollution prevention and control

The European Community has only relatively recently adopted a broadly 5.1.5
equivalent system to U.K. IPC, under the Directive 96/61 on integrated
pollution prevention and control (IPPC) which came into force on October
14, 1996. Member States must implement the Directive within three years
of that date, *i.e.* by October 14, 1999. Action to implement the Directive in
the United Kingdom is still to take place, and as such, a general discussion
of the changes which IPPC will bring is premature. In very general terms,
however, IPPC will cover a more extensive list of activities, and the concept
of "pollution" is extended to the effects of noise, heat and vibration, as well
as the effects of the discharge of physical substances. IPPC is focused on
installations rather than processes, and on inputs as much as outputs. It
covers the efficient use of energy, raw materials, noise, minimisation of
waste, safety, and points toward the need for future sustainability. Existing
installations must come into conformity with the new requirements by 2005.

SEPA — THE ENFORCING AUTHORITY

SEPA, established under the Part I of EA 1995, is now the sole agency 5.2.1
responsible for enforcing IPC in Scotland. It has subsumed the functions
formerly carried out by Her Majesty's Industrial Pollution Inspectorate
(HMIPI), and the River Purification Authorities (RPAs).

The costs of the enforcing authority are met from fees charged to those 5.2.2
regulated. Separate fees are charged for initial applications and applications

for variations, together with a "subsistence charge" paid annually to cover the costs of monitoring, etc. Separate fees are charged for each component of a process. Failure to pay the fees on time can, if the failure continues after a notice has been served, be followed by suspension or revocation of an authorisation.[1a]

THE BASICS OF IPC

5.3.1   The basic principle is contained in EPA 1990, s. 6(1) which states that no person shall, after certain prescribed dates, carry on a *prescribed process* except in accordance with the *conditions* of an *authorisation* granted by an enforcing authority. To do otherwise is an offence under section 23(1).

What processes come under IPC?

5.3.2   For the purpose of Part I of EPA 1990, processes are prescribed by the Environmental Protection (Prescribed Processes and Substances) Regulations 1991 (EP(PPS)R 1991), as amended.[2] Schedule 1 to the Regulations divides processes into six chapters covering broad industrial areas, each with subdivisions. Each process is categorised as either Part A or Part B. Part A processes are subject to IPC, but Part B processes are subject only to air pollution control. This chapter, therefore, does not cover Part B processes, although the rules are similar. Both Part A and B processes are regulated in Scotland by SEPA. Schedules 4, 5 and 6 to EP(PPS)R 1991 specify the prescribed substances whose release into the environmental media of air or water and on to land respectively must comply with the conditions of an authorisation. Schedule 2 to the Regulations deals with their interpretation. In particular, if Part A and B processes are carried on together, the whole operation falls under IPC. There are very limited exemptions under regulation 4 for vehicles, domestic activity and for cases where the amounts of substances released are trivial.

When does IPC apply to a process?

5.3.3   The dates at which the new IPC system came into force for various processes are laid down in Part III of Schedule 3 to EP(PPS)R 1991. All new processes were covered by IPC from April 1, 1992.

5.3.4   For existing processes, applications for authorisation had to be made in accordance with the timetable in paragraph 18 of Schedule 3 to the

---

[1a] Environmental Licences (Suspension and Revocation) Regulations 1996 (S.I. 1996 No. 508).

[2] S.I. 1991 No. 472, as amended by S.I. 1991 No. 836, S.I. 1992 No. 614, S.I. 1993 Nos. 1749 and 2405, S.I. 1994 Nos. 1271 and 1329, S.I. 1995 No. 3247, and S.I. 1996 No. 2678.

Regulations. The dates vary from April 1, 1992 for furnaces or boilers over 50 megawatts, to May 31, 1996 for processes under Chapter 6 of the Regulations, including paper and pulp manufacturing and coating. The date of compliance, however, is the date at which application for authorisation is refused or granted, so existing plant can continue to operate under any earlier provisions or licences after the dates on the timetable, provided application for their authorisation under IPC has been made at the time laid down (EP(PPS)R 1991, reg. 19).

An existing process is one which was carried on at some time in the 12   5.3.5
months up to April 1, 1992, or was to be carried on at works under construction or contracted for before April 1, 1992, and which has not ceased to be carried on for a period of 12 months between April 1, 1991 and the authorisation date (EP(PPS)R 1991, regs. 20 and 21).

AUTHORISATIONS

Obtaining an authorisation

The rules covering applications for authorisation are contained in Part I of   5.4.1
Schedule 1 to EPA 1990 and in the Environmental Protection (Applications, Appeals and Registers) Regulations 1991 (EP(AAR)R 1991), as amended.[3] Regulation 2 specifies the very full information which the applicant must supply. The enforcing authority can require further information to be furnished under EPA 1990, Sched. 1, para. 1. Failure to furnish information means that SEPA may refuse to proceed with the application. The appropriate fee must be paid with the application (EPA 1990, s. 6(2)).

Publicity is an important part of the scheme of EPA 1990. All applications   5.4.2
for authorisation must be advertised in the press,[4] and full details of any application with any further information supplied by the applicant are kept in a register which is open for inspection by the public (EPA 1990, s. 20). There is a general exemption from publicity for information affecting national security (EPA 1990, s. 21), but commercially confidential information has only limited protection (EPA 1990, s. 22). When applying, a claim must be made for confidentiality which is determined by SEPA or on appeal by the Secretary of State. If SEPA does not make a determination on commercial confidentiality within 14 days of the application, it is treated as having determined that the information is confidential, and it will be excluded from the register. If SEPA considers that information obtained otherwise than from the applicant or from the holder of an authorisation

---

[3] S.I. 1991 No. 507, as amended by S.I. 1991 No. 836, S.I. 1992 No. 614, S.I. 1993 No. 1749, S.I. 1994 No. 1271, S.I. 1996 Nos. 667, 979 and 2678, and EA 1995, s. 120 and Sched. 2.
[4] EP(AAR)R 1991, reg. 5.

might be confidential, it must notify the person to whom it relates, and give him an opportunity to object to its inclusion in the register (EPA 1990, s. 22(4)). There are only 21 days in which to appeal to the Secretary of State against a determination that information is not to be treated as confidential. The Secretary of State can direct that certain information, even if commercially confidential, will be included in the registers (EPA 1990, s. 22(7)). Time-limits affect confidential information excluded from the register; after four years, commercially confidential information will cease to be treated as such, unless the person who gave it applies to SEPA for it to remain confidential (EPA 1990, s. 22(8)).

5.4.3   While there is no requirement in the Act for holders of authorisations to have particular qualifications, SEPA must not grant authorisations unless it considers that the applicant will be able to comply with the conditions which would be imposed (EPA 1990, s. 6(4)). Previous difficulties or even convictions may not be relevant in deciding this, and the applicant for an authorisation is not required to be a "fit and proper person".[5]

5.4.4   As well as publicity by advertisement, there is a considerable list of persons and bodies who must be consulted about any application.[6]

Determination by the Secretary of State

5.4.5   The Secretary of State can issue directions to SEPA under section 6(5) of EPA 1990 requiring it to grant or refuse an authorisation. He can also call in an application for his decision (EPA 1990, Sched. 1, para. 3) in which case the applicant can require the Secretary of State either to hold a local inquiry or to let the applicant appear before a person appointed by the Secretary of State to state his case.[7]

Time-limits for decision

5.4.6   SEPA normally has four months in which to determine an application from the date it was received. The applicant can agree to a longer period (EPA 1990, Sched. 1, para. 5) unless the Secretary of State intervenes. If SEPA does not do so, the applicant can notify SEPA in writing that he is taking this as a deemed refusal, and appeal to the Secretary of State. If commercial confidentiality or national security matters have to be decided, the four-month period starts from the date on which those matters are finally disposed of.[8]

---

[5]   Contrast paras. 4.3.21–23.
[6]   EP(AAR)R 1991, reg. 4, implementing Sched. 1.
[7]   *ibid.* reg. 8.
[8]   Environmental Protection (Authorisation of Processes) (Determination Periods) Order 1991 (S.I. 1991 No. 513) (as amended by S.I. 1994 No. 2847), para. 2.

OUTLINE IPC AUTHORISATION PROCEDURE

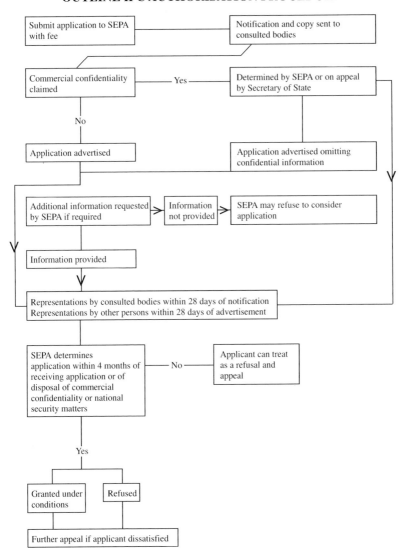

Conditions in authorisations

All authorisations are granted subject to conditions. These are critical for 5.4.7 the practical implementation of the system of IPC. Conditions, once imposed, however, do not last indefinitely. SEPA must review them not less often than every four years (EPA 1990, s. 6(6)). The Secretary of State may alter this four-year period by regulation (EPA 1990, s. 6(7)).

5.4.8   If a condition requires information to be supplied to the enforcing authority, application can be made for the information to be treated as commercially confidential, and thus be omitted from the public registers (EPA 1990, s. 22(2)).

5.4.9   Conditions can be considered in four categories.

(1)   The general condition requiring the process to be carried on using the best available techniques not entailing excessive cost (BATNEEC):

(a)   to prevent the release of prescribed substances, or to keep this to a minimum and render the released substances harmless;

(b)   to render harmless any other substance which might cause harm if released (EPA 1990, s. 7(4)).

This condition does not apply to matters where specific conditions regulate the operation of the process (EPA 1990, s. 7(6)).

(2)   Such specific conditions as SEPA considers appropriate in order to achieve the objectives in section 7(2) of EPA 1990, *i.e.*:

(a)   that BATNEEC will be used in carrying on the process;

(b)   to comply with E.C. or international law;

(c)   to comply with limits, standards, etc., set by the Secretary of State under other relevant enactments (EPA 1990, s. 7(12));

(d)   to comply with plans made by the Secretary of State under EPA 1990, s. 3(5).

(3)   Such conditions as the Secretary of State directs under section 7(3) of EPA 1990.

(4)   Such other conditions as SEPA thinks appropriate.

Best available techniques not entailing excessive cost (BATNEEC)

5.4.10 An understanding of BATNEEC is essential to understanding the role of conditions for IPC. Some explanation of both parts of the expression is required, which takes us back to the Dangerous Substances Directive,[9] which refers to the "best available technology". Use of the U.K. phrase "best available techniques" is intended to indicate that more than technology is

---

[9]   Directive 76/464.

required. A summary of the official view on the interpretation of BATNEEC appears in the Department of the Environment publication *Integrated Pollution Control — A Practical Guide*, section 7 (version issued in March 1996). This deals, in particular, with the position of existing plants.

"Techniques" refers to the plant or apparatus used in carrying on the 5.4.11
process, and also to other matters such as the way in which plant or apparatus is used and the staff employed, their level of training and supervision, and their methods of work. Items such as these can therefore be specified in a condition in an authorisation.

"Best available" indicates, first, that the technique is to be the most 5.4.12
effective in preventing, rendering harmless or minimising the emission of prescribed and other harmful substances, and, secondly, that the techniques, or more probably technology, are generally accessible. If the technology is available only from a monopoly supplier overseas, it is still "available", but the contrary would be the case if it could not be obtained by customers in general — for example, because it was a defence secret. It may be that two or more techniques are equally effective and, if so, each of them qualifies as the "best".

The phrase "not entailing excessive cost" naturally provides scope for 5.4.13
argument. "Excessive" is always a matter of opinion. It appears that there is a presumption that the best available techniques are to be used, but the cost to industry of upgrading existing plants is relevant where plants are to be upgraded in any case over a period of time. If an upgrade is to happen in the near future, it may well result in "excessive cost" to require the operator to bring the upgrade forward.

Whether or not an operator is permitted to use a cheaper technique which 5.4.14
is less effective is something which the applicant must negotiate with SEPA, and this will be a matter of degree. In some cases a technique at half the cost which is, for example, 75 per cent as effective as the best available, may be acceptable if the danger is not very great. In other cases, the substances involved may be considered so dangerous that the extra cost of the "best available" technique may be inescapable.

SEPA must also consider other factors, for example the length of time a 5.4.15
technique will be in use. An existing plant may not be capable of adaptation to use the best available techniques except at great expense, but the operator may intend to replace it in any case in a few years' time, when upgrading can readily take place. In such cases, the applicant may try to persuade the inspector that the existing arrangements should be allowed to continue. The economic position of an industry can apparently be taken into account: see *Integrated Pollution Control — A Practical Guide*, section 7.

Guidance

Under section 7(11) of EPA 1990, SEPA is obliged to have regard to guidance 5.4.16
issued by the Secretary of State. The current guidance notes issued by the

Environment Agency in England and Wales, but also used by SEPA, are *not* statutory guidance within the meaning of section 7(11), but these are of great practical importance in any negotiation with the enforcing authority. There are three types of guidance: (a) general guidance for certain industrial sectors; (b) process guidance offering more specific guidance for particular processes; and (c) technical guidance on matters such as monitoring, abatement and the best practicable environmental option.

5.4.17   The general guidance notes issued so far correspond to the first five chapters in Schedule 1 to EP(PPS)R 1992 and list the international obligations and E.C. directives applicable to those chapters, summarise the types of processes falling under the subdivisions of the chapters, and the reason for prescribing them. The notes also contain emission limits and advice on the requirement for sampling and monitoring.

5.4.18   More important are the process guidance notes which deal with various individual processes within the chapters of EP(PPS)R 1991, for example notes on the incineration of clinical, municipal and chemical waste. The notes contain details of the level of releases that may be permitted, and the practical requirements to achieve BATNEEC. Details of typical types of plant used and their relative advantages and disadvantages are given, together with notes on the techniques that may be used to avoid pollution, and for compliance monitoring. The notes also contain advice on the detail that must be provided when applying for an authorisation.

Best practicable environmental option

5.4.19 It is the purpose of IPC to look at potentially polluting processes "in the round". IPC covers cases where more than one environmental medium may be affected. In these cases, an additional requirement is imposed by EPA 1990, s. 7(7). BATNEEC has still to be applied to the process, but with the aim of minimising pollution to the environment as a whole by adopting the best practicable environment option (BPEO). BPEO is not defined in EPA 1990, but was discussed in the 12th Report of the Royal Commission on Environmental Pollution,[10] where it was defined as the option which provides "the most benefit or least damage to the environment as a whole ... in the long as well as the short term". Identification of the BPEO can only be made by careful consideration of all the factors affecting any process. The methodology for trying to decide on the BPEO is considered in technical guidance note E1, issued in 1995 by HMIPI, now the Environment Agency.

Content of conditions

5.4.20 In addition to the general purposes for which conditions are imposed —

---

[10] Cm. 310 (1987).

compliance with objectives, etc. — EPA 1990 contains a number of provisions which specify the matters which may be put in conditions.

(1) A condition may impose limits on the amount or composition of a substance used in, or produced by, a process over a period of time.

(2) A condition may require prior notification of any change in the way a process is carried on (EPA 1990, s. 7(8)).

(3) A condition may not be imposed purely for securing the health of persons at work (EPA 1990, s. 7(1)). In practice, however, this may be very hard to differentiate from more general aims to be achieved by imposing a condition.

(4) A condition may not regulate the final disposal of controlled waste by deposit in or on land (EPA 1990, s. 28(1)). Waste on land is generally dealt with in EPA 1990, Pt. II.[11] This may seem to be an area where IPC is less "integrated" than it could be. However, difficulties should be avoided because SEPA now acts as the waste regulation authority. Regulations under Part II of the Act (EPA 1990, s. 33(3)) may exempt certain plants from their scope, but, if this is done in relation to plants regulated under IPC, the conditions will still not regulate final disposal to land.

VARIATION OF AUTHORISATIONS

Numerous provisions in EPA 1990 deal with variation of authorisations, which must be considered against the background of the BATNEEC principle. If scientific knowledge or technology moves on, the original approval for the carrying on of a process may not meet new standards, and thus changes will have to be made. It is definitely not the case that once authorisation has been granted, an indefinite right to operate a process is acquired, notwithstanding that it has later been discovered, for example, to be more polluting than originally believed. Operators will also find new ways of carrying on processes, which will also require a change in the authorisation. Variations are in two broad categories: 5.5.1

(1) those imposed by SEPA (EPA 1990, s. 10); and

(2) those requested by the holder of an authorisation (EPA 1990, s. 11).

Variations imposed by SEPA as enforcing authority

Variations imposed by SEPA are promulgated by the service of a variation notice on the holder of the authorisation. A variation notice can itself be 5.5.2

---

[11] See Chap. 4.

varied by a further notice (EPA 1990, s. 10(3A)). A notice must specify the changes in the authorisation and the date or dates on which they are to take effect unless the notice is withdrawn (EPA 1990, s. 10(3)). A variation notice also specifies that the holder notify SEPA within a set period of the requirements necessary to comply, and requires the holder to pay a fee. Some variations may be minor, while others may involve a "substantial change" in the way in which the process is carried on. A "substantial change" is defined as a substantial change in the type, amount or any other characteristic of the substances released from the process (EPA 1990, s. 10(7)). It should be noted, however, that a small reduction in the permitted limit for emission of a prescribed substance may involve, for example, tearing down existing plant if it cannot be made to reach the standard laid down and its replacement with new equipment. The upheaval might be substantial but the change might not be substantial enough to require notification by SEPA.

5.5.3   If SEPA considers a change in the authorisation to involve such a "substantial change" that it must notify the holder (EPA 1990, s. 10(5)) it must also notify the consulted bodies (who are the same bodies as in relation to initial applications) of the actions which the holder must take in order to comply with the variation. The time-limit for notification is 14 days (EP(AAR)R 1991, reg. 4), and 28 days for responses by the consulted bodies (EPA 1990, Sched. 1, para. 6(7)). In "substantial change" cases, the holder must also advertise the action which he is to take, and a further 28 days are allowed after the advertisement for any representations to be made to SEPA. The Secretary of State has powers (EPA 1990, s. 10(6)) to direct SEPA as to the exercise of the variation powers.

5.5.4   If the holder appeals against a variation notice, this does not suspend operation of the notice pending the appeal (EPA 1990, s. 15(9)). The potential difficulty here is that the period within which action must be taken according to the notice may expire before the appeal is determined. While no offence is specified in EPA 1990, s. 23 for failure to obey a variation notice, if the holder has not altered the way in which his process is carried on accordingly, he will be operating in breach of a condition, and thus in breach of section 6(1).

Variation applied for by the holder of an authorisation

5.5.5   There are a number of possible routes for dealing with a variation applied for by the holder of an authorisation. Different rules apply depending on whether or not the process is in actual operation. A holder can apply for a determination as to whether or not a change will require a variation, or may apply directly for the variation.

5.5.6   Variation will probably be required where there is a "relevant change" in the manner of operating. A "relevant change" is one which is capable of altering the substances released or affecting the amount or any other characteristic of those substances (EPA 1990, s. 11(11)). There is nothing to say that a mere reduction in releases is not a "relevant change". Therefore, almost any significant alteration to the process will mean that the need for a variation must be considered.

If the process is not being carried on, the holder must apply directly for 5.5.7 a variation (EPA 1990, s. 11(5)), supplying such information as is prescribed, and paying the fee (EP(AAR)R 1991, reg. 3(3)(b) and (4)). This application includes an indication of the changes which the holder wishes SEPA to make to the authorisation. After consultation, and advertisement in the case of "substantial changes", SEPA may grant or refuse the variations.

If the process is being carried on, the holder can either apply directly for 5.5.8 a variation, if he is to make a "relevant change" which he considers will require variation (EPA 1990, s. 11(6)), or notify SEPA of the changes he proposes to make, and request it to determine whether or not the change will breach a condition (EPA 1990, s. 11(1) — an "application for a determination") and whether or not it would vary the conditions. SEPA may require further information to be furnished by the applicant (EPA 1990, s. 11(7)). SEPA must notify the holder:

(1) whether the change will breach a condition;
(2) if not, whether SEPA is likely to vary the conditions;
(3) if it would involve a breach, whether SEPA would consider varying the conditions;
(4) whether or not the proposed change is "substantial" (EPA 1990, s. 11(2)).

No time-limit is set down within which SEPA must respond to the applicant. 5.5.9

In any case where the conditions have to be varied to allow the change to proceed, SEPA notifies the holder of the variations which it is "likely to consider making" and the holder applies for the variation in the ordinary way. His application will be referred to consulted bodies and advertised if it is a "substantial change" (EPA 1990, s. 11(3), (4)–(8)).

If a holder applies directly for a variation, SEPA can treat that application 5.5.10 as an application for determination. This variation procedure applies to all other provisions of an authorisation, as well as actual conditions in an authorisation (EPA 1990, s. 11(10)).

The procedures for variations applied for by the holder are more easily 5.5.11 understood by using a diagram (see overleaf).

ENFORCEMENT PROCEDURES

As IPC deals with the processes most likely to cause environmental harm, 5.6.1 EPA 1990 provides a variety of increasingly strong powers which SEPA, as regulatory authority, may use to enforce compliance. In increasing order of severity, these are: enforcement notices, prohibition notices, and revocation of the authorisation. Failure to pay the prescribed fees can also result in an authorisation being suspended or revoked — see para. 5.2.2.

VARIATION APPLIED FOR BY HOLDER

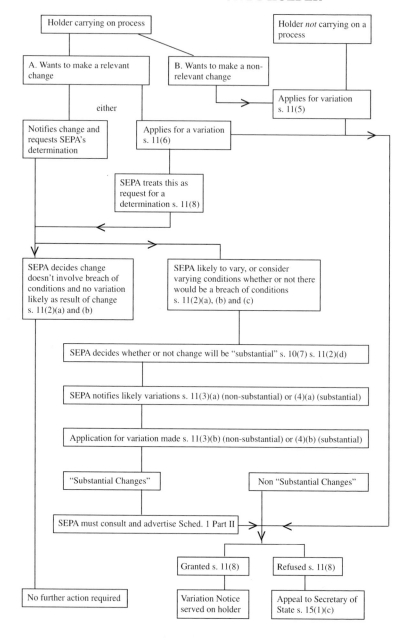

Enforcement notices

Enforcement notices may be served if SEPA, as enforcing authority, 5.6.2 considers that:

(1) a condition of an authorisation is likely to be breached by the person carrying on the process; or
(2) the condition is actually being contravened (EPA 1990, s. 13(1)).

The notice must state SEPA's opinion, namely, that there is a likelihood of a breach, or an actual breach, and specify the matter constituting the contravention or making it likely that a contravention will arise. The notice must also specify the steps to be taken to remedy the situation and the period within which this must be done. The Secretary of State may direct SEPA on the exercise of its powers under the enforcement notice procedure (EPA 1990, s. 13(3)). An enforcement notice may be withdrawn by SEPA after issue. It should be noted that an appeal against an enforcement notice does not suspend its operation (EPA 1990, s. 15(9)).

Prohibition notices

Prohibition notices are intended to cover situations where an imminent risk 5.6.3 of serious pollution exists. SEPA must serve a notice specifying:

(1) that it is of the opinion that an imminent risk exists;
(2) what the risk is;
(3) what must be done to remove the risk and the time allowed for so doing;
(4) that the authorisation is suspended, wholly or in part, until the prohibition notice is withdrawn — if the suspension is partial, the notice can specify conditions that apply to a part authorised to continue (EPA 1990, s. 14(3)).

Prohibition notices must be withdrawn in writing once the necessary 5.6.4 steps to comply have been taken (EPA 1990, s. 14(5)). As with enforcement notices, the Secretary of State has power to direct SEPA in performing its duties (EPA 1990, s. 14(4)).

Note particularly that a prohibition notice can be served whether or not 5.6.5 the holder is complying with the conditions of his authorisation, and may relate to aspects of the process not covered by conditions (EPA 1990, s. 14(2)). Appeal against a prohibition notice does not suspend its operation (EPA 1990, s. 15(9)).

Revocation of authorisation

SEPA may revoke an authorisation at any time (EPA 1990, s. 12(1)). 5.6.6 Revocation is also permitted if a process has not been carried on since the authorisation was granted, or if the process has been discontinued for a period of 12 months or more (EPA 1990, s. 12(2)). Once again, the Secretary of State has power to direct SEPA to revoke an authorisation (EPA 1990, s. 12(5)). Notice of revocation can take effect only on a date specified in, and at least 28 days following, the notice (EPA 1990, s. 12(3)). A revocation can be withdrawn before it takes effect (EPA 1990, s. 12(4)). An appeal against a revocation notice has the effect of suspending its operation (EPA 1990, s. 15(8)). In circumstances where a process ceases to be carried on, the power to revoke an authorisation has, in practice, been used by agreement as a way of removing the "unused" authorisation from the Registers.

5.6.7   Whether or not a process is being "carried on" is therefore important. A single instance of the carrying on of the operation may be insufficient to amount to "carrying on" the process.

APPEALS

5.7.1 An appeal to the Secretary of State is competent in eight cases (unless the decision made was by his direction) (EPA 1990, s. 15). Appeals are available against:

    (1) refusal to grant an authorisation;
    (2) conditions in an authorisation;
    (3) refusal of a variation of an authorisation sought by the holder;
    (4) revocation of an authorisation (the appeal suspends the revocation);
    (5) a variation notice;
    (6) an enforcement notice;
    (7) a prohibition notice;
    (8) refusal of commercial confidentiality for information (EPA 1990, s. 22(5)) — the information is not put on the Register pending determination of the appeal.
    (In cases (5) to (7) the appeal does not suspend operation of the notice.)

5.7.2   Appeals are heard either by the Secretary of State or by someone appointed to act in his place. Any matter involved in an appeal can be referred to an appointed person, along the same lines as a reporter in a planning appeal (EPA 1990, s. 15(3)).

Time-limits

5.7.3 The following is a summary of the time-limits within which notice of appeal must be given (EP(AAR)R 1991, reg. 10):

Cases referred to above	*Time*
Cases 1, 2 and 3	Within six months of decision or deemed refusal
Case 4	Before the revocation takes effect

Cases 5, 6 and 7   Within two months of the date of the
                                                notice
Case 8   Within 21 days of the determination

The Secretary of State can allow more time for notice of appeal to be submitted in cases 1, 2, 3, 5, 6 and 7.

Method of determining appeals

An appeal or appeals can be determined by written representations to the reporter appointed by the Secretary of State or by a hearing. The hearing may be held in public or private, or a mixture of both, as the inspector may decide (EP(AAR)R 1991, regs. 12 and 13). The Secretary of State, when deciding an appeal, can cancel, modify or impose conditions and can modify enforcement, etc., notices.   5.7.4

   Regulations 9 to 12 of EP(AAR)R 1991 contain further provisions concerning the conduct of appeals; content of notices of appeals, publicity where the appeal is to be by way of public hearing, notification of appeals to consulted bodies and those who made representations to SEPA, and on numerous other matters.   5.7.5

POWERS OF ENTRY, ETC.

Persons authorised by SEPA (the term "inspector" has been dropped) have extensive powers under sections 108 and 109 of EA 1995, including power to enter premises, to seize and destroy dangerous items, to make investigations and to take measurements and samples. Obstruction of authorised persons and failure to comply with their requirements are offences (EA 1995, s. 110). Intentionally or recklessly false statements may also lead to criminal conviction (EPA 1990, s. 23). The Secretary of State or SEPA for the performance of their duties may, by notice in writing, require any person to furnish information reasonably considered to be required (EPA 1990, s. 19). Failure to comply with the notice is an offence (EPA 1990, s. 23).   5.8.1

OFFENCES AND THE ONUS OF PROOF — OTHER REMEDIES

Offences are set out in section 23 of EPA 1990 and cover a wide variety — from carrying on a process without authorisation (which appears to be an offence of strict liability), to failure to comply with a court order under section 26 requiring a person convicted of breach of an authorisation to remedy that matter. In addition, under section 157 of the Act, any director, manager, secretary or other officer of a corporate body will also be criminally liable if his consent, connivance or neglect contributed to the commission of the offence.   5.9.1

Two other points should be particularly noted.

5.9.2　　(1)　SEPA, if it thinks the criminal sanctions inadequate to ensure compliance with the Act, may take proceedings, for example for interdict, in the Sheriff Court or Court of Session (EPA 1990, s. 24).

　　　　(2)　In a charge for failure to comply with the general condition in all authorisations under EPA 1990, s. 7(4), it is for the accused to show that there was no better BATNEEC than that actually used (EPA 1990, s. 25(1)). However, the general condition does not apply to matters which are regulated by specific conditions.

5.9.3　As well as criminal sanctions, the courts have power under section 26 to order anyone convicted of an offence to remedy the matter for which they were convicted. This could include changing working practices to avoid a repetition, or actually putting to rights the damage caused. Also, under section 27 SEPA may, with the approval of the Secretary of State, itself take measures to remedy any harm arising.

Penalties

5.9.4　On summary conviction the penalty can be a fine of up to £20,000 and/or three months' imprisonment. On conviction on indictment, the penalty can be an unlimited fine and/or two years' imprisonment.

TRANSFER OF AUTHORISATIONS

5.10.1　Authorisation relates to the manner of carrying on a process, rather than to an individual or company. As such, authorisations can be transferred to successors as owners or occupiers of a plant, and the transferee must notify SEPA in writing within 21 days of the fact of the transfer (EPA 1990, s. 9). Failure to do so is an offence, and since SEPA, as the regulatory authority, is directed by section 6(4) not to grant authorisations to persons who may be unable to implement the conditions of an authorisation, any intending transferee should investigate in advance with SEPA whether or not he is considered to be able to carry on the process in accordance with the authorisation. If SEPA does not consider that he is, it would be bound to revoke the authorisation.

CHAPTER SIX

CONTAMINATED LAND

INTRODUCTION

Contaminated land and the harm it may cause are of relevance in various 6.1.1
areas of environmental law. Contaminated land could result in pollution of
watercourses; it could be the cause of a criminal prosecution for the improper
deposit of waste on land or give rise to civil liability for environmental
harm; it could have an impact within planning law, and (as at the time of
writing (April 1997)) result in an action being taken for statutory nuisance.
All of these subjects are, however, discussed elsewhere within this book.
What this chapter seeks to do is describe the legal provisions introduced by
the Environmental Protection Act 1990 (EPA 1990) and the Environment
Act 1995 (EA 1995) which are specifically designed to introduce a statutory
regime dealing with contaminated land. It should be noted that as at the
time of writing no statutory regime has yet been brought into force with
respect to contaminated land in Scotland.

Before the drafting of EPA 1990 there were no specific statutory 6.1.2
provisions designed to address the problem of contaminated land. Local
authorities could and did, however, make use of the public nuisance
provisions contained within the Public Health (Scotland) Act 1897. These
provisions were, for example, made use of in the case of *Clydebank District
Council v. Monaville*,[1] which remains the best reported example of a case
relating to contaminated land. Asbestos had been deposited on a site in
Clydebank by a proprietor of the site who, subsequently, sold the site to
Monaville. The asbestos was not, however, properly covered over and was
creating a hazard to health. The provisions of the Public Health (Scotland)
Act 1897 permitted the local authority to apply to the sheriff court for an
order ordaining the "author of the nuisance" to take appropriate action to
prevent the continuation of a public nuisance, which was defined to include
any accumulation hazardous to public health. The Act made it clear that the
author of the nuisance was required to be the owner or occupier and,
accordingly, the court duly issued an order requiring Monaville to take
appropriate action to prevent the asbestos continuing to create a hazard to
health.

---

[1] 1982 S.L.T. (Sh. Ct.) 2.

6.1.3   In a practical case, therefore, the public nuisance provisions of the Public Health (Scotland) Act 1897 could be used to address a hazard created by contaminated land. It should be noted that the order did not require Monaville to take action to ensure that the land was no longer contaminated with asbestos — merely to take action to ensure that the hazard to health did not continue.

6.1.4   The Public Health (Scotland) Act 1897 provisions relative to statutory nuisance were not satisfactory, and were basically designed to deal with dirty ditches and cesspits. It was clear that modern legislation designed to address the issue of contaminated land was required.

ENVIRONMENTAL PROTECTION ACT 1990

6.2.1   When drafting EPA 1990 the Government wished to take some action to address the issue of contaminated land. The initial concern was to ascertain the precise nature of the problem. The Government wished to obtain accurate data as cheaply as possible and with as little effort as possible, relying on existing information. Accordingly, it was provided by section 143 of the Act that it would be the duty of each local authority as respects land in its area which was being or had been put to a contaminative use to maintain a register in a prescribed form and containing prescribed particulars.

6.2.2   Before section 143 could be brought into force, however, regulations were required to specify the form of the registers and the particulars to be included in them and, most importantly, to specify the contaminative uses which would cause land to be mentioned on the registers.

6.2.3   Following the passing of EPA 1990 there was extensive consultation regarding the content of these regulations. It became apparent that it would be possible for land to be listed on the register as having been put to a contaminative use which had not, thereby, been contaminated. It would also be possible for land to be contaminated but not mentioned in the register since it might be contaminated without there ever being any record of it being put to contaminative use. The Government also felt that since the register was a register of land which was being or had been put to a contaminative use, logic required that no area of land would ever be removed from the register even if it was cleaned up or could be proved never to have been contaminated in the first place. Extensive consultation revealed that there was a general fear that land would be blighted. The concern was that the register might be regarded as a register of "contaminated land" rather than being recognised merely as a register of land which was being or had been put to a contaminative use. It was ultimately recognised that this register might create more confusion than it solved. Accordingly, it was resolved that section 143 would not be brought into force.

6.2.4   Out of that extensive consultation procedure, however, flowed the provisions regarding contaminated land, which were introduced by EA 1995.

ENVIRONMENT ACT 1995

Policy background

In drafting the contaminated land provisions of EA 1995 the Government 6.3.1
was highly conscious that sweeping and radical contaminated land powers
might impose upon the U.K. economy a heavy financial burden. The
Government looked at the statutory regimes introduced in other countries
and made a positive decision to avoid a number of concepts used elsewhere.
Not surprisingly, given the basic philosophy of the Government, it avoided
any concept that clean-up should be carried out at the public expense. It
also avoided setting ambitious target values and requiring that land should
be cleaned up to the standards laid down by those target values.

The definition of contaminated land is drawn relatively narrowly. It is 6.3.2
clear from the terms of the Act, as expanded upon by the draft guidance
currently available (see para. 6.4.3) that the intention is that the contaminated
land powers will be used only where difficulties are being caused by the
land when it is put to its current use. It is intended that where the use of
land is to be changed then difficulties which would be caused by
contamination of that land when put to its new use will be dealt with in the
context of the planning regime.

The regime is very complex, and it will be difficult for local authorities 6.3.3
to use it to control contaminated land. The legislation also encourages
consultation with the parties affected by it. It is likely that a substantial
proportion of problems with contaminated land will be dealt with through
negotiation between the enforcing authorities and the parties which would
be affected by the statutory regime if it was enforced. It is also likely that
substantial amounts of contaminated land will be dealt with within the
context of the planning regime. At present, it would appear that the new
regime is likely to be used only in a relatively small number of cases.

Section 57

Under section 57 of EA 1995 there are inserted after section 78 of EPA 6.3.4
1990 new sections numbered 78A to 78YC inclusive (Part IIA). These
sections contain a substantial number of definitions which must be
understood if the contaminated land regime as a whole is to be understood.

Contaminated land

"Contaminated land" is defined by section 78A as any land which appears to 6.3.5
the local authority in whose area it is situated to be in such a condition, by
reason of substances in, on or under that land, that either (a) significant harm
is being caused or there is a significant possibility of such harm being caused,
or (b) pollution of controlled waters is being, or is likely to be, caused.

6.3.6   The statute makes it very clear that in determining whether any land appears to be contaminated land a local authority must act in accordance with guidance issued by the Secretary of State for Scotland. In particular, section 78A(5) provides that what harm is to be regarded as "significant", whether the possibility of significant harm being caused is "significant" and whether pollution of controlled waters is being or is likely to be caused, will be determined in accordance with guidance issued by the Secretary of State.

6.3.7   It is immediately apparent that the statutory guidance is critical. Only once the statutory guidance has been finalised and issued can the full meaning of "contaminated land" be appreciated. Further comments are made below regarding the drafts of the statutory guidance which are currently available (see paras. 6.4.1–9).

Special site

6.3.8   A "special site" is a sub-classification within "contaminated land". Section 78C of EPA 1990 provides that a special site is any contaminated land which accords with a description contained within regulations which are to be published by the Secretary of State. The Act does, however, provide by section 78C(10) that (without prejudice to the generality of the Secretary of State's power to prescribe any description of land for the purposes of designating special sites) the distinction should be that whereas land becomes contaminated land if "significant" harm is being caused or there is a significant possibility of such harm being caused or if pollution of controlled waters is being or is likely to be caused, contaminated land will be a special site if "serious" harm is being or might be caused or if serious pollution of controlled waters would be or would be likely to be caused. In other words, the difference between contaminated land and a special site is the presence or potential presence of serious rather than merely significant harm.

6.3.9   In broad summary, the difference created by designation of land as a special site is that whereas the local authority is the enforcing authority for most contaminated land, the Scottish Environmental Protection Agency (SEPA) is the enforcing authority for special sites.

Harm

6.3.10   "Harm" is defined by section 78A(4) of EPA 1990, and is harm to the health of living organisms or other interference with the ecological systems of which they form part and, in the case of man, includes harm to his property.

Appropriate person

6.3.11   "Appropriate person" is defined at length in section 78F of EPA 1990, and is a vital concept since it determines the identity of the party or parties who will actually pay for the remediation of contaminated land.

If it is possible to identify the person or any of the persons who caused or knowingly permitted the substances or any of the substances by reason of which the contaminated land in question is such land to be in, on or under that land then that person or persons is or are an appropriate person. A person shall only be an appropriate person with respect to substances which he caused or knowingly permitted to be present in, on or under the contaminated land. In other words (and as a gross simplification) this aspect of the definition of an appropriate person means the polluter. 6.3.12

Section 78F then goes on to specify that, if no such polluter has been found after reasonable inquiry, the appropriate person to bear responsibility for the things which are to be done by way of remediation will be the owner or occupier for the time being of the contaminated land in question. 6.3.13

The Act makes it very clear that the precise definition of appropriate person and the precise manner in which liability is to be divided among those who could be determined to be appropriate persons is to be governed by guidance to be issued by the Secretary of State. 6.3.14

Duty to inspect

A duty is imposed on every local authority (EPA 1990, s. 78B) to cause its area to be inspected from time to time for the purposes of (a) identifying contaminated land and (b) enabling the authority to decide whether any such land is required to be designated as a special site. If a local authority identifies any contaminated land in its area it must give notice of that fact to (a) SEPA, (b) the owner of the land, (c) any person who appears to the authority to be in occupation of the whole or any part of the land, and (d) any person who appears to the authority to be an "appropriate person". 6.3.15

As regards special sites, the Act provides that if at any time it appears to the local authority that any contaminated land in its area might be land which is required to be designated as a special site, the authority must decide whether or not the land is required to be so designated and, if it decides that the land does require to be so designated, it is required to give notice of that decision to the same persons to whom it requires to give notice that the land was "contaminated land" as itemised above. In the course of making these decisions the local authority will be required to take account of the wide variety of guidance available, and will also be required to consult with SEPA and the Secretary of State. 6.3.16

Consultation

Provision is made by section 78H to the effect that the enforcing authorities must reasonably endeavour to consult with the persons who will be affected before a remediation notice is served. 6.3.17

Remediation notices

6.3.18 The enforcing authority (*i.e.* the local authority with respect to contaminated land other than special sites, and SEPA with respect to special sites) must serve on each person who is an "appropriate person" a notice (known as a "remediation notice") specifying what that person is to do by way of remediation and the periods within which he is required to do each of the things so specified (EPA 1990, s. 78E). Remediation notices requiring the remedying of different things may be served on several persons due to the presence of different substances in, on or under any land or waters. If two or more people are appropriate persons in relation to any particular thing which is to be carried out by way of remediation, the notices served on them will state the proportion of the cost of remediation which each of them will have to bear. Remediation is defined widely by section 78A(7) as not only carrying out works to restore land or waters to prevent, minimise, remedy or mitigate the effect of harm or pollution of waters, but also carrying out appropriate steps to assess the condition of land or controlled waters and carrying out subsequent inspections to review the condition of land or waters.

Rights of entry

6.3.19 Section 78G provides a right of access to carry out works and provides for compensation for the exercise of that right of access.

Appeal

6.3.20 Provision is made by section 78L for appeals to the sheriff court against the service of remediation notices. Most of the details regarding the appeal procedure and, in particular, the grounds on which appeals may be made, will be as specified in regulations which have still to be made.

Failure to comply with the remediation notice

6.3.21 Failure to comply with the remediation notice is a criminal offence under section 78M.

6.3.22   Where a person on whom a remediation notice has been served fails to comply with any of the requirements of the notice (and in certain other circumstances) the enforcing authority will be entitled to do what is appropriate by way of remediation to the relevant land (EPA 1990, s. 78N). The enforcing authority can then recover the reasonable costs incurred in carrying out this remediation from the appropriate person or, if there are two or more appropriate persons, from those persons in the proportion as determined in the same manner as they would be determined in drafting the original remediation notice. In deciding whether to recover the cost (and how much of the cost it is entitled to recover) the enforcing authority must have regard to any hardship the recovery will cause to the person from whom the cost is recoverable and any guidance issued in this respect (EPA 1990, s. 78P).

Registers

In terms of section 78R every enforcing authority must maintain registers 6.3.23 open for public inspection with respect to numerous notices, etc., served in terms of Part IIA. Matters can be excluded from the public register if required for reasons of national security if it is commercially confidential information.

GUIDANCE

The provisions of EPA 1990, as amended by EA 1995, relating to 6.4.1 contaminated land cannot be brought into force until the guidance notes referred to so often have been brought into force. Following the publication of various preliminary drafts during 1996, final drafts of the guidance notes and regulations were issued for consultation inviting comment by December 18, 1996. As at the time of writing (April 1997) final issue of these guidance notes and regulations is still awaited and, accordingly, a definite date for introduction of the whole contaminated land regime cannot be specified.

The final drafts issued for consultation were, however, very complex 6.4.2 documents. Because of the numerous issues addressed, the draft guidance was printed in three different typefaces. Material in one typeface represents factual narrative or description of statutory provisions or policy background and does not form part of the statutory guidance. Material in another typeface represents guidance, in the normal grammatical sense of material to which the enforcing authority must have regard. Material in a third typeface indicates that the enforcing authority is required to act in accordance with the guidance, *i.e.* it is easier to regard this as subsidiary legislation than guidance in the true sense.

The draft guidance casts substantial light on a number of issues. The 6.4.3 definition of contaminated land is extensively explained, and is intended to embody the concept of risk assessment. Before any enforcing authority can identify any land as contaminated land it must show evidence of (1) a contaminant or potential pollutant, (2) a receptor or target, and (3) a pathway by which the contaminant can reach the receptor. The relationship between a contaminant, a pathway and a receptor is termed "a pollutant linkage". A significant pollutant linkage is one which is causing significant harm to a receptor, or presents a significant possibility of significant harm being caused to a receptor, or is causing the pollution of controlled waters which constitute the receptor or is likely to result in such pollution.

6.4.4   One ground for establishing land as contaminated land is that significant harm is being caused. The guidance notes contain a table listing types of receptor opposite descriptions of harm. The guidance notes state that harm should be regarded as significant only if that type of harm is being caused to a type of receptor shown opposite that type of harm in the table.

6.4.5   A second ground establishing land as contaminated land is if there is a significant possibility of significant harm being caused. The description of this ground in the guidance notes is, to say the least, more difficult to understand. In this respect, however, the guidance notes provide a second table giving descriptions of significant harm to receptors and, opposite those descriptions, conditions for there being a significant possibility of significant harm. The guidance notes then state that the possibility of significant harm being caused should be regarded as significant in respect of the descriptions of significant harm to receptors in the relevant column of the table in the cases where the conditions specified in the second column of that table against that description will be fulfilled within a time-scale which the enforcing authority has decided is appropriate for assessing the possibility of significant harm in relation to that land.

6.4.6   The third ground on which land can be defined as contaminated land is that pollution of controlled waters is being or is likely to be caused. Section 78A(9) of EPA 1990 defines the pollution of controlled waters as the entry into controlled waters of any poisonous, noxious or polluting matter or any solid waste matter, and the guidance notes point out that this definition follows the provisions of Part II of the Control of Pollution Act 1974 (see para. 3.5.9). Accordingly, little further guidance is given.

6.4.7   The draft guidance contains extensive provision relative to exclusion from liability in terms of the Act of a person who would otherwise be responsible for remediation costs by reason of his having caused or knowingly permitted the presence of a significant pollutant. These tests are concerned with establishing whether, in relation to other members of the liability group, it is fair that he should bear any part of that responsibility. It should be noted, however, that after the tests have been applied and any exclusions made, at least one member of a liability group should remain to bear responsibility for each significant pollutant linkage.

> *Test 1*   may exclude those identified as having caused or knowingly permitted the land to be contaminated solely through having carried out certain listed actions, such as providing financial assistance, withholding financial assistance, carrying out any action necessary for underwriting an insurance policy, providing legal financial engineering, scientific or technical advice to another person, etc.
>
> *Test 2*   may exclude from liability those who have already, in effect, paid some other member of the liability group to carry out adequate remediation.

Test 3 may exclude from liability anyone who has knowingly caused or permitted the presence of significant pollutants and who has sold the land or let it on a long lease and has ensured that the purchaser or lessee had information on the presence of those pollutants and thus had the opportunity to take that into account in agreeing the price.

Test 4 may exclude from liability those who are members of a liability group solely because they caused or knowingly permitted the presence in, on or under the land of a substance which has only led to the creation of a significant pollutant linkage because another substance which interacted with the earlier substance was later introduced to the land, or because the actions of another person who caused or knowingly permitted the presence of a significant pollutant have caused physical changes to any of the properties of the substance.

Test 5 may exclude from liability those who would otherwise be liable for the remediation of contaminated land which has become contaminated as a result of the escape of substances from other land where it can be shown that another person who caused or knowingly permitted the presence of a significant pollutant was actually responsible for that escape.

Test 6 may exclude from liability those who would otherwise be liable solely because of the subsequent introduction by others of the relevant pathways or receptors forming part of the significant pollutant linkage.

These tests must be treated with extreme care. It would be dangerous, for 6.4.8 example, to assume that Test 3 will necessarily relieve a person from liability because he has provided certain information regarding contamination to a purchaser or lessee. All six tests are long and complex and the full detailed rules of the tests must be satisfied if they are to be relied upon.

The owner or occupier for the time being of the contaminated land in 6.4.9 question may be an appropriate person with respect to that land if no "polluter" can be found. The guidance gives an indication as to the division of responsibility between owners and occupiers. The guidance provides a test, the purpose of which is to exclude from liability those who do not have an interest in the capital value of the land in question. Where two or more persons have been identified as liable to meet remediation costs solely by reason of ownership or occupation of the land in question, the guidance provides that the authority should exclude such of those persons as occupy the land under a licence which has no marketable value, or who are liable to pay a rent equivalent to the full market rent for such of the land in question as they occupy and hold no interest in the *dominium utile* over the land in question.

SUMMARY

6.5.1 In summary, the system we are left with is that local authorities must identify "contaminated land" and particular types of contaminated land, called "special sites". The enforcing authority for contaminated land is the relevant local authority, and the enforcing authority for special sites is SEPA. Once these sites have been identified the enforcing authorities must then identify who should be made to remediate the sites. The people who are required to remediate the sites are the polluters, in accordance with the degree of their pollution, whom failing the owners or occupiers. Appeal procedures are available against notices requiring people to carry out remediation. In addition, fallback powers allow the enforcing authorities to carry out remediation and recover the costs of carrying out such remediation. This system is not yet in force; it will be brought into force only once the necessary guidance has been finalised and issued.

6.5.2   The system is very complex and makes provision for extensive consultation. It is likely that a substantial amount of clean-up will be carried out through consultation and negotiation, rather than by use of the remediation notice powers. It is also likely that a substantial amount of clean-up will be carried out in the context of the planning regime when sites are redeveloped.

6.5.3   Only once the guidance has been finalised and issued and the system brought fully into force can we really know how the system will operate in practice.

CHAPTER SEVEN

PLANNING LAW

INTRODUCTION

Environmental protection has always been an important focus of the 7.1.1
planning process; however, it has never been its sole concern. The Scottish
Development Department (SDD), in its *Review of the Management of
Planning* (1977) emphasised the broad scope of the process. Planning "was
initially, and is still mainly, a means of controlling and guiding the use of
land and the processes of change in the environment". This remains an
adequate statement of its objectives. Environmental protection is one factor
to be taken into account in controlling and guiding the use of land and the
processes of change. Other factors, such as economic considerations, are
also taken into account.

In practice, environmental considerations have enjoyed a high profile in 7.1.2
the planning process. Indeed, it is probably fair to suggest that, until recently,
the process was the most comprehensive and sophisticated of the regimes
dealing with environmental protection. Until the early 1990s, other
environmental legislation had a relatively limited impact. Much of it, for
example statutory nuisance, was essentially corrective in its approach. The
planning process, by contrast, was, and still is, essentially an anticipatory
or preventative process.

However, recent legislation, and in particular the Environmental 7.1.3
Protection Act 1990 (EPA 1990), has given environmental protection a
higher profile, and there are signs that the role of the planning process in
this sphere is changing (a theme which is returned to later in this chapter).
Nonetheless, a clear endorsement of the continuing role of the planning
system in environmental protection is to be found in National Planning
Policy Guideline 1, "The Planning System", issued by the Scottish Office,
which states at paragraph 11:

> "Across Scotland, the quality of the environment will be main-
> tained and enhanced by consistently applying policies which seek
> to protect the identified assets of the natural, cultural and built
> environment, which encourage environmental improvement
> wherever development is to take place, and which promote the
> re-use of formerly developed urban land. One of the key func-
> tions of the planning system is to improve environmental qual-
> ity".

7.1.4   Underlying the statement from the Review referred to above is an acknowledgment that the market, if left to itself, will not allocate land in a way which adequately safeguards the environment. The abuses of the industrial revolution provided ample evidence of that; intervention is required. This has been achieved in regard to the planning process by appropriating to the state the right to develop land. Since 1948[1] a landowner has enjoyed no more than the right to carry on the existing use of the land. Development can be carried out only if a licence (a grant of planning permission) is first obtained from the planning authority. When deciding whether to grant planning permission, the authority will have regard, amongst other considerations, to the likely effect of the proposal on the environment. If the likely effects are regarded as unacceptable, the development may not be allowed to proceed. The planning authority will have to balance the environmental consequences with other relevant considerations. In the event of refusal, the landowner is not entitled to compensation.

7.1.5   To ensure that planning decisions reflect national and local policy and to bring a measure of consistency and continuity to the process, decisions are made within a framework of policy guidance. However, the process is flexible. Although policy guidance carries very considerable weight in day-to-day decisions (see below), it is not binding, and each proposal is considered on its merits.

7.1.6   The planning process is not intended to be wholly reactive. Planning authorities are intended to guide the processes of change in the environment. The policy guidance referred to above has an important role to play in this. Planning authorities also have powers to enter the market and acquire land to implement policy. However, a mixture of ideological and resource constraints have severely limited the use of these powers in recent years, and this description of planning law focuses mainly on the control of development proposals.

7.1.7   There is a tendency to regard the development control process as a largely negative function. This is too simplistic. Planning authorities have a role to play in ensuring that development happens in an environmentally acceptable way. Negotiations between a developer and the authority to put a proposal into an acceptable form are a key part of the process; and conditional consents and planning agreements are intended to ensure that development remains that way.

7.1.8   The process outlined above is what is sometimes referred to as "mainstream planning control", which is the subject of this chapter. However, the new trilogy of planning Acts — the Town and Country Planning (Scotland) Act 1997; the Planning (Listed Buildings and Conservation Areas) (Scotland) Act 1997; and the Planning (Hazardous

---

[1]   The year when comprehensive planning control was first introduced in Scotland.

Substances) (Scotland) Act 1997 — also incorporate a number of special regimes of control having implications for the environment. The felling of trees, for example, although subject to control in the context of a development proposal, is not itself regulated by mainstream planning control. Nonetheless, because of their contribution to the landscape, trees can be the subject of a separate system of control.[2] Proposals to alter or extend buildings of architectural or historic interest or groups of such buildings may be subject to mainstream control, but because of the importance attached to safeguarding the nation's supply of interesting buildings, they are subject also to a concurrent system of control.[3] Mineral working differs from other forms of development in that it is essentially destructive of land and, because of this, it is subject not only to mainstream control but to additional controls.[4] Advertisements may have an impact on the landscape or townscape out of proportion to their size and are subject to a separate regime of control.[5] For reasons of safety, provisions exist for subjecting the introduction of hazardous substances on to land to an additional system of control.[6] Finally, where the condition of land adversely affects amenity, planning authorities have power to secure the abatement of these adverse effects.[7] Such action is beyond mainstream control.

Although some of these controls may, at times, offer important 7.1.9 environmental safeguards, limitations on space preclude a description of such controls in this chapter. What follows is a description of mainstream planning control.

ADMINISTRATION

Overall responsibility for the administration of the town and country 7.2.1 planning legislation in Scotland rests with the Secretary of State for Scotland, who acts in planning matters through the Scottish Office Development Department (SODD). The day-to-day operation of the legislation rests, for the most part, with the local authorities.

---

[2] Town and Country Planning (Scotland) Act 1997, ss. 159–178; Town and Country Planning (Tree Preservation Order and Trees in Conservation Areas) (Scotland) Regulations 1975 (S.I. 1975 No. 1204), as amended.

[3] Planning (Listed Buildings and Conservation Areas) (Scotland) Act 1997; Town and Country Planning (Listed Buildings and Buildings in Conservation Areas) (Scotland) Regulations 1987 (S.I. 1987 No. 1529); Historic Scotland Circular 1/1973 and the *Memorandum of Guidance on Listed Buildings and Conservation Areas* (Historic Scotland, 1993).

[4] 1997 Act, ss. 74 and 84; Environment Act 1995, s. 96, and Scheds. 13 and 14; Town and Country Planning (Compensation for Restrictions on Mineral Workings) (Scotland) Regulations 1987 (S.I. 1987 No. 433); SODD Circular 34/1996, *Guidance on the Review and Updating of Old Mineral Permissions*.

[5] 1997 Act, ss. 182–187; Town and Country Planning (Control of Advertisements) (Scotland) Regulations 1984 (S.I. 1984 No. 467), as amended.

[6] Planning (Hazardous Substances) (Scotland) Act 1997.

[7] 1997 Act, ss. 179–181.

7.2.2   The Secretary of State's role in planning falls into two parts. First, he secures a measure of consistency and continuity in the operation of the planning process in Scotland; and secondly, he ensures that planning is administered in line with national policy.

7.2.3   The Secretary of State has a number of instruments at his disposal to fulfil his role. He has extensive power under the Town and Country Planning (Scotland) Act 1997 (the 1997 Act) to make subordinate legislation, and has used this power to adjust the scope of planning (see paras. 7.4.13–14) and to prescribe procedures. He issues national planning policy guidelines, circulars and other forms of guidance (see paras. 7.3.2–6) on matters of policy and procedure. He determines appeals against planning authority decisions and, in this way, is the final arbiter on matters of planning merit. Structure plans, the top tier of the development plan, are subject to his approval. Finally, he has the power under the 1997 Act to issue directions to planning authorities with regard to a wide range of planning matters. Directions may be specific or general in their application.

7.2.4   Below the Secretary of State are the 32 local authorities — the planning authorities. The Local Government etc. (Scotland) Act 1994 (the 1994 Act) introduced a unitary system of local government into Scotland with effect from April 1, 1996. It repealed the earlier two-tier structure with its complex arrangements for the discharge of planning functions which had operated in much of Scotland under the Local Government (Scotland) Act 1973 (the 1973 Act). Under the 1994 Act each authority is an all-purpose planning authority, although in some parts of Scotland authorities are required to work together in the preparation of the structure plan (see para. 7.3.11).

7.2.5   A planning authority may delegate planning functions to a committee or sub-committee of the council, to an officer of the authority or to another local authority under section 56 of the 1973 Act.

PLANNING POLICY

7.3.1   The essential characteristic of Scottish planning is that it is a system of discretionary development control operating within a framework of indicative policy guidance. Those involved in the development control process will wish to know where to find such guidance, which is issued at the national and local levels.

National policy guidance

7.3.2   The Secretary of State is under no obligation to issue statements of national policy on planning matters, but in order to fulfil his role in the planning system he often does so. The principal sources at the present time are national planning policy guidelines, circulars and planning advice notes.

7.3.3   National planning policy guidelines (NPPGs) are replacing the earlier series of national planning guidelines. NPPGs provide statements of government policy on nationally important land uses and other planning matters, supported, where appropriate, by a locational framework. At the time of writing, what appear to be the key guidelines are almost complete. Eleven NPPGs have been issued, focusing on such key issues as *The Planning System*, *Land for Housing* (subsequently revised), *Land for Business and Industry*, *Retailing* and *Planning and Waste Management*. A draft NPPG has also been issued, entitled *Transport and Planning*.

Circulars are used to explain new legislation and to deal with procedural matters. Occasionally they have been used to offer an interpretation of the law on such matters as the use of planning conditions and agreements. 7.3.4

Planning advice notes (PANs) set out advice on good planning practice on specific issues. For example, PAN 51, *Planning and Environmental Protection* gives advice on the role of the planning system in controlling pollution and its relationship to a number of environmental regimes. 7.3.5

Copies of relevant national policy guidance may be obtained on request from the Scottish Office Development Department, Victoria Quay, Leith, Edinburgh, EH6 6QQ. 7.3.6

Local authority policy guidance

Unlike the Secretary of State, planning authorities are required by Part II of the 1997 Act to prepare planning policy statements for their area, which are prepared in two tiers and are together referred to as the development plan. The top tier is a strategic land use plan, referred to as the structure plan. These plans may cover the whole or part of an authority's area and, as a result of changes introduced in the 1994 Act, in some cases will now cover all or part of the area of more than one authority. Structure plans are not map-based but contain an indicative "key diagram". They set out strategic guidance on land use allocations in the plan area. The bottom tier comprises one or more local plans, which cover a smaller area than the structure plan. They are map-based and, as a consequence, are much more detailed in terms of land use allocations. The local plans should provide a firm framework on which development control decisions can be based. 7.3.7

Structure and local plans are expected to play a part in achieving environmental goals. Indeed, increasing recognition is being given to environmental protection in the formulation of policy. Specifically, this is reflected in the requirement for structure and local plans to include measures for the conservation of the natural beauty and amenity of land and for the improvement of the physical environment and the management of traffic (1997 Act, ss. 7(1)(a) and 11(3)(a)). More generally, there are two ways in which development plans are expected to make a contribution. First of all, they bring together and integrate land use policy with other policies; for example, NPPG 10, *Planning and Waste Management*, states that "the waste management industry needs the assurance of clear, comprehensive and up-to-date development plans that take account of the wider waste management 7.3.8

picture". To aid this process, structure and local plans are now required to include policies in respect of suitable waste disposal sites or installations.[8] Secondly, recent NPPGs have emphasised the importance of development plans helping to find the appropriate balance between environmental and other considerations; for example, NPPG 4, *Mineral Working*, and NPPG 12, *Skiing*, give general guidance to planning authorities on the extent to which environmental protection should be traded for the economic benefits which can result from mineral working and skiing. Planning authorities are expected to reflect this general guidance in specific policies for their area in the development plan.

7.3.9   The Government has signalled its intention that development plans should have a higher profile in the planning process than hitherto. Section 25 of the 1997 Act[9] provides that decisions must be made in line with the development plan unless material considerations indicate otherwise. In *St Albans District Council v. Secretary of State for the Environment*[10] the English High Court held that the corresponding provision in the English legislation now created a presumption in favour of the development plan. However, the court went on to reject the submission that the plan should prevail unless strong planning considerations to the contrary could be shown. It was enough that material considerations existed which "indicated otherwise". Whatever view the courts may take of the interpretation of section 25 as a matter of law, the Secretary of State has indicated in paragraph 44 of NPPG 1 that, as a matter of policy, determinations should depart from the provisions of up-to-date structure and local plans only if there are compelling reasons.

7.3.10   The two tiers are now considered in more detail.

Structure plans[11]

7.3.11   Under section 5 of the 1997 Act the Secretary of State has power to designate structure plan areas in respect of which planning authorities are to prepare structure plans. The district of every planning authority is to be included in a structure plan area, but any such area may extend to only part of the district of an authority or may extend to the district of more than one authority.[12] The Secretary of State designated 17 structure plan areas in

---

[8]   Waste Management Licensing Regulations 1994 (S.I. 1994 No. 1056), reg. 19 and Sched. 4, para. 7.

[9]   Formerly s. 18A of the Town and Country Planning (Scotland) Act 1972, added by the Planning and Compensation Act 1991, s. 58.

[10] [1993] 1 P.L.R. 88.

[11] For further information about structure plans, see the 1997 Act, ss. 6–10; Town and Country Planning (Structure and Local Plans) (Scotland) Regulations 1983 (S.I. 1983 No. 1590); PAN 37 (revised 1996).

[12] 1997 Act, s. 5(2) and (3).

September 1995.[13] Of these, 11 coincide with the boundaries of the new authorities; the remaining six areas cross the boundaries of two or more of the new authorities. Concern has been expressed over the efficiency and, indeed, the prospects for harmony of joint working arrangements. The legislation anticipates possible problems by providing that, at the request of the constituent authorities, or of his own volition, the Secretary of State may establish a joint board to discharge structure plan functions.[14]

The structure plan is intended to be problem-orientated, singling out for consideration in the plan those issues which are significant at the national or strategic level and in respect of which action is required. The structure plan is not map-based, comprising, instead, a written statement supplemented by diagrams.[15]   7.3.12

The stages in the preparation of a structure plan are as follows: 7.3.13

(1) survey of the plan area, if considered appropriate by the authority, and preparation of report;
(2) consultation with specified bodies;
(3) opportunity for the public to participate in the formulation process;
(4) making of the plan and submission to the Secretary of State for approval;
(5) opportunity for objection;
(6) at the discretion of the Secretary of State, examination in public of selected key issues by invited parties led by a person appointed by the minister;
(7) rejection or approval of the plan by the minister in whole or in part. Approval may be with or without modifications or reservations.

The intention is that the structure plan should be kept up-to-date. With this in mind, authorities are required to monitor and review the plan and may submit proposals for alteration from time to time.   7.3.14

Local plans

The second tier of the development plan for an area comprises one or more local plans, which must be prepared by planning authorities for all parts of their area.[16] Two or more planning authorities may make a joint local plan extending to parts of each of their districts. This process has taken longer   7.3.15

---

[13] Designation of Structure Plan Areas (Scotland) Order 1995 (S.I. 1995 No. 3002).
[14] 1994 Act, Sched. 4, para. 3.
[15] 1997 Act, s. 7; Town and Country Planning (Structure and Local Planning) (Scotland) Regulations 1983 (S.I. 1983 No. 1590).
[16] 1997 Act, s. 11(1).

than expected and is still under way. A local plan consists of a map and a written statement.[17] A local plan must conform generally to the relevant structure plan (1997 Act, s. 11(5)(b)).

7.3.16   The stages in the preparation and adoption of a local plan are as follows:

(1) survey of the plan area, in so far as this has not already been done;

(2) consultation with specified bodies;

(3) opportunity for the public to participate in the formulation exercise;

(4) preparation of plan and opportunity for objection;

(5) consideration of objections by planning authority — an objector may require to be heard at a public inquiry;

(6) adoption by planning authority of the plan as originally prepared or as modified to take account of objections.

7.3.17   The intention is that the local plans should be kept up-to-date. With this in mind, planning authorities are required to monitor and review their local plan or plans and may make proposals for alteration from time to time.

OBTAINING PLANNING PERMISSION

7.4.1 Planning permission must be obtained for the development of land (1997 Act, s. 28(1)). "Development" is, therefore, a key word in the development control process. If an activity is not development it is beyond the control of the planning authority.

7.4.2   "Development" is defined in section 26(1)) of the 1997 Act as:

"the carrying out of building, engineering, mining or other operations in, on, over or under land, or the making of any material change in the use of any buildings or other land."

7.4.3   Certain activities are specifically excluded from the definition by section 26(2). These include:

(1) works which affect only the interior of a building or which do not materially affect the external appearance of a building;

(2) the use of any buildings or other land within the curtilage of a dwelling-house for any purpose incidental to the enjoyment of a dwelling;

---

[17] For further information about local plans, see the 1997 Act, ss. 11–19; Town and Country Planning (Structure and Local Plans) (Scotland) Regulations 1983 (S.I. 1983 No. 1590); PAN 49.

(3) the use of land for the purpose of agriculture or forestry;
(4) the demolition of any description of building specified in a direction given by the Secretary of State — the demolition of a building is treated as a building operation, but the minister has directed that the demolition of a building that does not contain a dwelling should not constitute development[18];
(5) a change from one use to another within the same class specified in an order made by the Secretary of State.

Under the Town and Country Planning (Use Classes) (Scotland) Order 1989,[19] article 3 provides that where a building or other land is used for a purpose in one of the 16 classes specified in the Schedule to the Order, the use of that building or land for any other purpose in the same class is not to be taken to involve development. The classes group broadly similar uses of land together, for example shops (class 1), general industrial (class 5).   **7.4.4**

It is generally easy to determine when an activity will fall within the scope of the first part of the definition of development. However, determining when a material change of use has taken place can be more difficult. The change must be "material", *i.e.* it must be of some substance and not merely trivial in planning terms.   **7.4.5**

Where multiple uses are being carried out on land, it is necessary to distinguish between the primary use (or uses) and uses which are merely ancillary. Ancillary uses may vary, and do not constitute development. In considering whether a proposed change would be material, it must be judged against the primary use.   **7.4.6**

Where multiple uses occur it is helpful in determining whether a proposed change in one of the uses is material to identify the planning unit, which is the area of land to be looked at when considering the materiality of the proposed change. The answer to the question "is the change material?" may depend on the area selected for consideration. The planning unit is generally taken to be the unit of occupation — the area occupied as a single holding by an occupier or occupiers. However, where, within that unit, two or more physically separate areas are occupied for different primary activities, the planning unit is the unit of activity: *Burdle v. Secretary of State for the Environment.*[20]   **7.4.7**

The mere discontinuance of a use is not development. Even if the intention is to abandon the use, it seems that the planning permission for that use may be reactivated at a later stage (*Pioneer Aggregates (U.K.) Ltd v.*   **7.4.8**

---

[18] Town and Country Planning (Demolition which is not Development) (Scotland) Direction 1994, annexed to Scottish Office Environment Department (SOEnvD) Circular 15/1995.
[19] S.I. 1989 No. 147; and see SDD Circular 1989/6.
[20] [1972] 1 W.L.R. 1207.

Secretary of State for the Environment[21]) provided it has not been extinguished in the meantime by the commencement of some other use.

Development not requiring planning permission

7.4.9 Certain activities, although constituting development within the meaning of section 26 of the 1997 Act, do not require planning permission.

    (1) Where an enforcement notice (see para. 7.6.3) is served in respect of unauthorised development, the resumption of the immediately preceding lawful use does not require planning permission (1997 Act, s. 28(4)).

    (2) Development by the Crown on Crown land (as defined in section 242(1) of the 1997 Act) does not require planning permission. Instead, an informal consultation procedure set out in SDD Circular 21/1984 is followed. In March 1994 the Government announced that it intends to legislate to remove the Crown exemption from the need to apply for planning permission.

Deemed planning permission

7.4.10 In certain cases, planning permission may be deemed to be granted for an activity. These cases include:

    (1) development by a local authority of land in respect of which it is the planning authority. The authority must follow a separate procedure prescribed in the Town and Country Planning (Development by Planning Authorities) (Scotland) Regulations 1981,[22] completion of which confers a deemed planning permission;

    (2) certain cases, for example, the construction of a power station or the laying of a cross-country pipeline, where a public body or utility is required to obtain an authorisation for development under some other statutory procedure.

Enterprise zones

7.4.11 An enterprise zone scheme, made by the Secretary of State under the Local Government, Planning and Land Act 1980 for a period of 10 years to encourage economic development in certain areas of physical and economic

---

[21] [1985] A.C. 132.

[22] S.I. 1981 No. 829, as amended by the Town and Country Planning (Development by Planning Authorities) (Scotland) Amendment Regulations 1984 (S.I. 1984 No. 238); and see also the Town and Country Planning (Notification of Applications) (Scotland) Direction 1995 and SODD Circular 26/1995.

decline, will grant a general planning permission for specified activities within the enterprise zone. Other activities in the zone will require a grant of planning permission in the normal way. Five such zones have been designated in Scotland, and three have now reached their term date.

Simplified planning zones

In similar fashion, a simplified planning zone made by a planning authority 7.4.12 under powers conferred by the Housing and Planning Act 1986 will grant a general planning permission for specified activities within the zone. At the time of writing only four such zones have been made. The more relaxed planning regime of the zone is intended to encourage investment in an area identified as suitable for development.

Development orders

Planning permission may be granted by development order under 7.4.13 subordinate legislation made by the Secretary of State under sections 30 and 31 of the 1997 Act. An order may be special in the sense that it applies to a defined area. Examples are the special development orders made for five of the six new town development corporations in Scotland which granted planning permission for development within the new town area in accordance with the new town master plan.

Alternatively, an order may have general application throughout Scotland. 7.4.14 Article 3 of the Town and Country Planning (General Permitted Development) (Scotland) Order 1992[23] grants planning permission for the activities listed in the 25 Parts of Schedule 1 to the Order. These include development within the curtilage of a dwelling-house, certain agricultural and forestry buildings and operations, industrial and warehouse development and mineral exploration. The permission granted by the order may be conditional and may be subject to tolerances. The purpose of the order is to remove from planning control certain categories of relatively minor development or development carried on by bodies having a public character, such as statutory undertakers.

Making a planning application

An application for planning permission is made to the appropriate planning 7.4.15 authority. It must be accompanied by: the appropriate fee[24]; a certificate

---

[23] S.I. 1992 No. 223, as amended by S.I. 1992 Nos. 1078, 2084, S.I. 1993 No. 1036, S.I. 1994 Nos. 1442, 2586 and 3294. See also (1996) 56 S.P.E.L. 74.
[24] Town and Country Planning (Fees for Applications and Deemed Applications) (Scotland) Regulations 1997 (S.I. 1997 No. 10).

stating that the applicant is the owner or that the owner and any agricultural tenant has been notified; and a certificate that neighbours[25] have been notified.

7.4.16 An application for operational development (but not for a material change of use) may be made in outline or for full planning permission. An outline planning permission settles the principle of the proposed development but reserves for later approval certain matters of detail.

Environmental impact assessment

7.4.17 E.C. Directive 85/337 on the assessment of the effects of certain public and private projects on the environment has been implemented for the purpose of development control by the Environmental Assessment (Scotland) Regulations 1988 (the 1988 Regulations).[26] The Regulations, which are explained in SDD Circular 13/1988, require that an environmental assessment should accompany a planning application for one of the 10 categories of development listed in Schedule 1. These are large, complex developments, such as crude oil refineries, thermal power stations, integrated chemical installations and waste disposal installations. A planning authority must not grant planning permission for such development unless it has first taken account of the assessment.

7.4.18 Schedule 2 to the 1988 Regulations lists 14 categories of development where the planning authority has a duty to consider whether significant environmental effects are likely to arise, and a discretion to request an environmental assessment before determining a planning application. An applicant may seek a direction from the Secretary of State that no assessment is required. The categories in Schedule 2 include certain agricultural developments, some of the activities undertaken by the extractive and energy industries, wind generators, coast-protection works, the processing of metals, some infrastructure projects, and certain activities associated with the chemical and food industries.

7.4.19 SDD Circular 13/1988 states that the purpose of environmental assessment is to draw together expert quantitative analysis and qualitative assessment of the likely environmental effects of the proposed development in a systematic way so that these effects may be properly evaluated by the planning authority. Information about the content of an environmental statement is provided in Schedule 3 to the 1988 Regulations. The information

[25] Defined in art. 10 of the Town and Country Planning (General Development Procedure) (Scotland) Order 1992 (S.I. 1992 No. 224).
[26] S.I. 1988 No. 1221, as amended by the Environmental Assessment (Scotland) Amendment Regulations 1994 (S.I. 1994 No. 2012). A further Directive 97/11 upgrading the arrangements for environmental assessment was issued on March 3, 1997.

contained in an environmental statement must be taken into account by a planning authority before determining a planning application, and the authority must confirm that it has done so when notifying its decision on the application.[27]

The 1988 Regulations also apply to certain electricity, road and land 7.4.20 drainage projects. SOEnvD Circular 26/1991 and General Order No. 27A also apply the spirit of the 1988 Regulations to provisional orders made under the Private Legislation Procedure (Scotland) Act 1936, which authorise the carrying out of works. Other regulations require environmental assessment to be undertaken in connection with appeals against enforcement notices and prior to the carrying out of prescribed activities which are beyond planning control. These are the Environmental Assessment (Afforestation) Regulations 1988,[28] the Environmental Assessment (Salmon Farming in Marine Waters) Regulations 1988,[29] and the Electricity and Pipeline Works (Assessment of Environmental Effects) Regulations 1990.[30] At the time of writing a draft Directive has been issued by the European Commission proposing the extension of environmental assessment from projects to land use plans.

Consultations

The Town and Country Planning (General Development Procedure) 7.4.21 (Scotland) Order 1992[31] requires a planning authority to consult with specified bodies where appropriate, and to have regard to their response when determining a planning application. Statutory consultees include Scottish Natural Heritage and SEPA. Community councils must also be supplied with weekly lists of planning applications.

Publicity

Apart from the requirement on the applicant to notify owners of the subject 7.4.22 land and neighbours, the planning authority must give public notice of the following applications:

(1) those which fall within one of the 15 classes of "bad neighbour development". This is a term generally applied to the classes

---

[27] Information on environmental assessment must be taken into account and the planning authority must confirm that this has been done when notifying the decision (see S.I. 1988 No. 1221 and S.I. 1994 No. 2012).
[28] S.I. 1988 No. 1207.
[29] S.I. 1988 No. 1218.
[30] S.I. 1990 No. 1442.
[31] S.I. 1992 No. 224.

listed in Schedule 2 to the Town and Country Planning (General
Permitted Development) (Scotland) Order 1992 and may involve
development which would be likely to have an adverse environmental impact;

(2) those which constitute a departure from the development plan[32];

(3) those which affect the character of a conservation area or affect
the setting of a listed building.

The planning authority must have regard to any response. All planning
applications must also be deposited in the planning register maintained by
the planning authority, which is open for public inspection.

Call-in

7.4.23   The Secretary of State has required planning authorities to notify him of
certain planning applications[33] so that he can decide whether to issue a
direction calling them in from the planning authority with a view to making
the decision himself. These are applications which, for the most part, raise
issues of national importance.

Determination of an application

7.4.24   When determining an application, the planning authority must have regard
to the development plan, so far as material, and to any other material
consideration (1997 Act, s. 37(2)). As already indicated, the determination
will have to be made in accordance with the development plan unless
material considerations indicate otherwise (1997 Act, s. 25; and see para.
7.3.9).

7.4.25   Nonetheless, the process is discretionary. Each application must be
considered on its merits against the background of relevant policy, and the
planning authority may depart from its development plan where material
considerations "indicate otherwise". Before doing so, however, the authority
must follow certain procedures which are designed to ensure that it does
not ride roughshod over plans which have been subject to the discipline of
public participation and a merit-testing procedure.[34]

7.4.26   The term "material considerations" is not defined in the 1997 Act, and
the scope of the term has given rise to considerable uncertainty. In *Stringer v.*

---

[32] For departure procedures, see the Town and Country Planning (Development Contrary to
Development Plans) (Scotland) Direction 1996, annexed to SODD Circular 10/1996 and
PAN 41 *Development Plan Departures* (revised 1997).

[33] Town and Country Planning (Notification of Planning Applications) (Scotland) Direction
1997, annexed to SODD Circular 4/1997.

[31] *ibid.*

Minister of Housing and Local Government[35] Cooke J. defined these other considerations as "any consideration which relates to the use and development of land". He went on to say that "whether a particular consideration falling within that broad class is material in any given case will depend on the circumstances". These two tests provide no more than very general guidance. The initial decision as to the materiality of a consideration and the weight to be given to it rests with the planning authority and with the Secretary of State on appeal.

The list of material considerations is open-ended and much will depend 7.4.27 on the particular circumstances of a case. Environmental factors are, of course, often important in the determination of planning applications. By way of illustration of more specific factors, the following considerations have, in particular circumstances, been held to be material:

(1) compatability with other uses;
(2) the effect on private interests;
(3) the desirability of retaining the existing use;
(4) the risk of creating an undesirable precedent;
(5) circulars and other policy statements;
(6) the need for the development in economic terms;
(7) the financial consequences of the development;
(8) the availability of alternative sites;
(9) the lack of infrastructure;
(10) personal circumstances.

In the specific context of planning proposals which raise environmental 7.4.28 protection issues, PAN 51, *Planning and Environmental Protection*, paragraph 54 suggests that the following considerations might be regarded as material by a planning authority:

(1) the sensitivity of the area as reflected in landscape, agricultural land and soil quality, nature conservation or archaeological designations;
(2) the visual impact of the development;
(3) the hours of operation proposed for the development and the consequences for neighbours;
(4) the possibility that the release of smoke, fumes, gases, dust, steam, smell or noise might result in nuisance or loss of amenity.

A question which has caused some difficulty in recent years is how far 7.4.29 planning authorities may take into account in the development control process matters which may have to be considered later by the appropriate environmental protection agency. The law is now reasonably clear. A

---

[35] [1970] 1 W.L.R. 1281.

principle is applied in interpreting legislation to the effect that general powers in an Act should not derogate from powers granted specifically in other legislation. In other words, if there is a specific power in an Act to deal with a particular manner, it should not be dealt with under a general power in some other Act. However, powers will not often be truly concurrent because different Acts have different purposes and contexts. Certainly, as far as planning and other statutes are concerned, the courts have shown little inclination to construe different statutes as if Parliament had allocated mutually exclusive areas of jurisdiction to them.[36] This is borne out by two recent cases which focus on the overlap between planning and environmental matters.

7.4.30　　　In *Aberdeen District Council v. Secretary of State for Scotland*[37] a decision letter on an appeal stated that as the dropping of litter was dealt with under other legislation it was not a proper reason for refusing planning permission. The decision was challenged by the planning authority. The court held that as the principal issue in the appeal was the prospect of a serious loss of amenity, the problem of litter was a material consideration which should have been taken into account.

7.4.31　　　In *Gateshead Metropolitan Borough Council v. Secretary of State for the Environment*[38] an outline application for a clinical waste incinerator was refused and an appeal was lodged with the Secretary of State. The inspector recommended refusal because although the plant could meet emission limits the impact of the proposal on air quality was insufficiently defined. The recommendation was rejected by the Secretary of State, who concluded that the emission would be controlled by other environmental legislation and that it was not the role of the planning system to duplicate those controls. Accordingly, he granted planning permission for the incinerator, a decision which was upheld in the English Court of Appeal.

7.4.32　　　In the High Court the deputy judge laid down some useful guidelines for resolving demarcation problems:

- the planning authority must have regard to the provisions of the development plan and to any other material considerations;
- the environmental impact of emissions into the air is a material consideration;
- the existence of stringent pollution control legislation is also a material consideration;
- the weight to be given to a material consideration is a matter for the discretion of the decision-maker and the courts will not disturb this in the absence of *Wednesbury* unreasonableness.[39]

---

[36] *Esdell Caravan Parks Ltd v. Hemel Hempstead R.D.C.* [1996] 1 Q.B. 895; *Ladbroke (Rentals) Ltd v. S. of S. for the Environment* [1981] J.P.L. 427.

[37] 1993 S.L.T. 1325.

[38] [1995] J.P.L. 432.

[39] *Associated Provincial Picture Houses v. Wednesbury Corp.* [1948] 1 K.B. 223.

The Secretary of State has given guidance, as a matter of policy (rather 7.4.33 than as a matter of law), on this exercise of discretion where planning and other environmental controls overlap. NPPG 1, *The Planning System*, for example, states at paragraph 49 that "planning powers should not normally be used to secure objectives which can be achieved under other legislation". NPPG 4, *Mineral Working*, is more specific about this relationship, and states:

> "The main factors to be considered are visual intrusion, noise, blasting and vibration, dust, pollution of water courses and transport issues. Apart from visual intrusion, these considerations are also covered by other legislation specifically related to pollution control. Planning authorities should not, therefore, seek to control through planning measures matters that are the proper concern of the pollution control authority, except where planning interests can be clearly distinguished."

PAN 51, *Planning and Environmental Protection*, indicates at paragraph 47 7.4.34 the circumstances in which it may be appropriate to rely on planning control:

> "There may be circumstances where the environmental protection body is satisfied that their requirements in relation to a proposed development can be satisfied, but the planning authority takes the view that, because of the particular characteristics of an area, the development is unacceptable on environmental protection grounds and planning permission may have to be refused. In such cases, which are only likely to arise in exceptional circumstances, the planning authority will need to demonstrate the land use planning reasons which have led them to conclude that the proposed development is unacceptable."

Conditions

The planning authority may grant planning permission unconditionally, subject 7.4.35 to conditions, or it may refuse permission (1997 Act, s. 37). The power to impose conditions is expressed in very wide terms; the authority may impose such conditions as it thinks fit. For the avoidance of doubt, section 41 of the 1997 Act makes clear that conditions may regulate the development or use of land under the control of the applicant, whether or not it is part of the application site, and may require the carrying out of works.

Although the power is expressed in very broad terms, the courts require 7.4.36 that conditions should serve a planning purpose, be fairly and reasonably related to the subject-matter of the application, and should not be unreasonable in the administrative law sense: *Newbury District Council v. Secretary of State for the Environment*.[40] Conditions must also be sufficiently certain.

---

[40] [1981] A.C. 578.

7.4.37   In addition to the qualifications laid down by the courts, the Secretary of State has given policy guidance on the scope of the power to impose conditions. SDD Circular 18/1986 states that, in deciding whether to impose a condition, the planning authority should consider whether it would refuse the application without it. If it would not, the condition requires some special justification. The Circular lays down the following tests which a condition should satisfy: necessity; relevance to planning; relevance to the development in question; enforceability; precision; and reasonableness in all other respects. The Circular goes on to give guidance on the use of conditions to deal with particular circumstances such as restrictions on occupancy and the future management of the development.

7.4.38   In practice, conditions are extensively used by planning authorities to control a wide range of matters relating to the environment. Conditions may be used, for example, to secure landscaping and tree planting, to monitor and control various aspects of pollution, and to safeguard environmentally important aspects of a site. Conditions also have an important role to play (together with agreements — see below) in ensuring that historic contamination is tackled so that land will be fit for its proposed use.

7.4.39   A condition will be unreasonable if it requires the fulfilment of some obligation which is beyond the control of the applicant, for example the provision of landscaping on land outwith the application site which is not controlled by the applicant. However, in *Grampian Regional Council v. Secretary of State for Scotland*[41] it was held that a condition could properly be imposed which made the commencement or occupation of the development contingent on the happening of a specified event. The condition will be valid even if there is little or no prospect of the contingency being fulfilled.[42] Such a negatively worded condition could enable permission to be granted, for example, where it would otherwise have to be refused because of the lack of off-site landscaping.

Planning agreements

7.4.40   Section 75 of the 1997 Act enables a planning authority to enter into an agreement with any person interested in land with a view to restricting or regulating the development or use of the land. If it is recorded in the Register of Sasines or in the Land Register for Scotland, such an agreement will be enforceable at the instance of the planning authority against singular successors.

7.4.41   Planning agreements are almost invariably triggered by a planning application, and are used by planning authorities to enhance their

---

[41] 1984 S.C. (H.L.) 58; 1984 S.L.T. 197.
[42] *British Rail Board v. S. of S. for the Environment* [1994] J.P.L. 32.

development control powers, including the control of matters of environmental concern. Planning agreements overcome limitations on the control that can be secured by condition, and open up the prospect of alternative and possibly more effective enforcement mechanisms.

Until recently, considerable uncertainty existed over the legitimate scope of planning agreements. Matters have now been clarified up to a point by the decision of the House of Lords in *Tesco Stores Ltd v. Secretary of State for the Environment*.[43] The case involved competing applications for superstores on sites at Witney, Oxfordshire. The applications were the subject of a conjoined inquiry. Tesco offered to pay £6.6 million towards the cost of funding the construction of a new link road to the west of Witney if planning permission were granted. The Secretary of State rejected his inspector's recommendation to grant planning permission to Tesco, and instead granted planning permission to a competitor. In doing so the Secretary of State accepted the inspector's conclusion that the relationship between Tesco's proposed superstore and the need for the link road was no more than tenuous. That being so, the Secretary of State considered that the offer should be given no weight in the decision. Tesco challenged the decision principally on the ground that the Secretary of State had failed to have regard to a material consideration — the offer to fund the link road. The House of Lords upheld the Secretary of State's decision. Four points emerge from this decision:

- for it to influence the decision, there must be some relationship, however tenuous, between the obligation and the proposed development;
- if such a relationship exists, regard must be had to the obligation;
- the weight to be attached to the obligation in making the decision on the application is entirely a matter for the decision-maker, and the courts will not disturb this in the absence of *Wednesbury* unreasonableness;
- the decision-maker may be influenced by the extent to which the obligation is fairly and reasonably related to the proposed development, or by the extent to which it provides public benefits.

Policy advice on the scope of planning agreements can be found in SODD Circular 12/1996, which steers planning authorities away from a public benefits approach and advises that obligations in agreements should be reasonably related to and in proportion to the requirements of the proposed development.

7.4.42

7.4.43

---

[43] [1995] 1 W.L.R. 759; [1995] J.P.L. 581.

Planning authority's decision

7.4.44 The period within which the planning authority is to give notice of its decision is two months. The period may be extended by agreement with the applicant.

7.4.45   A planning permission enures for the benefit of the land (unless, exceptionally, the permission is personal to the applicant). However, it must be acted upon within five years of the grant or such other period specified in the grant, otherwise it lapses. The time-limit is slightly different where planning permission is granted in outline (see para. 7.4.16) (1997 Act, s. 59). Mineral permissions have a defined life, which, unless otherwise stated, will be 60 years.

7.4.46   A grant of planning permission for development may bring about a change in the character of the locality; therefore what might previously have been regarded as a nuisance will not be seen as out of place. In *Gillingham Borough Council v. Medway (Chatham) Dock Co.*[44] a grant of planning permission for the conversion of the former naval dockyard to a container port resulted in an increase in disturbance to residents from lorry traffic. The increased activity was not regarded by the court as out of place in the vicinity of a container port and could not, therefore, be restrained as a nuisance.[45]

Revocation and discontinuance

7.4.47 A planning authority may, by order, revoke or modify a planning permission at any time before it is implemented (1997 Act, s. 65). Where a permission has been implemented, the authority may, by order, require the discontinuance of the use or the alteration or removal of buildings or works (1997 Act, s. 71). Except for an unopposed revocation order, both types of order require confirmation by the Secretary of State, although it should be noted that the power to revoke a planning permission is exercised when the order is made. In both cases, there is provision for objection, for a hearing before a person appointed by the Secretary of State, and for compensation for loss arising from the order.

7.4.48   Revocation and discontinuance orders are rarely employed in practice because planning authorities are not well-placed to buy environmental improvements. In this respect the decision in *R. v. Exeter City Council, ex p. Thomas*[46] is of interest. Planning permission was granted for substantial residential development in the vicinity of two factories. Permission was

---

[44] [1995] Env. L.R. 98.
[45] See also *Wheeler v. J.J. Saunders* [1995] Env. L.R. 286.
[46] [1990] 3 All E.R. 413.

granted notwithstanding objections from the operators of the factories that the uses would be incompatible. The report of the decision shows that the planning authority wanted to secure the relocation of the factories which, because of the way the area had developed over a period of years, were now non-conforming uses. The authority had no resources to use the discontinuance procedure and, in granting planning permission for housing, was well aware that the consequence might be a nuisance action by incoming householders against the established industrial uses and the latters' consequent forced relocation. The decision was challenged on the grounds that the authority had acted on an improper motive and that the decision was unreasonable in that it failed to pay sufficient regard to the established uses. The challenge failed. The court concluded that the authority had been motivated by proper planning considerations.

Compensation and purchase notices

No compensation is payable for a refusal of planning permission or for the imposition of onerous conditions.   7.4.49

However, the legislation recognises that the effects of regulation can sometimes be every bit as severe as expropriation, and provision is made in such cases for the service of a purchase notice (1997 Act, s. 88). In order to serve a purchase notice following an adverse planning decision, it is necessary to show that the land is incapable of reasonably beneficial use in its existing state, and that it cannot be put to reasonably beneficial use by implementing any permission that has been granted or which is promised. It is not enough that land is of less use or value as a result of an adverse planning decision which will often be the case. The test is whether it is incapable of reasonably beneficial use: *R. v. Minister of Housing and Local Government, ex p. Chichester Rural District Council.*[47]   7.4.50

The purchase notice procedure operates like an inverse compulsory purchase order. The notice must be served within 12 months of the adverse decision. If the notice is resisted by the planning authority, it is referred to the Secretary of State for a decision. If the notice is accepted or confirmed, the authority must buy the subject land at its market value.   7.4.51

APPEAL

An applicant may appeal to the Secretary of State against a refusal of planning permission or against the imposition of onerous conditions. An applicant may also appeal against a deemed refusal if the period for giving a decision has passed (see para. 7.4.44) and no decision has been given.   7.5.1

---

[47] [1960] 1 W.L.R. 587.

The appeal must be made within six months of the decision or within six months of the expiration of the period for giving the decision, as appropriate. There is no right of appeal against a grant of planning permission.

7.5.2   The appeal is an administrative rather than a judicial procedure. Although certain procedures must be followed to ensure fairness, the decision-maker is free to consider the evidence led against the background of national or local policy.

7.5.3   An appeal may be pursued through written submissions (essentially an exchange of correspondence), or, at the request of the appellant or the planning authority, by way of a public inquiry. In an effort to speed up the proceedings, most appeals are now dealt with by written submissions. The appeal process is conducted by a reporter from the Scottish Office Inquiry Reporters' Unit and, in the great majority of appeals, the decision has been delegated to the reporter as an "appointed person", again with a view to speeding up the process. With a few appeals raising issues of national importance, the process will culminate in a report to the Secretary of State, who will make the decision.

7.5.4   The conduct of appeals is governed by procedural rules. For inquiries where the decision is to be made by the Secretary of State, the relevant rules are the Town and Country Planning (Inquiries Procedure) (Scotland) Rules 1997.[48] Where the decision following an inquiry is delegated to an appointed person, the rules are the Town and Country Planning Appeals (Determination by Appointed Person) (Inquiries Procedure) (Scotland) Rules 1997.[49] Written submission appeals are governed by the Town and Country Planning (Appeals) (Written Submissions Procedure) (Scotland) Regulations 1990.[50]

7.5.5   Planning appeals often deal with matters of interest not just to the appellant and the planning authority but to the wider public. This is particularly the case where a proposed development raises issues of environmental concern. Persons falling within certain prescribed categories who have made representations on the appeal or application have a right to be heard. The person conducting the appeal has a discretion to hear other interested third parties and, in practice, they will be heard if they have something relevant to say.

ENFORCEMENT

7.6.1   Part VI of the 1997 Act makes provision for the enforcement of planning control. A breach of planning control occurs when development is carried out without planning permission or when there is a failure to comply with

---

[48] S.I. 1997 No. 796.
[49] S.I. 1997 No. 750.
[50] S.I. 1990 No. 507.

a condition subject to which planning permission has been granted (1997 Act, s. 123). A breach of planning control is not automatically an offence. Formal enforcement action begins with a notice procedure designed to secure compliance. Criminal sanctions may be invoked only if the notice procedure fails to remedy the position.

There are two separate notice procedures. First, where there is a breach 7.6.2 of a condition, the authority may service a "breach of condition notice" requiring compliance with the condition. There is no appeal against such a notice and failure to comply within the time allowed will render the responsible person guilty of an offence punishable on conviction by a fine.

Secondly, in respect of any breach of control, the planning authority 7.6.3 may serve an "enforcement notice". This also requires compliance within a specified time. There is a right of appeal to the Secretary of State on prescribed grounds against such a notice (1997 Act, s. 130), and the consequence of an appeal is to suspend the effect of the notice pending final determination of the matter. Failure to comply with an enforcement notice is an offence, and the penalties were considerably enhanced by the Planning and Compensation Act 1991. The planning authority may also be in a position to take direct action to secure compliance.

The consequence of a breach of control in terms of pollution, hazard or 7.6.4 effect on landscape or nature conservation may be so serious that the planning authority will want to bring it to a halt straightaway rather than waiting for the outcome of an appeal against an enforcement notice. In such a case, the authority may serve a stop notice after the enforcement notice requiring specified activity to stop until such time as the outcome of the enforcement notice is determined (1997 Act, s. 140). There is no appeal against a stop notice, and failure to comply is an offence. The penalties following conviction were substantially enhanced by the Planning and Compensation Act 1991. However, if the stop notice is withdrawn or if an appeal against the related enforcement notice succeeds on one of the legal grounds in section 130 of the 1997 Act, the planning authority may have to compensate for any loss resulting from the service of the stop notice. The prospect of a compensation claim inhibits the use of a stop notice.

Whether or not it has exercised, or proposes to exercise, any of the powers 7.6.5 under Part VI, a planning authority may seek to restrain or prevent an actual or anticipated breach of control by means of an application for an interdict (1997 Act, s. 146).

THE ROLE OF THE COURT OF SESSION IN PLANNING CONTROL

Any person aggrieved by a decision of the Secretary of State on an 7.7.1 application for planning permission which he has called in for decision or on appeal against a refusal of planning permission, the imposition of onerous conditions, the service of an enforcement notice or by certain other decisions and orders under the 1997 Act, may apply to the Court of Session under section 239 of the 1997 Act for the order or decision to be quashed. The validity of structure and local plans may also be challenged by way of application under section 238.

7.7.2   Exactly who is encompassed by the term "aggrieved person" is not clear, but it is likely that in the context of appeal decisions it would include not only owners and tenants of the subject land, the appellant and the planning authority who are directly affected by the decision, and also anyone who took part in the appeal process or who, for some reason, was denied the opportunity to take part.

7.7.3   The application must be made within six weeks of the date of the decision in question. There are two possible grounds on which the application may be made: first, that the decision was outwith the powers of the Act; and, secondly, that there has been a failure to comply with a procedural requirement which has caused substantial prejudice to the appellant. The courts have adopted a broad approach in interpreting the scope of the statutory grounds of challenge. Between them they encompass the full range of the *ultra vires* principle.

7.7.4   A successful application under sections 238 or 239 may result in the order, plan or decision in question being quashed. The court will not substitute its own decision; it will be for the decision-maker to make a fresh decision.

7.7.5   Planning actions and decisions which are not subject to the statutory application procedure in sections 238 and 239 are subject to the general supervisory jurisdiction of the Court of Session and may be the subject of an application for judicial review. However, a person contemplating such an application must qualify title and interest.

BLIGHT

7.8.1   Blight is generally taken to refer to the depressing effect on the value of property resulting from proposals which imply either the public acquisition of the property or disturbance of the existing use. For example, a proposal to build a major road, extend an airport or construct a high-speed rail link will have a depressing effect not only on the value of property to be acquired for the work but on property nearby which will suffer serious disturbance, including environmental disturbance such as noise, fumes, dust, etc., from the construction and subsequent use of the work.

7.8.2   The 1997 Act, in Part V, Chap. II makes some provision for alleviating hardship on the part of those whose property is earmarked for eventual acquisition. A person who can show that the proposed works are sufficiently advanced in their planning to cast a blight on the value of his property may serve a "blight notice" on the responsible body. He must, however, have an interest which qualifies for protection.[51] The provisions do not protect everyone suffering from blight; only the most serious cases.

---

[51]   1997 Act, s. 100.

If the blight notice is accepted or confirmed on a reference to the Lands   7.8.3
Tribunal for Scotland, the responsible body must acquire the property at its
market value — ignoring the effects of the blight.

Owners of property not required for the works who will suffer disturbance   7.8.4
from its construction and use have three possible remedies: first, the
responsible body may be empowered to buy up the interests of those who
are most seriously disturbed[52]; secondly, the responsible body may be in a
position to take steps to mitigate the effects of disturbance by, for example,
noise insulation[53]; and, thirdly, those disturbed may qualify for compensation
equal to the depreciation in the value of their property.[54]

---

[52] Land Compensation (Scotland) Act 1973, s. 24, as amended by the Planning and
Compensation Act 1991, s. 76.
[53] Land Compensation (Scotland) Act 1973, s. 18; and see the Noise Insulation (Scotland)
Regulations 1975 (S.I. 1975 No. 460).
[54] Railways Clauses Consolidation (Scotland) Act 1845, s. 6, as applied by the Acquisition of
Land (Authorisation Procedure) (Scotland) Act 1947; see also the Land Compensation
(Scotland) Act 1973, Pt. I.

Chapter Eight

NOISE

INTRODUCTION

8.1.1 Noise is a pollutant which has traditionally failed to attract and sustain much public attention. This is due to a variety of reasons. Noise is invisible; furthermore, unlike other forms of pollution, such as hazardous waste or harmful chemicals, noise has no "fall-out" factor. There has never been, nor will there be, a noise disaster of similar proportions to Bhophal or Seveso. Indeed, writing in 1994, the author, somewhat dismissively, described noise as a "Cinderella" pollutant.[1] The lowly status which noise has enjoyed as an environmental pollutant is reflected in its piecemeal development in the United Kingdom. Indeed, before the passage of the Noise Abatement Act 1960[2] there was no specific national legislation dealing with noise.

8.1.2 In recent years, however, noise has assumed a higher profile in the mind of both the public and the Government which seems more willing to respond to noise-related issues than in the past. Both the Noise and Statutory Nuisance Act 1993 and the Noise Act 1996 (which does not apply to Scotland) have been introduced as a speedy response to public pressure against different types of noise problems.

8.1.3 Noise can be controlled by either:

(a)   the common law; and/or
(b)   under a number of unconnected statutes.

The main controls are now discussed.

COMMON LAW

8.2.1 The most important branch of the common law which can be invoked to deal with unwanted noise is the law of nuisance (see paras. 9.2.1–39).

Elements of nuisance

8.2.2 Essentially, the courts will protect the enjoyment of occupied land from any form of unreasonable interference by others. In order to ascertain

---

[1]   Adams and McManus, *Noise and Noise Law* (1994), p. 151.
[2]   Repealed by the Control of Pollution Act 1974.

whether a nuisance exists in law the courts take a variety of factors into account. None of these factors is *per se* conclusive, nor is the list discussed below exhaustive. Furthermore, the courts do not give one factor prominence over another in determining whether any given state of affairs constitutes a nuisance.

Types of noise nuisance

A wide variety of noise sources have been held to constitute a nuisance in law. The list includes noise from printworks,[3] building works,[4] a sawing mill,[5] singing,[6] domestic birds,[7] cattle,[8] horses,[9] a power station,[10] an unruly family,[11] power boats,[12] a children's playground,[13] a military tattoo,[14] and the firing of guns.[15]   8.2.3

Social utility of the defender's conduct

The court takes into account the value of the defender's conduct to society in general. The more socially useful the defender's conduct is, the less likely the court would consider his conduct unreasonable.[16] The courts have, however, carefully avoided constructing a hierarchy, in terms of social worth, of the various activities which have been the subject of nuisance actions. While the courts recognise the social utility of, for example, manufacturers, it is impossible to predict whether the courts would regard an opera house as more valuable to society than, *e.g.*, a cinema or swimming pool, and so be less willing to regard noise from the opera house a nuisance than noise from a cinema or swimming pool.[17]   8.2.4

Motive of the defender

The courts take into account the extent to which, if any, the state of affairs complained of is motivated by spite. If spite is present the courts readily   8.2.5

---

[3] *Rushmer v. Polsue and Alfieri* [1906] 1 Ch. 234.
[4] *Andreae v. Selfridge & Co. Ltd* [1938] Ch. 1.
[5] *Gilling v. Gray* [1910] T.L.R. 39.
[6] *Motion v. Mills* (1897) 13 T.L.R. 427.
[7] *Leeman v. Montague* [1936] 2 All E.R. 167.
[8] *London Brighton and South Coast Railway v. Truman* (1886) 11 App.Cas. 45.
[9] *Ball v. Ray* (1873) 8 Ch. App. 467.
[10] *Allen v. Gulf Oil Refining Ltd* [1981] A.C. 1001.
[11] *Smith v. Scott* [1973] Ch. 314.
[12] *Kennway v. Thompson* [1981] Q.B. 88.
[13] *Dunton v. Dover D.C.* (1978) 76 L.G.R. 87.
[14] *Webster v. Lord Advocate*, 1984 S.L.T. 13.
[15] *Hollywood Silver Fox Farm Ltd v. Emmett* [1936] 2 K.B. 468.
[16] *Harrison v. Southwark and Vauxhall Water Co.* [1891] 2 Ch. 409.
[17] See Whitty in *The Laws of Scotland: Stair Memorial Encyclopaedia*, Vol. 14, para. 2072. See also, *London Borough of Lewisham v. Fenner* (1995) 248 *ENDS Report* 44.

incline to the view that a nuisance exists. The leading cases on the significance of spite in the law of nuisance all relate to noise. In *Christie v. Davie*[18] the plaintiff's family annoyed the defendant by frequently playing musical instruments. The defendant decided to retaliate by banging tin trays on the party wall. It was held that the defendant had created a nuisance. Furthermore, in *Hollywood Silver Fox Farm Ltd v. Emmett*[19] the plaintiff's company bred foxes on his land. The defendant objected to this practice and therefore decided to create a cacophony by shooting along the boundary which separated his property from that of the plaintiff.[20] The plaintiff succeeded in a nuisance action.

Locality

8.2.6 The nature of the relevant locality where the alleged nuisance exists is taken into account. The leading case is *Inglis v. Shotts Iron Co.* where the Lord Justice-Clerk stated[21]: "Things which are forbidden in a crowded community may be permitted in the country. What is prohibited in enclosed land may be tolerated in the open." The rationale of such a judicial approach can be explained on the grounds that courts expect people who live in localities where a certain state of affairs is commonplace to have become habituated to it. For example, the noise from the unloading of ships in a port is less likely to constitute a nuisance than a similar level of noise from a newly established discotheque situated in the same locality. However, the nature of the locality is relevant only when the adverse state of affairs complained of solely affects the plaintiff's comfort.[22] The locality principle, therefore, becomes redundant when physical damage accrues as a result of the alleged nuisance complained of.[23] For example, if noise and vibration from factory operations damaged the foundations of a nearby building it would be irrelevant that the defender's factory was situated in an industrial area. There is no authority, however, on how the courts would apply the locality principle if the defender's factory were situated in an industrial area but the pursuer's premises were situated in a residential area. In the absence of authority, it is suggested that if, in such a case, the locality test were applicable, the relevant locality would be that of the pursuer.

---

[18] [1893] 1 Ch. 316.
[19] [1936] 2 K.B. 468.
[20] The effect of loud noises on vixen is to deter mating, whelping and to provoke infanticide! See also, *Western Silver Fox Ranch Ltd v. Ross and Cromarty C.C.*, 1940 S.C. 601.
[21] (1881) 8 R. 1006 at p. 1021. See also *Bamford v. Turnley* (1862) 31 L.J.Q.B. 286; and *Swinton v. Pedie* (1837) 15 S. 775.
[22] *St Helen's Smelting Co. v. Tipping* (1865) 11 H.L. Cas. 642.
[23] *Lord Advocate v. Reo Stakis Organisation*, 1982 S.L.T. 140; 24 [1996] Env. L.R. 138.

Nature of the adverse state of affairs

There is now English authority to the effect that in considering if the adverse 8.2.7
state of affairs complained of constitutes a nuisance, the nature and character
of the nuisance must be taken into account. The more unusual the state of
affairs is, the more likely the court will incline to the view that it constitutes
a nuisance in law. The leading case on this point is *Hunter v. Canary Wharf
Ltd & London Docklands Development Corporation*.[24] The plaintiffs claimed
damages for interference over a period of years with the reception of
television broadcasts at their homes. The interference was said to have been
caused by the existence of the Canary Wharf Tower. It was held by the
Court of Appeal that the interference with the television reception did not
constitute an actionable nuisance in law. One of the factors which influenced
Pill L.J. in coming to his decision in favour of the defendants was that tall
and bulky buildings have become a feature of urban landscapes.

Hunter is not binding, however, on the Scottish courts. Furthermore, to 8.2.8
what extent, if any, the reasoning of Pill L.J. on this point will be followed
as far as other types of alleged nuisances are concerned, is difficult to predict,
in other words the factor under discussion may assume relevance only in
relation to interference with television signals.

Duration and intensity

The length of time the relevant state of affairs lasts and its intensity are 8.2.9
taken into account.[25] The dissenting but authoritative judgment of Pollock
C.B. in *Bamford v. Turnley* is worthy of repetition:

> "A clock striking the hour or a bell ringing for some domestic pur-
> pose may be a nuisance, if unreasonably loud and discordant of which
> the jury alone must judge; but although not unreasonably loud if the
> owner for some whim or caprice, made the clock strike the hour every
> ten minutes or the bell ring continually, I think a jury would be satis-
> fied in considering it to be a very great nuisance."[26]

Time of day

The time of day when the state of affairs complained of exists is taken into 8.2.10
account. Therefore, noise which is created during the night is more likely
to constitute a nuisance than noise which occurs during the day.[27] It is

---

[24] [1996] 2 W.L.R. 348; affirmed by House of Lords, *The Times*, April 25, 1997.
[25] *Harrison v. Southwark and Vauxhall Water Co.* [1891] 2 Ch. 409.
[26] (1862) 31 L.J.Q.B. 286 at 346.
[27] *Bamford v. Turnley* (n. 21 *above*).

unlikely that the time of day is relevant in relation to alleged nuisances other than noise.

Sensitivity of the pursuer

8.2.11   The courts are not indulgent to the over-sensitive. This general rule is well illustrated in nuisance law in the case of *Heath v. Brighton Corporation*[28] where the plaintiff, who possessed hypersensitive hearing, failed in his nuisance action since it was proved that a person of normal hearing would not have been affected in the circumstances.

A state of affairs

8.2.12   The pursuer must show that the enjoyment of his property is prejudiced by a state of affairs, *i.e.* the alleged nuisance must have some flavour of permanence. Therefore, the alleged nuisance cannot be transitory in nature.[29] This requirement is normally satisfied automatically as far as noise nuisance is concerned.

Fault required

8.2.13   Whereas in English law liability for nuisance is strict,[30] in Scots law the pursuer requires to prove *culpa*, or blame, on the part of the defender.[31] The concept of *culpa*, however, is wider than that of negligence at common law.[32] Unfortunately, the concept of *culpa* in terms of the law of nuisance is not adequately articulated by way of decided cases. As far as noise nuisance is concerned, while there seems little doubt that the requirement of *culpa* would be satisfied if, for example, a "ghetto-blaster" was played very loudly, in reckless disregard of the comfort of the next-door neighbour, would the requirement of *culpa* be satisfied if one were to organise a barbeque in one's garden in the knowledge that the noise from the guests would possibly discomfit a neighbour? This question cannot be answered with certainty at present.

Who is liable?

The author

8.2.14   Generally, the person who creates a nuisance is liable at common law. Such a person does not need to have a proprietary interest in the land on which

---

[28]   (1909) 98 L.T. 718.
[29]   *Spicer v. Smee* [1946] 1 All E.R. 489.
[30]   *Cambridge Water Co. v. Eastern Counties Leather plc* [1994] 2 A.C. 264.
[31]   *RHM Bakeries v. Strathclyde R.C.*, 1985 S.L.T. 214; *Kennedy v. Glenbelle*, 1996 S.C.L.R. 411.
[32]   *Kennedy v. Glenbelle*, above.

the adverse state of affairs exists.[33] Therefore, musicians who use unoccupied premises for band practice could be successfully sued if they caused undue annoyance to adjoining proprietors.

The occupier

The occupier of the premises concerned will normally be the relevant   8.2.15
defender in a noise nuisance action.[34] In practice, the author of the nuisance
and the occupier will usually be the same individual.

The landlord

A landlord of premises is not liable for every nuisance which emanates   8.2.16
from the premises during the appropriate lease.[35] A landlord is only liable
for any nuisance, for example a noise nuisance, which emanates from the
relevant premises, provided such a state of affairs is the ordinary and
necessary consequence of granting the lease.[36] If, however, the source of
the nuisance is created by the landlord prior to the property concerned being
let, the landlord is solely liable for the manifestation of that nuisance during
the currency of the lease.[37]

The licensor of the nuisance

The person who authorises a nuisance will normally be liable, especially if   8.2.17
he makes no effort to abate the nuisance concerned. The leading case is
now *Webster v. Lord Advocate*,[38] where the Lord Ordinary, Lord Stott, in
the Outer House of the Court of Session held the Secretary of State for
Scotland liable for authorising the holding of the Edinburgh Military Tattoo,
the noise from which *inter alia* was alleged to cause a nuisance. It was held
to be irrelevant that the contract between the Secretary of State and the
Tattoo Policy Committee included a condition that no nuisance was to be
created, since no effort had been made by the former to monitor the activities
of the licensees or to enforce the condition of the licence. It is possible that
the court may adopt a different attitude if it were satisfied that the licensor
was capable of making, and, in fact, did make a genuine effort to ensure
that his licence did not create a nuisance. This point can only be clarified
by future decision.

---

[33] *Slater v. McLellan*, 1924 S.C. 854.
[34] See *Sedleigh-Denfield v. O'Callaghan* [1940] A.C. 880.
[35] *Smith v. Scott* [1973] Ch. 314.
[36] *Tetley v. Chitty* [1986] 1 All E.R. 202.
[37] *Metropolitan Properties Ltd v. Jones* [1939] 2 All E.R. 202.
[38] 1984 S.L.T. 13; 1985 S.L.T. 61.

Defences, etc.

Statutory authority

8.2.18 It is possible for Parliament to sanction the creation and continuance of a nuisance. The leading case is *Allen v. Gulf Oil Refining Ltd*,[39] where occupiers of property which was situated in the vicinity of a huge oil refinery were affected *inter alia* by oil smut and noise emanating from the plant. A private Act of Parliament had authorised the establishment and operation of the plant. The House of Lords[40] held that the oil company had a complete defence since the Act had sanctioned the existence and operation of the refinery, the inevitable consequence of which was the creation of the nuisance. Whether any statute authorises a nuisance, therefore, depends on its construction. The court in such circumstances would have to satisfy itself that the defender conducted his activities without negligence and, furthermore, took reasonable measures to mitigate the relevant nuisance.[41]

Prescription

8.2.19 The law will not allow the pursuer to succeed in a nuisance action if he has acquiesced to the nuisance for 20 years or more.[42] Furthermore, the nuisance must remain substantially constant in nature over the period and constitute an actionable nuisance.[43] In practice, the defence is applicable mainly to noise nuisance actions. The leading case is now *Webster v. Lord Advocate*[44] where Lord Stott stated *obiter* in relation to the noise from the performance of the Edinburgh Military Tattoo that, while the programme of events varied in detail, the sound content of the Tattoo was broadly similar each year and, therefore, the defence of prescription would possibly have been appropriate.

Coming to a nuisance

8.2.20 It is no defence that the pursuer has come to a nuisance and thereby implicitly accepted its very presence at the outset. The leading case is, again, *Webster v. Lord Advocate*[45] where the pursuer moved into a flat adjoining the Edinburgh Castle esplanade in the knowledge that by so doing she would be within earshot of the noise from the performance of the Tattoo. The Lord Ordinary

---

[39] [1981] A.C. 1001.
[40] Lord Keith dissented.
[41] See also *Department of Transport v. North West Water Authority* [1984] A.C. 336.
[42] Prescription and Limitation (Scotland) Act 1973, s. 8.
[43] *Sturges v. Bridgman* (1879) 11 Ch. D. 852.
[44] 1984 S.L.T. 13; 1985 S.L.T. 361.
[45] *ibid.*

accepted the view of both counsel in the case that it was immaterial that the pursuer had come to the nuisance.[46]

Common law remedies

Damages

The court has power to award damages to compensate the pursuer for the **8.2.21** infringement of the enjoyment of his property. The court can take into account the extent to which the pursuer has been discomfited, as well as the physical injury caused to the property of the pursuer.

Interdict

The court can grant an interdict to prevent either the occurrence or recurrence **8.2.22** of the noise nuisance in question. It is a discretionary remedy, *i.e.* the pursuer does not have a right to be granted the remedy. No interdict will be granted to restrain minor interference with the pursuer's rights.[47] The interdict is a flexible tool which can be used to abate the nuisance in question but, at the same time, allow the operations from where the nuisance emanates to continue. Such flexibility is illustrated by the following nuisance cases, which all concern the English equivalent to the interdict (the injunction), to which similar principles apply. In *Dunton v. Dover District Council*[48] the plaintiff sought an injunction to combat the cacophany from a children's playground. The injunction restricted the opening of the playground to between 10 a.m. and 1 p.m., and then only to children under the age of 12. In *Kennaway v. Thompson*[49] the noise nuisance in question was generated by power boats operating on the lake which adjoined the plaintiff's premises. The Court of Appeal granted an injunction which prevented the defendant boat club from holding more than one international event, two national events and three club events per racing season. In addition, no boat capable of creating more than 75 dB(A) was to be used on the club's water. The injunction also restricted the use of motorboats employed to pull waterskiers to the extent that not more than six could be used at any one time.

As a general rule, the terms of the interdict are required to be precise **8.2.23** and must leave the defender in no doubt as to what requires to be done in order to comply with its terms.[50]

---

[46] 1984 S.L.T. 13 at p. 14.
[47] *Ankerson v. Connelly* [1907] 1 Ch. 678.
[48] (1978) 76 L.G.R. 87.
[49] [1981] Q.B. 88.
[50] *Webster v. Lord Advocate*, 1985 S.L.T. 361.

Declarator

8.2.24 In some cases a pursuer who alleges that he has been or is being affected by a nuisance may apply to the court for a declarator that his legal rights are being infringed. For example, the court could make a declaration to the effect that the defender, a factory occupier, had created a sufficient level of noise to constitute a nuisance in law.

Abatement

8.2.25 Scots law allows an individual to abate a nuisance without first enlisting the help of the courts. However, the doctrine is not well developed by way of judicial decision. In the English case of *Lemmon v. Webb*[51] it was held lawful for the occupier of land, without notice, to cut off the overhanging branches of his neighbour's trees. Again, in *Butler v. Standard Telephones*[52] it was held lawful for the plaintiff to sever the roots of the trees situated in an adjoining property. This form of remedy, however, seems to have found little favour with the courts in Scotland.[53]

STATUTORY CONTROL OF NOISE

8.3.1 A number of statutory controls exist dealing with the subject of noise. This area of environmental law has been described by the author as a "mosaic of legislative provisions".[54] The first statutory controls directed at the problem of noise took the form of local authority byelaws, which remained the main legislative source of noise control until Parliament, prompted by the then fledgling Noise Abatement Society, passed the Noise Abatement Act 1960, which gave local authorities in the United Kingdom the power to suppress noise nuisances in their areas. The 1960 Act was repealed by the Control of Pollution Act 1974 (COPA 1974) which, in turn, was substantially amended by the Environmental Protection Act 1990 (EPA 1990), the Noise and Statutory Nuisance Act 1993 and the Environment Act 1995. The relevant provisions of these Acts are discussed below in relation to:

- neighbour noise;
- construction noise;
- loudspeakers in streets; and
- noise abatement zones.

---

[51] [1895] A.C. 1.
[52] [1940] 1 K.B. 555. See also, *Co-operative Wholesale Society Ltd v. British Railways Board, The Times*, December 20, 1995.
[53] *Glasgow and Carlisle Road Trustees v. White* (1828) 7 S. 115.
[54] Adams and McManus, *Noise and Noise Law* (1994), p. 161.

Neighbour noise

Capacity of premises to resist noise

In Scotland, Part III of EPA 1990 deals with general nuisances, including 8.3.2
noise nuisance. The relevant provisions are discussed with special reference
to noise. At the outset it should be stressed that the courts give the expression
"nuisance" as used in statute its ordinary common law meaning.[55] In other
words, when a court has to determine if a given state of affairs constitutes a
nuisance in terms of a statute, it takes into account the same factors as those
discussed above.[56]

Section 79(1) of EPA 1990 places a duty on a local authority to cause its 8.3.3
area to be inspected from time to time to detect statutory nuisances and,
furthermore, to investigate complaints of statutory nuisances made by
persons living within its area, where this is reasonably practicable. Section
79(1)(a) provides that "any premises in such a state as to be prejudicial to
health or a nuisance" constitutes a statutory nuisance for the purpose of the
Act.

In *Southwark London Borough Council v. Ince*[57] the occupiers of 8.3.4
dwelling-houses successfully brought an action under section 92(1)(a) of
the Public Health Act 1936[58] against the owners of the houses on the grounds
that noise and vibration from passing trains and traffic was a nuisance and
prejudicial to health in terms of the section. It was held that it was legitimate
for the court to take into account external factors when considering whether
the state of the premises flouted the provisions of the section. The court
went on to determine, on the facts of the case, that the noise did not constitute
a nuisance but was prejudicial to health.

Other noise nuisances

Section 79(1)(g) of EPA 1990 provides that "noise emitted from premises 8.3.5
so as to be prejudicial to health or a nuisance" constitutes a statutory nuisance
for the purpose of the Act. The word "noise" is defined as including vibration.
The general utility of the subsection is to some extent circumscribed by the
fact that the relevant noise is required to emanate from premises.[59] Noise
emanating from streets and other public places would not, therefore,
normally fall within the scope of the section.

---

[55] See, *e.g. A Lambert Flat Management Ltd v. Lomas* [1981] 2 All E.R. 280. See also, *East Northamptonshire D.C. v. Fossett* [1994] Env. L.R. 388.
[56] See paras. 8.2.2.–13.
[57] *The Times*, May 16, 1989.
[58] Repealed by EPA 1990.
[59] *Tower Hamlets L.B.C. v. Manzoni and Walder* [1984] J.P.L. 437.

8.3.6 While, as stated above, it must be shown that a given state of affairs constitutes a nuisance in terms of section 79 of EPA 1990, it is not necessary for the local authority to adduce evidence to the effect that a specific individual was affected by the noise in question.[60] It is sufficient for the prosecution to rely solely on other evidence, including expert evidence.[61] By virtue of section 79(6) of EPA 1990, subsection 1(g) does not apply to noise caused by aircraft other than model aircraft.

Noise from car radios, stereos, etc.

8.3.7 It is indisputable that noise from car radios and stereos presents a perennial problem not only for those using roads and pavements, but also householders. The Noise and Statutory Nuisance Act 1993 introduces a new paragraph (ga) to section 79(1) of EPA 1990 to the effect that noise which is prejudicial to health or a nuisance which is emitted from or caused by a vehicle, machinery or equipment in a street, ranks as a statutory nuisance. However, under the new section 79(6A), section 79(1)(ga) does not apply to noise made:

  (a) by traffic;
  (b) by any naval, military or airforce of the Crown or by a visiting force (as defined in section 79(2) of EPA 1990); or
  (c) by a political demonstration or a demonstration supporting or opposing a cause or campaign.

Abatement procedure for nuisances

8.3.8 Under section 80(1) of EPA 1990 a duty is placed on a local authority, if it is satisfied that a nuisance exists, or is likely to occur or recur in its area, to take proceedings to abate the nuisance or to prohibit its occurrence or recurrence. Under section 80(2) the relevant abatement notice must be served on the person responsible for the nuisance. The expression "person responsible" is defined in section 79(7) as the person to whose act, default or sufferance the nuisance is attributable, and, in relation to a vehicle, includes the person in whose name the vehicle is registered and any other person who is the driver of the vehicle. In relation to machinery or equipment, the expression includes any person who is the operator of the machinery or equipment. Furthermore, where the nuisance arises from any defect of a structural character, the notice must, under section 80(2), be served on the owner of the premises. However, where the person responsible

---

[60] *Wellingborough B.C. v. Gordon* [1993] 1 Env. L.R. 218.
[61] *Cooke v. Adatia* (1989) 153 J.P. 129.

for the nuisance cannot be found or the nuisance has not yet occurred, the notice must be served on the occupier of the premises.

The terms of the abatement notice are required to be precise and 8.3.9 practicable in their terms.[62] However, it is sufficient if the recipient of the notice knows what is wrong from the terms of the notice, taking all the relevant circumstances of the case into account.[63] The relevant notice can be worded to take immediate effect.[64] Whereas section 80(1) of EPA 1990 requires the notice to specify the time or times within which the notice is to be complied with, it has been held that it is not necessary for the relevant notice to specify a time-limit for the prohibition of the recurrence of the nuisance.[65] Under section 80(4) if a person on whom an abatement notice is served, without reasonable excuse, contravenes or fails to comply with any requirement or prohibition imposed by the notice, he commits an offence. In *Wellingborough Borough Council v. Gordon*[66] it was held that holding a birthday party did not provide a reasonable excuse for breach of a noise reduction notice in terms of a notice served in terms of section 58(4) of COPA 1974 (now repealed).

The abatement of street noise falling within the scope of section 79(1)(ga) 8.3.10 of EPA 1990 is now dealt with specifically by section 80A(1) of the Act.

Statutory defences

Under section 80(7) of EPA 1990 the defence of best practicable means is 8.3.11 available in proceedings relating to the abatement of statutory nuisances under the Act. Section 79(9) provides that the expression "best practicable means" is to be interpreted by reference to *inter alia* the following provisions:

(a) "practicable" means reasonably practicable having regard, among other things, to local conditions and circumstances, to the current state of technical knowledge and to the financial implications;

(b) the means to be employed include the design, installation, maintenance and manner and periods of operation of plant and machinery, and design, construction and maintenance of buildings and structures.

However, by virtue of section 80(8) as far as proceedings in respect of noise are concerned, the defence of best practicable means applies only in respect of

---

[62] *Strathclyde R.C. v. Tudhope*, 1983 S.L.T. 22; 1982 S.C.C.R. 286. See also, *R. v. Fenny Stratford Justices, ex p. Watney Mann (Midlands) Ltd* [1976] 1 W.L.R. 1101.

[63] *Myatt v. Teignbridge D.C.* [1994] Env. L.R. 18.

[64] *Strathclyde R.C. v. Tudhope* (n. 62 *above*).

[65] *R. v. Birmingham Justices Clerk, ex p. Guppy* (1988) 86 L.G.R. 264. See also, *R. v. Tunbridge Wells Justices, ex p. Tunbridge Wells B.C.* [1996] Env. L.R. 88.

[66] [1993] 1 Env. L.R. 218.

noise from industrial, trade or business premises or in respect of vehicles used for such purposes. The defence must be established on the balance of probability. It was further held that if the accused has taken all possible steps to secure planning permission for measures to reduce the effect of noise from the relevant premises, and thereby allow the provisions of the relevant abatement notice to be complied with, the defence of best practicable means could succeed.[67]

Appeals against notice

8.3.12   A person served with an abatement notice may, in Scotland, appeal against the notice to the sheriff within 21 days from the service of the notice (EPA 1990, s. 80(3)). The grounds on which notice of appeal can be served are specified in the Statutory Nuisance (Appeals) (Scotland) Regulations 1996.[68] It has been held that failure to appeal against an abatement notice deprives the accused of the right to challenge the terms of the notice at any subsequent trial.[69]

Summary proceedings by private individuals

8.3.13   Section 82(2) of EPA 1990 empowers a sheriff court to make an order if it is satisfied on a complaint made by a person alleging that he is aggrieved by a statutory nuisance:

(a)   requiring the defender to abate the nuisance within the time specified in the order, and to execute any works necessary for that purpose; and

(b)   prohibiting a recurrence of the nuisance, and requiring the defender, within a time specified in the order, to execute any works necessary to prevent the recurrence.

There is no authority as to the meaning of the word "aggrieved" as used in the section. However, it is suggested that the word simply means adversely or prejudicially affected by the relevant nuisance. Under section 82(8) a person who, without reasonable excuse, contravenes such an order, commits an offence under the Act. The defence of best practicable means is available in respect of proceedings under the section (EPA 1990, s. 80(10)).

Audible intruder alarms

8.3.14   The use of audible intruder alarms is becoming more common in premises. Section 9 of the Noise and Statutory Nuisance Act 1993 makes special provision for such alarms, including the requirement that an audible alarm

---

[67]   *Chapman v. Gosberton Farm Produce* [1993] 1 Env. L.R. 191.

[68]   S.I. 1996 No. 1076.

[69]   *Stagecoach Ltd v. McPhail*, 1988 S.C.C.R. 289.

installed in or on any premises, must comply with any prescribed standards.[70]
The provisions contained in section 9 come into effect only if the local
authority so resolves.

Construction site noise

Noise from construction sites presents an obvious potential problem for 8.3.15
those residing in close proximity to such sites. Building site noise is usually
generated by machinery which is employed in excavating, lifting, cutting,
demolishing, etc., as well as by site traffic. The capacity of building sites to
generate noise complaints is increased by the fact that people tend to be
more adversely affected by noise to which they are unaccustomed. Since
building site operations are generally of only temporary duration the
residents in the vicinity of the site do not have time to become habituated to
the relevant noise and are, therefore, more predisposed to being discomfited.

Section 60 of COPA 1974 confers wide and detailed powers on local 8.3.16
authorities in relation to noise from construction sites. The section applies
to:

> "(a) the erection, construction, alteration, repair or maintenance of
>   buildings, structures or roads;
> (b) breaking up, opening or boring under any road or adjacent land
>   in connection with the construction, inspection, maintenance or
>   removal of works;
> (c) demolition or dredging work; and
> (d) (whether or not also comprised in paragraph (a), (b) or (c) above)
>   any work of engineering construction."

Under section 60(2) a local authority is empowered to serve a notice
imposing requirements on the way in which the works are to be carried out.
An important point is that the section does not lay down any requirement
that a nuisance should exist before notice is served.

The terms a local authority can stipulate in the notice are required to be 8.3.17
both practical and precise.[71] Under section 60(3) the notice may specify the
plant or machinery which is, or is not, to be used, and the hours during which
the works may be carried out. Importantly, the notice may also specify the
level of noise which may be emitted from the premises. In *Adam (Scotland)
Ltd v. Bearsden and Milngavie District Council*[72] it was held by the sheriff
that a local authority could, by a notice served under the section, require a

---

[70] Sched. 3. See also, Control of Noise (Code of Practice on Noise from Audible Intruder
   Alarms) Order 1981 (S.I. 1981 No. 1829).
[71] *Strathclyde R.C. v. Tudhope* (n. 62 above).
[72] 1996 S.L.T. (Sh. Ct.) 21.

construction firm not to permit noise emanating from the site to travel further than the relevant site boundary. Under section 60(4) the local authority must have regard to the provisions of any code of practice[73] issued under Part III of the Act, and the best practicable means to minimise the noise.

8.3.18   The relevant notice is required to be served on the person who appears to the local authority to be carrying out, or going to carry out, the works, and on such other persons appearing to the local authority to be responsible for, or to have control over, the carrying out of the works as the local authority thinks fit (COPA 1974, s. 60(5)). Therefore, notice could be served on the relevant building contractor as well as the person commissioning the works (if they are different persons) such as the owner or occupier of the land concerned. The notice may specify the time within which its terms are to be complied with, and may require the person on whom notice is served to execute works as opposed, simply, to refrain from creating noise (COPA 1974, s. 60(6)). The person served with a notice under section 60 may appeal against the notice, as far as Scotland is concerned, to the sheriff court within 21 days from the service of the notice (COPA 1974, s. 60(7)). It is a defence in relation to proceedings under section 80 of EPA 1990 (which deals with summary proceedings for noise nuisances) to prove that the alleged offence is covered by a notice served under section 60 of COPA 1974.[74]

8.3.19   It can be seen, therefore, that the possibility of the appropriate local authority serving notice under section 60 of COPA 1974 could constitute a constant threat to a building contractor who requires to know at the outset how long the building works will be in progress and the type of machinery he will employ on site. Section 61, therefore, allows a person who intends to carry out building works to apply to the local authority for consent. If, as in most cases in Scotland, the relevant building works require a warrant in terms of section 6 of the Building (Scotland) Act 1959, the request for approval must be made at the same time as application for building warrant. The application must contain particulars of the works and the method by which they are to be carried out and, perhaps more importantly, the steps proposed to be taken to minimise the noise resulting from the works. Under section 61(4), if the local authority considers that it would not serve a notice under section 60, it must give its consent to the application. A local authority, when considering whether to grant consent, must address its mind to the provisions of section 60(4). If consent is, in fact, granted, the local authority can reduce the nuisance potential of the site by attaching relevant conditions to a consent and limiting or qualifying the consent to allow for any change of circumstances and limiting the duration of the consent.

8.3.20   The applicant can appeal to the sheriff court against any condition or qualification attached to the consent. It is in the interests of a person who

---

[73] See Control of Noise (Codes of Practice for Construction and Open Sites) Order 1984 (S.I. 1984 No. 1992).

[74] EPA 1990, s. 80(9).

intends to carry out building works to obtain consent under section 61 of COPA 1974 since, in any proceedings for an offence under section 60(8) of the Act, it is a defence to prove that the alleged contravention amounted to the carrying out of works in accordance with consent given under section 61. A further consequence of a consent given under section 61 is that it precludes a local authority from serving notice under section 80 of EPA 1990 (which deals with the abatement of noise nuisances) (EPA 1990, s. 80(9)). Consent under section 61 of COPA 1974 does not, however, preclude an occupier aggrieved by an alleged noise nuisance, taking action against the contractor, etc., under section 82 of EPA 1990.

Noise in streets

Street noise received express legislative attention for the first time in 1960 when it came within the ambit of the Noise Abatement Act 1960. Section 62(1)[75] of COPA 1974 (which, in effect, repeals and re-enacts the appropriate provision of the 1960 Act) proscribes the use of a loudspeaker in a street between 9 p.m. and 8 a.m. for any purpose. It is also made an offence to use a loudspeaker in a street at any other time for the purpose of advertising any trade or business. Under section 62(1A) of COPA 1974 power is now given to the Secretary of State to amend the times specified above, by order. However, no order may amend the times so as to permit the operation of a loudspeaker in a street[76] at any time between the hours of 9 p.m. and 8 a.m.[77]   8.3.21

Section 62(2) exempts from the provisions of section 62(1) of COPA 1974 certain types of loudspeaker, including those used by the police, fire brigade and ambulance service. Also exempt is the use of a loudspeaker (*e.g.* a loudspeaker which is part of a car radio system) to entertain or communicate with the occupant of a vehicle, provided the loudspeaker is not operated so as to give reasonable cause for annoyance to persons in the vicinity. Another important exemption, in practical terms, is that made in respect of the operation of a loudspeaker between 12 p.m. and 7 p.m. on the same day, provided the loudspeaker is fixed to a vehicle used for the purposes of sale of a perishable commodity (*e.g.* ice cream) for human consumption and is operated so as not to give reasonable cause for annoyance to persons in the vicinity.[78]   8.3.22

---

[75] s. 62 is amended by the Noise and Statutory Nuisance Act 1993.
[76] "Road" in Scotland.
[77] COPA 1974, s. 62(1B).
[78] *ibid.*, s. 62(3). See Control of Noise (Code of Practice on Noise from Ice Cream Van Chimes etc.) Order 1981 (S.I. 1981 No. 1828).

8.3.23   Under section 62(3A) of COPA 1974 power is given to the relevant local authority to give consent to the operation of a loudspeaker in terms of Schedule 2 to the Noise and Statutory Nuisance Act 1993, in which case the provisions of section 62(1) do not apply. However, the provisions of the Schedule only come into operation if the local authority passes a resolution to that effect.

Noise abatement zones

8.3.24 COPA 1974 introduces a new concept in noise control by way of noise abatement zones. Under section 63 a local authority is empowered to designate all or any of its area as a noise abatement zone. The relevant order must specify the classes of premises to which it applies. Local authorities, therefore, have considerable discretion as to both the nature and scope of the zone they institute.

8.3.25   The procedure for setting up a noise abatement zone is set out in Schedule 1 to COPA 1974. Prior to initiating such a scheme the local authority need not make a prior inspection of the area concerned, although such an inspection would be administratively prudent.[79] Provision is made in Schedule 1 for the proposals to be adequately publicised to allow individuals who have a proprietary interest in the relevant premises to make objections to the local authority concerned. In turn, the local authority must consider objections prior to making the appropriate order under section 63.

8.3.26   Following the establishment of the noise abatement zone the local authority is required to measure the level of noise emanating from the premises concerned and record this in the noise level register, which must be kept by the authority.[80] After recording the noise level the local authority must serve a copy of that record on the owner and occupier concerned (COPA 1974, s. 64(3)). Any person on whom a notice is served can appeal to the Secretary of State against the notice, who has complete powers of review and can give such directions to the local authority as he thinks fit. In turn, the local authority must comply with the directions (COPA 1974, s. 64(4)). Under section 65(1) the level of noise recorded in the noise level register in relation to any premises must not be exceeded except with the written consent of the local authority concerned. The local authority's consent may be given conditionally (COPA 1974, s. 65(2)). An applicant for consent may appeal to the Secretary of State against the local authority's decision within three months of the date of the decision (COPA 1974, s. 65(4)). Again, the Secretary of State may review the local authority's

---

[79] *Morganite Special Carbons Ltd v. Secretary of State for the Environment* (1980) 256 E.G. 1105.

[80] See the Noise Level (Measurements and Registers) (Scotland) Regulations 1982 (S.I. 1982 No. 660).

decision. It is an offence to emit noise from any premises in contravention either of section 65(1) or of a condition attached to a consent (COPA 1974, s. 65(5)). The sheriff court, when convicting a person of such an offence, if it is satisfied that the offence is likely to recur, may make an order requiring the execution of any works necessary to prevent it continuing or recurring. It is an offence to contravene such an order without reasonable excuse (COPA 1974, s. 65(6)). Default powers are given to the local authority if the order is contravened by the relevant individual failing to carry out the necessary works (COPA 1974, s. 69).

Section 66(1) of COPA 1974 gives a local authority power to reduce the 8.3.27
level of noise emanating from any premises situated in a noise abatement zone if the noise is of such a level that it is not acceptable having regard to the purposes for which the order was made, and that a reduction in that level would afford a public benefit. The noise reduction notice may specify particular times or particular days, during which the noise level is to be reduced, and may require the noise level to be reduced to different levels for different times or days. In Scotland, a person served with a noise reduction notice can appeal to the sheriff against the notice. It is an offence to contravene a noise reduction notice without reasonable excuse.[81] Section 69(2) gives a local authority power to carry out works in default of the person on whom a noise reduction notice is served.

Under section 67(1) of COPA 1974 if it appears to the local authority 8.3.28
that a new building is going to be constructed in a noise abatement zone or that the use of an existing building will be changed by reason of which, in either case, the terms of the noise abatement order will apply, the local authority may, either on its own initiative or on the application of the owner or occupier of the premises or a person who satisfies the local authority that he is negotiating to acquire an interest, determine the level of noise which will be acceptable from those premises. Appeal against this predetermined level can be made to the Secretary of State within three months of the date the applicant owner or occupier is notified of the decision of the local authority concerned (COPA 1974, s. 67(3)).

Miscellaneous provisions

Section 68 of COPA 1974 allows the Secretary of State to make regulations 8.3.29
to reduce noise from plant or machinery and limit the level of noise which may be caused by any plant or machinery used in connection with building works. Under section 71 the Secretary of State may issue codes of practice for minimising noise.[82]

---

[81] See n. 60 above for the meaning of "reasonable excuse".
[82] See the Control of Noise (Code of Practice for Construction Sites) (Scotland) Order 1982 (S.I. 1982 No. 601) and the Control of Noise (Codes of Practice for Construction and Open Sites) (Scotland) Orders 1985 (S.I. 1985 No. 145) and 1987 (S.I. 1987 No. 1730).

OTHER STATUTORY CONTROLS

Town and Country Planning (Scotland) Act 1997

8.4.1 Planning law and its effect on the environment is dealt with elsewhere in this work.[83] Therefore, only brief mention can be made here of its significance in the context of noise. First, the relevant development plan made under the Act can be used to encourage the location of potential noise sources, such as factories, to be a sufficient distance from premises whose occupants could be adversely affected. Secondly, as far as the grant of planning permission is concerned, considerations of noise can rank as a material consideration to which the relevant planning authority must address its mind.[84] Thirdly, effective prophylactic measures against the source of environmental noise can often be taken at the development stage of the relevant building by the appropriate planning authority imposing conditions on the granting of planning permission under section 37(1)(a) of the 1997 Act.[85]

Civic Government (Scotland) Act 1982

8.4.2 Under section 49(1) of the Civic Government (Scotland) Act 1982 it is an offence *inter alia* for any person to suffer or permit any creature in his charge to give a person reasonable cause for annoyance. Section 54(1) makes it an offence for any person who:

   (a) sounds or plays any musical instrument;
   (b) sings or performs; or
   (c) operates any radio or television receiver, record player, tape-recorder or other sound-producing device,

so as to give any other person reasonable cause for annoyance, to fail to desist on being required to do so by a constable in uniform. Section 49(3) makes exceptions in relation to certain types of vehicles and loudspeakers, for example loudspeakers used by the police or fire brigade.

Byelaws

8.4.3 Since Victorian times local authorities have used their various byelaw-making powers to deal with the problem of noise nuisance. The famous

---

[83] See Chap. 7.
[84] See, *e.g. British Airports Authority v. Secretary of State for Scotland*, 1979 S.C. 200; 1979 S.L.T. 197.
[85] See Planning and Noise Circular 23/73, which is currently under review. For England and Wales, see PPG 24, *Planning and Noise* (1994). See Stein and Humber, "Planning, Pollution and Noise Control" (1995) S.J. 12.

case of *Kruse v. Johnston*[86] centred on the legality of a byelaw which purported to make certain types of street music illegal. As far as Scotland is concerned, local authorities have power under section 201(1) of the Local Government (Scotland) Act 1973 to make byelaws *inter alia* for the prevention and suppression of nuisances. Such a power could be used to make byelaws to suppress noise nuisances.

Health and safety at work

Under section 3 of the Health and Safety at Work etc. Act 1974 a duty is placed on every employer to conduct his undertaking in such a way as to ensure, so far as is reasonably practicable, that persons not in his employment are not exposed to risks to their health or safety. Clearly, therefore, such a duty would cover risks posed to occupiers of land by noise and vibration from industrial and commercial premises.
8.4.4

Licensing (Scotland) Act 1976[87]

Section 38(1)(f) of the Licensing (Scotland) Act 1976 allows a licensing board to make byelaws for the setting out of conditions which may be attached to licences for the improvement of standards of, and conduct in, licensed premises. The appropriate board could, therefore, make conditions relating to noise from licensed premises. Under section 38(3) the board, when granting a licence, may attach to the licence any condition set out in a byelaw. Such a power would be particularly relevant in relation to premises incorporating, for example, discotheques and juke boxes.
8.4.5

Aircraft noise

The relevant controls over aircraft noise can be roughly divided into those which relate to the control of noise from the flight or navigation of aircraft and those which specifically relate to the control of noise from aerodromes.
8.4.6

Flight noise

Under section 76(1) of the Civil Aviation Act 1982 no action may lie *inter alia* in respect of nuisance by reason only of the flight of the aircraft over any property, as long as the provisions of any air navigation order and any order made under section 62 (which relates to orders made during times of war and emergency) have been complied with, and, furthermore, there is no breach of section 81 (which proscribes dangerous flying).
8.4.7

---

[86] [1898] 2 Q.B. 91.
[87] Amended by the Licensing (Amendment) (Scotland) Act 1996.

8.4.8   Section 60(2) of the 1982 Act allows Orders in Council to be made *inter alia* to regulate air navigation. Under section 60(3)(e) the order may specify *inter alia* the conditions under which aircraft may fly from one part of the United Kingdom to another. Therefore, conditions could be imposed, for example, to control the effect of noise from aircraft on residents of premises in the relevant flight paths. Under section 60(3)(e11) the order may also prohibit aircraft flying over such areas (*e.g.* congested areas) in the United Kingdom, as may be specified in the order. Under article 3(1) of the Aircraft Navigation Order 1989[88] an aircraft may not fly over the United Kingdom unless it is registered in the manner prescribed by the Order. Article 95(1) of the Order allows the Civil Aviation Authority (CAA) to direct the operator or commander of any aircraft not to make a particular flight, etc., if the aircraft would be flown in such a way that article 3 would be contravened.

8.4.9   The noise from low flying aircraft presents an obvious problem. Regulation 5(1) of the Rules of the Air Regulations 1991[89] prohibits low flying (an expression which is defined by the Regulations) by aircraft. No aircraft, other than a helicopter, is allowed to "low fly" over any congested area of a city, town or settlement. Regulation 5(c) prohibits low flying by a helicopter except with the permission in writing of the CAA.

8.4.10   While potential noise problems from aircraft can be reduced by controlling the flight of aircraft flying over Britain, much more important is the need to reduce the noise from aircraft at source. As far as the United Kingdom is concerned, this issue is addressed by a system of noise certification.[90] Under article 5(1) of the Air Navigation (Noise Certification) Order 1990[91] no aircraft to which the Order applies may take off or land in the United Kingdom unless a noise certificate has been granted in relation to the aircraft. Article 5(2) makes certain exceptions to this requirement. Article 6 requires the CAA to issue a noise certificate if it is satisfied that the aircraft complies with the appropriate standards specified in the article in relation to noise made by aircraft. The CAA is empowered to direct the appropriate operator or commander not to make a particular flight if the provisions of article 5 would be infringed.

Aerodrome noise[92]

8.4.11   Section 77(1) of the Civil Aviation Act 1982 allows provision to be made by way of an appropriate air navigation order, for regulating the conditions

---

[88] S.I. 1989 No. 2004, amended by S.I. 1990 No. 2154 and S.I. 1991 No. 1726.
[89] S.I. 1991 No. 2437.
[90] See Adams and McManus, *Noise and Noise Law* (1994), pp. 183–184 for relevant background to the noise certification system.
[91] S.I. 1990 No. 1514, made under s. 60 of the Civil Aviation Act 1982.
[92] See, generally, Bigham in Johnson (ed.), *Aviation, the Environment and the Planning Law* (1995).

under which noise and vibration may be caused by aircraft on aerodromes. Under section 77(2) no action may lie in respect of nuisance by reason only of the noise and vibration caused by aircraft on an aerodrome as long as the provisions of the order are complied with. The appropriate current Order is the Air Navigation Order 1989.[93] Under section 78(1) of the Act, the Secretary of State may designate certain aerodromes in relation to which certain requirements concerning the minimisation of noise and vibration, apply.[94] Under section 78(3) the Secretary of State can prohibit aircraft taking off or landing at a designated aerodrome during certain periods. Under section 78(6) he can give to the person managing a designated aerodrome appropriate directions for the purpose of avoiding, limiting or mitigating the effect of noise and vibration connected with the taking-off or landing at the aerodrome. The duties imposed by the aforementioned subsections are enforceable by order of the Court of Session.

Under section 79 of the Act, the Secretary of State may, by statutory instrument, make a scheme requiring a person managing a designated aerodrome to make a grant towards the cost of insulating such buildings, or part of such buildings, against noise.

8.4.12

Military aircraft

Noise from military aircraft, especially low flying aircraft, presents a particular problem, which is aggravated by the fact that military aircraft are designed in such a way that they have more capacity to create noise than civil aircraft. Furthermore, the legal controls discussed above are largely inapplicable to military aircraft. The Crown is generally immune from civil action in respect of noise from military aircraft.[95] However, the Ministry of Defence keeps noise from military aircraft under constant review by its Noise Panel, which has no statutory status. The Ministry also provides noise compensation schemes for those in the vicinity of military airfields. These *ex gratia* compensation schemes are comparable to those in operation for aerodromes designated by the Secretary of State under section 78 of the Civil Aviation Act 1982. Furthermore, the Ministry is also prepared to compensate financially owners of dwellings which have depreciated in value as a result of noise and other physical factors resulting from the creation of new airfields or the extension of existing airfields.

8.4.13

---

[93] S.I. 1989 No. 2004.
[94] The Civil Aviation (Designation of Aerodromes) Order 1981 (S.I. 1981 No. 651) made under s. 29B of the Civil Aviation Act 1971 (now s. 80 of the Civil Aviation Act 1982) does not designate any Scottish airport.
[95] Crown Proceedings Act 1947, s. 11.

Traffic noise

8.4.14   Section 41(1) of the Road Traffic Act 1988 allows the Secretary of State to make regulations governing *inter alia* the use of motorvehicles on roads and the conditions under which they can be used. Power is also given to make regulations relating to the construction and equipment of vehicles. Under section 41(2)(c) such regulations can make provision *inter alia* for noise. Section 42 makes it an offence for a person to fail to comply with any regulations made under section 41. The Road Vehicles (Construction and Use) Regulations 1986[96] presently govern the construction and use, etc., of vehicles. Under regulation 54 every vehicle propelled by an internal combustion engine requires to be fitted with an exhaust system including a silencer, both of which are required to be maintained in good and efficient working order. Regulations 56 to 58 inclusive make provision in respect of noise limits which vehicles must not exceed. Under regulation 97 no motor-vehicle may be used in such a manner as to cause any excessive noise which could have been avoided by the exercise of reasonable care on the part of the driver. Under section 54 of the 1988 Act the Secretary of State is empowered to make regulations requiring the type approval of vehicles with regard to their design, construction and equipment. If he approves a vehicle as a type he must issue a certificate stating that the vehicle complies with the relevant type approval. A plethora of type approval regulations have been made. The contents of the vast majority of this legislation have no bearing on noise. However, the Motor Vehicles (Type Approval) (Great Britain) Regulations 1984[97] make provision relating to noise and silencers in respect of vehicles.

8.4.15   Brief mention should be made here of section 56(1) of the Countryside (Scotland) Act 1967[98] which allows a local authority to make byelaws *inter alia* requiring the use of effectual silencers on pleasure boats. Byelaws can also be made to control the use on land or waterways of vehicles including hovercraft and boats, as well as the landing and taking-off of aircraft.

Land Compensation (Scotland) Act 1973

8.4.16   Section 18(1) of the Land Compensation (Scotland) Act 1973 allows the Secretary of State to make regulations imposing a duty or conferring a power on responsible authorities to insulate buildings or make grants in respect of such insulation against noise caused or expected to be caused by the construction or use of public works. Under regulation 3(1) of the Noise

---

[96]   S.I. 1986 No. 1078, as amended. See also, the Motor Cycle Act 1987 and the Motor Cycle Silencer Regulations 1995 (S.I. 1995 No. 2370).
[97]   S.I. 1984 No. 981, as amended.
[98]   Amended by s. 11 of the Countryside (Scotland) Act 1981.

Insulation (Scotland) Regulations 1975,[99] where the use of a highway first open to the public after October 16, 1972 (or in respect of which an additional carriageway has been or is to be constructed since that date) causes or is expected to cause noise at a level not less than the level specified in the Regulations, the appropriate highway authority is required either to carry out or to make the appropriate grant in respect of relevant insulation work. Subject to certain exceptions, grants may only be made under regulation 7 in respect of dwellings and other buildings used for residential purposes.

Noise from household appliances, etc.

Regulation 3 of the Household Appliances (Noise Emission) Regulations 8.4.17 1990[1] prohibits the manufacturer or importer of an appliance manufactured or imported by him on or after February 28, 1980 from marketing any appliance unless the provisions of regulation 4 are complied with. Regulation 4 provides that where a manufacturer or an importer of an appliance takes any steps to inform any person to whom the appliance is to be or may be marketed, of the level of airborne noise emitted by the appliance, the level requires to be determined in accordance with Article 6(1) of the E.C. Directive set out in the Schedule to the Regulations.[2]

Building Standards (Scotland) Regulations 1990

The Building Standards (Scotland) Regulations 1990[3] apply to the 8.4.18 construction of new buildings as well as those being refurbished. Part H of the Regulations is intended to protect occupants of dwellings from excessive noise transmitted from other parts of the building by imposing requirements as to the structural design of such buildings. The standards which are imposed by Part H are the same for new and old buildings. Part H does not, however, deal with external noise sources such as that generated by road traffic, nor does it apply to a wholly detached dwelling.

E.C. NOISE POLICY[4]

To date, the European Community has not made a significant contribution 8.5.1 to noise control. This "hands-off" approach has been attributable largely to

---

[99] S.I. 1975 No. 460, as amended by S.I. 1994 No. 1386.
[1] S.I. 1990 No. 161. See also the Lawnmowers (Harmonisation of Noise Emission Standards) Regulations 1992 (S.I. 1992 No. 168).
[2] Directive 86/594.
[3] S.I. 1990 No. 2179.
[4] See Burns and McManus, "Noise" in Holder (ed.), *The Impact of E.C. Environmental Law in the United Kingdom* (1997), Chap. 11.

the fact that noise was perceived as a local problem and, therefore, best dealt with solely by Member States. However, in a recently published Green Paper[5] (which is the first stage in the development of a noise abatement programme to meet the targets outlined in the 1993 Fifth Action Programme[6]), the Commission, after commencing in a penitent mood for its past "sins" of omission, goes on to indicate that it wishes to give noise a much higher profile in the E.C. agenda than it has assumed to date. A new framework directive is proposed. The main area for Community involvement will remain linked to the reduction of noise from products, for example noise from road traffic, rail and aircraft, and so-called "outdoor equipment", for example construction machinery and garden equipment. Increasing use will be made of economic instruments to control noise. Finally, a new directive is proposed to harmonise the methods of assessment of noise exposure in the Community.

---

[5] *Future Noise Policy*, COM (96) 540 final, November 4, 1996.
[6] See paras. 12.2.2–4.

CHAPTER NINE

CIVIL LIABILITY FOR ENVIRONMENTAL HARM

INTRODUCTION

Civil liability for environmental harm may arise either at common law or 9.1.1
under statute. Under the common law, liability for damages in respect of
environmental harm is most likely to arise under the law of delict, although
where pollution or other harm occurs in breach of an agreement, liability
may arise in contract. Regard must be had to land law in the context of
determining riparian rights, and rights to draw water and make deposits
into rivers, although the common law rights are subject to statutory
regulation of polluting activities. Drainage rights are also determined by
land law in the form of servitudes. The following discussion of the common
law refers to environmental harm which infringes the rights of individuals
as opposed to the world at large.

The relevant areas of delict are primarily nuisance and negligence. 9.1.2
Historically, the law of nuisance was mobilised in towns against polluting
industrial processes. Statutory regulation of nuisance followed, and the
control of various forms of nuisance came within the remit of local
authorities. However, the common law continues to apply. It remains the
case that individuals who are affected in their heritable property by pollution
or other sources of environmental harm may seek damages or interdict under
the common law. However, in practice it may prove more expedient to
complain to the relevant authority when the source of the harm complained
of falls within the scope of statutory nuisance and the authority is empowered
to deal with the problem. Unlike statute, the common law does not recognise
defined categories of nuisance; the primary concern is with the interest
invaded rather than the source of the harm.[1]

Where damages are sought in respect of environmental harm manifested 9.1.3
in some form of legally recognisable loss to an individual, it may be
appropriate to raise an action of negligence, which is less restricted in scope
than nuisance, not being associated necessarily with the use or enjoyment

---

[1] Burn-Murdoch, *Interdict* (1933), p. 221: "[S]ince conduct becomes an actionable nuisance,
not because of itself, but because of its results". Whitty in *The Stair Memorial Encyclopaedia
of the Laws of Scotland* (1988), Vol. 14, *Nuisance*, para. 2005: "The modern approach in
Scots law is that nuisance has reference to the invasion of an interest rather than to the
thing, condition or activity causing the invasion".

of land. Negligence is the appropriate form of action where the source of harm can be directly attributed to a failure to comply with a legally required standard of care in circumstances where harm to the pursuer was reasonably foreseeable. The point is trite, but recent Scots case law indicates some difficulty in distinguishing negligence and nuisance and in determining the respective requirements of the relevant pleadings.

9.1.4   The availability of interdict in nuisance renders that remedy of practical significance in respect of environmental harm which affects individuals on their land or in their dwellings or other buildings. Accordingly, this chapter gives nuisance particular attention. Nuisance is generally recognised as a difficult area of the common law,[2] and its treatment here is far from comprehensive. This chapter seeks to provide an introduction to nuisance, focusing, in particular, on the nature and definition of common law nuisance, on recent developments concerning the requirement to establish fault on the part of the defender, and on the distinction between nuisance and negligence. After a brief consideration of the relevance of contract, civil liability under statute is outlined.

NUISANCE

Nature of nuisance in modern Scots law

9.2.1   The common law confers upon the owners or occupiers of land the right to comfortable enjoyment of their property free of material damage or substantial interference.[3] Conversely, the law of nuisance operates to restrict the freedom of proprietors to use their land in whatever way they please.[4] A violation of the right to comfortable enjoyment of heritable property may give rise to an action in nuisance in which either interdict or damages is sought. In some circumstances it will be more appropriate to raise an action in negligence. It should be noted that not all interference with a neighbour's enjoyment of property is actionable as nuisance. The interference must be more than reasonably tolerable.[5] For example, in *Cumnock and Doon Valley District Council v. Dance Energy Associates Ltd*[6] the sheriff court refused interim interdict against the promoter of a rave on grounds that the noise nuisance over a limited period was not such as to create inconvenience beyond a reasonable level of tolerance, taking account of the facts that the proposed rave was a one-off event and that few people were likely to be

[2] Smith admitted mystification, *A Short Commentary on the Law of Scotland* (1961), p. 531.
[3] See paras. 8.2.1–25.
[4] See Rankine, *The Law of Land Ownership in Scotland* (4th ed., 1909), p. 387; Smith, *op. cit.*, p. 533; *Watt v. Jamieson*, 1954 S.C. 56.
[5] *Watt v. Jamieson*, above; *Kennedy v. Glenbelle*, 1996 S.C.L.R. 411.
[6] 1992 G.W.D. 25–1441.

disturbed. Further, it should be noted that some forms of harm emanating from neighbouring property must be borne according to rules of property law.[7]

Common law nuisance protects the immediate environment of a person's **9.2.2** home or other premises from noise, smells, vibration, interference with support, smoke or other sources of damage or discomfort. The common law provides a potentially useful supplement to statutory regulation inasmuch as individuals are not restricted to circumstances defined by statute in mobilising the law on their own behalf. Common law remedies are available at the suit of the aggrieved parties, whereas statute empowers regulatory bodies.[8]

Definition of nuisance

The first problem in undertaking nuisance arises from the loose way in **9.2.3** which the term is used. As Whitty writes[9]: "an occupier may be liable in nuisance for maintaining a nuisance emitting nuisances by which a nuisance occurs to the nuisance of the pursuer". Thus, the word is used in a variety of different senses. A further source of confusion is a tendency, most often found in England, to describe a source of harm as a nuisance where the basis of liability is negligence.[10]

Lord Migdale said of nuisance[11]: "It is not easy to define that term and it **9.2.4** may be that it is not capable of one comprehensive definition". The definition most often quoted in modern texts[12] is that of Lord President Cooper in *Watt v. Jamieson*[13]:

> "[T]he proper angle of approach to a case of alleged nuisance is rather from the standpoint of the victim of the loss or inconvenience than from the standpoint of the alleged offender; and that if any person so uses his property so as to occasion serious disturbance or substantial inconvenience to his neighbour or material damage to his neighbour's property, it is in the general case irrelevant to plead merely that he was making a normal and familiar use of his property. The balance in all such cases has to be held between the freedom of a proprietor to use his property as he pleases, and the duty on a proprietor not to inflict material loss or

---

[7] *e.g.* floodwater not attributable to the fault of the defender. See, for example *Logan v. Wang (U.K.) Ltd*, 1991 S.L.T. 580.

[8] Although see para. 9.4.5.

[9] Whitty, *op. cit.*, n. 1, para. 2003.

[10] *e.g. Bolton v. Stone* [1951] A.C. 850.

[11] *Central Motors (St. Andrews) Ltd. v. Magistrates of St. Andrews*, 1961 S.L.T. 295.

[12] See, *e.g.* Thomson, *Delictual Liability* (1994), p. 159; Stewart, *Delict* (2nd ed., 1993), p. 20.

[13] *Watt v. Jamieson* (n. 4 above), p. 57.

substantial inconvenience on adjoining proprietors or adjoining property, and in every case the answer depends on considerations of fact and degree … The critical question is whether what he was exposed to was *plus quam tolerabile* when due weight has been given to all the surrounding circumstances of the offensive conduct and its effects."

9.2.5   The view that nuisance is seen from the standpoint of the victim, may serve to provide a starting-point for distinguishing the focus of inquiry in a nuisance action from negligence. In nuisance the concern is with the interest invaded; in negligence it is with the conduct of the defender.[14] On the other hand, for liability in damages to arise the defender must be found to be at fault.[15] This must involve some inquiry into the wrongfulness of the defender's activities. Given the arguments in *Watt*, a better interpretation of the point may be that what is a reasonable use of property is seen from the point of view of the pursuer or victim, rather than the defender or user. In nuisance, there has been some recent confusion concerning the extent to which pursuers must aver and prove specific fault,[16] whereas in negligence, the breach of duty must be averred and proved explicitly. This point is developed further below. It is clear from Lord President Cooper's opinion that nuisance is to be understood in terms of a balance of competing proprietory interests. Thus, in Scotland nuisance is generally understood to arise between neighbouring proprietors.[17]

9.2.6   Lord President Emslie referred to the dictum of Lord President Cooper as "the best of the most recent descriptions of our law of nuisance".[18] However, Lord Fraser said of *Watt v. Jamieson*[19]: "All that the case decided was that it was not a relevant defence to say that the defender's use of property was a normal and familiar one".

9.2.7   There may be limitations on the extent to which Lord President Cooper's dictum, without further comment, should be relied upon for a definitive statement. Most importantly, a modern definition now has to take account of the requirement to aver and prove fault where damages are sought. Another potentially important issue is whether reasonable user may be a

---

[14]   See Buckley, *The Law of Nuisance* (1981), p. 3; although the point is not so made in the second edition.

[15]   *RHM Bakeries (Scotland) Ltd v. Strathclyde R.C.*, 1985 S.L.T. 214.

[16]   See para. 9.2.19 below for the view of Lord Fraser in *RHM Bakeries (Scotland) Ltd v. Strathclyde R.C.*, above.

[17]   Although there have been exceptions. See *Slater v. MacLellan*, 1924 S.C. 854; *McColl v. Strathclyde R.C.*, 1983 S.C. 225.

[18]   *Lord Advocate v. Reo Stakis Organisation*, 1982 S.L.T. 140 at 143.

[19]   *RHM Bakeries (Scotland) Ltd v. Strathclyde R.C.* (n. 15 above), p. 218. In fact Lord President Cooper was following authorities cited in Salmond on *Torts*, (11th ed.) (1953), p. 259; *Bamford v. Turnley* (1862) 3 B. & S. 66; *Rheinhardt v. Mentasti* (1889) 42 Ch. D. 685; *Broder v. Saillard* (1876) 2 Ch. D. 692; *Vanderpant v. Mayfair Hotel Co.* [1930] 1 Ch. 138; and Burn-Murdoch, *op. cit.*, n. 1, p. 228; *Shotts Iron Co. v. Inglis* (1882) 9 R. (H.L.) 78.

relevant defence when taken into account along with other considerations, particularly where the loss complained of is interference with comfortable enjoyment rather than material damage.[20]

The most recent authoritative description of nuisance is to be found in 9.2.8 the opinion of Lord President Hope in *Kennedy v. Glenbelle*[21]:

> "A claim for damages for nuisance is a delictual claim as it does not depend for its existence on any contract. It arises where there is an invasion of the pursuer's interest in land to an extent which exceeds what is reasonably tolerable. The *plus quam tolerabile* test is peculiar to the liability in damages for nuisance. Where that test is satisfied and culpa is established, the requirements for the delictual liability are fulfilled."

Differences between the laws of Scotland and England

In considering common law nuisance, care must be taken when seeking 9.2.9 guidance from English authorities and texts. It is suggested that the points of congruence and divergence between the two jurisdictions are inadequately understood. This section alerts the reader to some points which suggest that equivalence between Scots and English nuisance should not be taken for granted.

The most readily recognised difference is the lack of any distinction in 9.2.10 Scotland between public and private nuisance. "The only useful distinction in Scots law is between nuisance at common law, and nuisance by statute, local or general."[22] Despite attempts to define nuisance in Scots law to contemplate what the English would recognise as private and public nuisance,[23] it is not entirely clear that there is any such thing as public nuisance in Scotland[24] although violation of rights of access to public places,

---

[20] A distinction between the two categories of harm was drawn in *St. Helen's Smelting Co. v. Tipping* (1865) 11 H.L.C. 642, the defence of reasonable user being relevant to interference with comfortable enjoyment, but not to material damage. See Burn-Murdoch, *op. cit.*, n. 1, p. 228: "This defence [reasonable user] verges, however, on what, in matters of mere annoyance or disturbance, is a recognised criterion for assessing what must reasonably be borne."

[21] 1996 S.C.L.R. 411 at 414F; 1996 S.L.T. 1186 at 1188K.

[22] Rankine, *op. cit.*, n. 43, p. 386.

[23] See: Bell, *Prin.,* (10th ed., Guthrie), 974; Burn-Murdoch, *op. cit.*, n. 1, p. 202; Whitty *op. cit.*, n. 1, para. 2002.

[24] After all, if nuisance is defined in terms of certain invasions amounting to interference with the enjoyment of heritable property rights, then interference with or damage to persons in public places cannot be the same thing. If, on the other hand, nuisance is understood in terms of wrongful use of land by the defender, then the problem does not arise. See Cameron, "Nuisance in the Common Law of Scotland", 1997/8 S.L.P.Q. (forthcoming). On invasions on the use of public places see Whitty, *op. cit.*, n. 1, paras. 2159–2168.

and the right not to be harmed whilst there, are protected by other grounds of action, for example negligence.[25]

9.2.11   English authorities have played a substantial role in the development of nuisance in Scots law.[26] Indeed, there is eminent judicial dicta to the effect that the principles of nuisance are the same in Scotland and England.[27] However, it appears that the differences between the two jurisdictions have not been submitted to the kind of rigorous judicial or academic scrutiny which would enable clear conclusions to be drawn with confidence. Smith was adamant on the point[28]: "This much may be said: the tort of nuisance in England is no part of the law of Scotland".

9.2.12   In Scotland, nuisance is analysed in terms of a balance of proprietorial interests[29] and, while the view has been put forward that the essence of nuisance consists in the interest invaded,[30] it is uncertain whether Scottish courts would admit a claim of common law nuisance where the harm complained of arose from any source other than the wrongful use of neighbouring or adjoining land in the occupation or control of the defender. There is a clear suggestion, in the opinion of Lord President Hope in *Kennedy v. Glenbelle*,[31] that the liability of the reclaimers was to be dependent upon establishing that their presence in the relevant property was "more than merely transitory".[32] This approach should be contrasted with a dictum of Devlin L.J. in *Southport Corporation v. Esso Petroleum*,[33] paraphrased by Mahon J. in the Supreme Court of New Zealand: "It is clear that to give a cause of action for private nuisance the matter complained of must affect the property of the plaintiff. But I know of no principle that it must emanate from land belonging to the defendant."[34]

9.2.13   The extent to which Devlin L.J.'s view represents the law of England is arguable,[35] although it was founded on in New Zealand to allow

---

[25] *McQueen v. Glasgow Garden Festival (1988) Ltd*, 1995 S.L.T. 211 is an example of such an action. It was analysed in terms of negligence. See also *Glasgow Corporation v. Barclay Curle & Co.*, 1923 S.C. (H.L.) 78; *Fergusson v. Pollok* (1900) 3 F. 1140.

[26] See Whitty, *op. cit.*, n. 1, paras. 2015–2016.

[27] *Fleming v. Hislop* (1886) 13 R. (H.L.) 43 at 48, *per* Lord Fitzgerald; *Slater v. MacLellan*, 1924 S.C. 854 at 857, *per* Lord President Clyde; *Gourock Rope Works v. Greenock Corporation*, 1996 S.L.T. 125 at 127, *per* Lord Fraser.

[28] Smith, *op. cit.*, n. 2, p. 534. This view may be overly robust, but *cf.* Gordon, *Scottish Land Law* (1989), p. 836: "as it is not clear that Scots law and English law use 'nuisance' to mean the same thing, although it is sometimes said that the law is the same in both countries".

[29] *Watt v. Jamieson* (n. 4 above). The law has been described in terms of a relationship between two principles: *qui jure suo utitur neminem laedit*; and *sic utere tuo ut alienum non laedas*. See Burn-Murdoch (n. 1 above), p. 206; Rankine (n. 4 above), p. 368; and Smith (n. 2 above), p. 530.

[30] See n. 1.

[31] n. 21 above.

[32] n. 21 above, p. 417D. It is not entirely clear whether the concern here was with occupation or responsibility.

[33] [1953] 2 All E.R. 1204 at 1207.

[34] *Paxhaven Holdings Ltd v. Att.-Gen.* [1974] 2 N.Z.L.R. 185 at 188; See also *Clearlite Holdings Ltd v. Auckland City Corporation* [1976] 2 N.Z.L.R. 729 at 736.

[35] See Buckley, *The Law of Nuisance* (2nd ed., 1996), pp. 4–5.

nuisance claims in two cases where the source of harm was on the plaintiffs' own land.[36] In England, a *quia timet* injunction was granted in *Khorasandjian v. Bush* in respect of nuisance in the form of telephone harassment, without any apparent concern whether the harm emanated from the use of land.[37] The definition of nuisance adopted by the Court of Appeal in *Khorasandjian v. Bush* made no reference to use of land by the defendant.[38] This demonstrates flexibility, but does not correspond well with a Scottish analysis. Underlying any consideration of the convergence or divergence of the laws in Scotland and England is the historical point that in England nuisance has always been a tort, while in Scotland it appears bound up in land law[38a] and only really appears as a delict where damages are sought.

Interdict

Two forms of remedy are available in respect of nuisance. Damages may be sought where the pursuer seeks reparation in respect of loss suffered. Interdict must be regarded as the primary remedy where nuisance arises from environmental pollution,[39] and is sought in order to put a stop to interference amounting to nuisance which is continuing in nature. There is no requirement on the petitioner to establish fault. Interdict is available in respect of existing and anticipated nuisance,[40] and is also available to prevent an increase in an existing source of harm or discomfort.[41] 9.2.14

Courts cannot order the cessation of operations without reference to the extent of the right to be protected. The legal standard of comfort to which a 9.2.15

---

[36] *Paxhaven* and *Clearlite* (n. 34 above). These decisions create scope for confusion between the torts of nuisance and trespass. See Chambers, "Nuisance-Judicial Attack on Orthodoxy" (1978) N.Z.L.J. 172.

[37] [1993] Q.B. 727. Indeed, if telephone harassment gives rise to a civil remedy, should it make a critical difference according to whether the phone calls were made from the defendant's (defender's) own home or from a public call box?

[38] *Clerk and Lindsell on Torts* (16th ed., 1989), p. 1354, per Dillon L.J. in *Khorasandjian* at p. 481: "The essence of nuisance is a condition or activity which unduly interferes with the use or enjoyment of land". This may be compared with an earlier English definition *per* Talbot J. in *Cunard v. Antifyre* [1933] 1 K.B. 551 at 556–7: "[P]rivate nuisances, *at least in the vast majority of cases*, are interferences for a substantial length of time by owners or occupiers of property with the use or enjoyment of neighbouring property" (emphasis added).

[38a] Nuisance is presented in early nineteenth century Scots texts as operating to restrict absolute rights of property ownership: Bell, *Prin.*, 240 (10th ed., 973); Hume, *Lectures on the Law of Scotland* (ed. Paton, Stair Society), Vol. 3, p. 207.

[39] Although material damage, for example to crops or shrubs, may be incidental to pollution causing substantial discomfort. See, *e.g.* *Hart v. Taylor* (1827) 4 Mur. 313; *Chalmers v. Dixon* (1876) 3 R. 461.

[40] On anticipated nuisance, see *Gavin v. Ayrshire C.C.*, 1950 S.C. 197.

[41] See, *e.g.* *Fleming v. Hislop* (1886) 13 R. (H.L.) 43.

property holder is entitled in England is determined by answering a question posed in *Walter v. Selfe*[42]:

> "[O]ught this inconvenience to be considered in fact as more than fanciful, more than one of mere delicacy or fastidiousness, as an inconvenience materially interfering with the ordinary comfort physically of human existence, not merely according to elegant or dainty modes of living, but according to plain and sober and simple notions among the English people?".

9.2.16   This point is addressed in modern Scots law by the requirement that the harm or interference complained of must be *plus quam tolerabile*. It is in the context of interdict that this requirement seems most likely to come into play, since the argument that the interference is no more than must reasonably be borne, hardly arises where reparation is sought for material damage to property, such as that caused by flooding. On the other hand, its relevance may be in establishing a prima facie case. Nevertheless, it seems a curious requirement. Plainly the law does not recognise trifling or minor matters of inconvenience (*de minimis non curat lex*). Establishing that a source of discomfort or annoyance is more than reasonably tolerable merely goes to show that it is material. In *Fleming v. Hislop* Lord Bramwell said[43]:

> "The word 'material' is one used continually in endeavouring to explain to a jury what it is which would constitute a nuisance, as distinct from something which might indeed be perceptible but not of such a substantial character as to justify the interference of the court or allow the maintenance of an action in conformity with the legal maxim '*lex non favet delicatorum votis*'."[44]

9.2.17   Determining whether a particular source of annoyance is actionable depends on all the facts and circumstances of the case.[45] The nature of the locality is a relevant consideration.[46] Accordingly, what must reasonably be borne may differ from location to location, although zoning of land for different types of use makes this point less significant than it was when industrial operations and residences were more often to be found in proximity. It is no defence to state that the petitioner came to a pre-existing nuisance.[47] Where operations are found to cause a nuisance it is not

---

[42] (1851) 4 De G. & S. 315 at 322, *per* V.C. Sir J.L. Knight-Bruce.
[43] n. 41 above, at 47.
[44] The law does not favour the wishes of the fastidious.
[45] *Watt v. Jamieson* (n. 4 above).
[46] *Anderson v. The Aberdeen Agricultural Hall Co. Ltd* (1879) 6 R. 901; *Inglis v. Shotts Iron Co.* (1888) 8 R. 1006; *Maguire v. Charles McNeil Ltd*, 1922 S.C. 174.
[47] *Fleming v. Hislop* (n. 41 above), at 49, *per* Lord Halsbury; *Webster v. Lord Advocate*, 1984 S.L.T. 13; 1985 S.L.T. 361.

necessarily the case that courts will ban further activities altogether. The terms of interdict may be framed so as to allow the continuation of the operation, but to prohibit it from being carried out in such a way as to give rise to nuisance.[48]

Damages

Damages will only be awarded in circumstances where the pursuer avers 9.2.18 and proves fault on the part of the defender.[49] This requirement has given rise to much difficulty and the specification of pleadings required to establish a relevant case in nuisance has provided the focus of debate in a number of cases.

In *RHM Bakeries v. Strathclyde Regional Council* Lord Fraser stated[50]: 9.2.19

"The view that I have expressed does not by any means imply that, in a case such as this, a pursuer cannot succeed unless he avers the precise nature of the fault committed by the defender which caused the accident. It would be quite unreasonable to place such a burden on the pursuer, who in many cases will have no knowledge, and no means of obtaining knowledge of the defender's fault. As a general rule it would be relevant for a pursuer to make averments to the effect that his property has been damaged by a flood caused by an event on the defender's land, such as the collapse of a sewer which it was the defender's duty to maintain, that properly maintained sewers do not collapse, and that the collapse is evidence that the defender had failed in his duty to maintain the sewer. The onus will then be on the defender to explain the event in some way consistent with absence of fault on his part. As a general rule the defences available will be limited to proving that the event was caused either by the action of a third party for whom he was not responsible, as the defender did in *Gourock Ropework Co. Ltd v. Greenock Corporation*,[51] or by a damnum fatale."

This dictum was bound to give rise to controversy. It is clear that in 9.2.20 Lord Fraser's view the requirements of pleadings in nuisance are less onerous than those in negligence. However, scope for confusion between nuisance and negligence arises from Lord Fraser's reference to breach of a duty as the basis for liability. Moreover, the dictum suggests that pursuers have very little to aver before the onus of proof passes to defenders. Lord Fraser appears to have stated the law on *res ipsa loquitur*. The distinction between

---

[48] *Fleming v. Hislop* (n. 41 above); *Webster v. Lord Advocate* (n. 47 above).
[49] *RHM Bakeries (Scotland) Ltd v. Strathclyde R.C.*, 1985 S.L.T. 214.
[50] *ibid.* at 219.
[51] 1966 S.L.T. 125.

nuisance and negligence appears to have been clarified by the First Division in *Kennedy v. Glenbelle*.[52] However, before considering that case it is useful to look briefly at intervening decisions.

9.2.21   The danger of relying on averments drafted exactly as Lord Fraser suggested was demonstrated in *Argyll & Clyde Health Board v. Strathclyde Regional Council*.[53] In this case the pursuers had suffered damage to property as a result of a burst water pipe in the control of the defenders. The pursuers claimed damages, averring that properly maintained water mains do not burst. The Lord Ordinary (McCluskey) took the view that a bare averment of fault was not relevant. The basis of the pursuers' case appeared to be that the defenders were at fault in not properly maintaining the water main, but in the absence of any averments indicating the standard of maintenance which would have been proper, possible or reasonably practicable, the claim failed.

9.2.22   Lord McCluskey made some important points on the issues of relevancy and the burden of proof. He stated[54]:

> "[I]n order to pass the test of relevancy the pursuers must give adequate notice in their pleadings of facts which either infer a specific fault or are so eloquent of some unspecified fault on the part of the defenders that, in the absence of any acceptable alternative explanation (alternative in the sense of excluding fault), *res ipsa loquitur*, and the court would be entitled to infer that the cause of the loss, injury and damage must have been some fault on the part of the defenders ... The onus does not pass to the defenders until the pursuers aver facts and circumstances from which, at least, fault appears the best explanation of the defect, in the absence of any better one."

Thus, the rules of *res ipsa loquitur* are preserved, but they do not apply especially to cases of nuisance, a view made arguably tenable by Lord Fraser's observations in *RHM Bakeries*[55] (see para. 9.2.19).

9.2.23   *Noble's Trustees v. Economic Forestry (Scotland) Ltd*[56] concerned a claim for damages in respect of harm to a hydro-electric scheme operated by the pursuers. The action was brought against contractors and two neighbouring landowners, upon whose land the contractors had carried out operations resulting in an increase in the flow of surface water off the land onto the pursuer's land to the harm of the pursuer. The pursuer averred that the defenders were at fault. However, in the absence of any averment either that the operations instructed were inherently dangerous or that they required

---

[52] 1996 S.C.L.R. 411; 1996 S.L.T. 1186.
[53] 1988 S.L.T. 381.
[54] *ibid.* at 384.
[55] n. 49 above.
[56] 1988 S.L.T. 662.

particular precautions to be taken, or indeed that the defenders knew or ought to have known that the operations might have been harmful, the pursuer failed to make a relevant case in nuisance against the second and third defenders. The fate of the action against the first defenders is not recorded in the report.

Observations were made by Lord Jauncey in *Noble's Trustees* which have since proved influential. He said[57]:   9.2.24

> "A landowner will be liable if he carries out operations on his land which could or are likely to cause damage to his neighbour's land however much care is exercised. Similarly will a landowner be liable in respect of operations carried out either by his own hand or at the hand of the contractor, if it is necessary to take steps in the carrying out of those operations to prevent damage to a neighbour, and he, the landlord, does not take or instruct those steps. In the former case *culpa* lies in the actual carrying out of his operations in the knowledge, actual or implied of their likely consequences. In the latter case *culpa* lies in not taking steps to avoid consequences which he should have forseen would be likely to flow from one method of carrying out the operation."[58]

Those responsible for drafting pleadings appear to have been slow to learn the lessons of the preceding cases. In *Borders Regional Council v. Roxburgh District Council*[59] Lord Dervaird dismissed the case brought in nuisance against the first defenders. The averments did not allow an inference of knowledge of risk. The decision in *Logan v. Wang (U.K.) Ltd*,[60] so far as that case concerned damages in respect of nuisance, was similar. Lord Prosser stated[61]:   9.2.25

> "[T]he case based on nuisance contains no averments of fault beyond the description of the nuisance as 'created by the fault' of the defenders in question ... I am satisfied that where fault is alleged to arise in relation to the presence of a major development such as this, some specification and notice would be essential."

RHM Bakeries established that fault must be averred, and *Argyll* established that, in addition, sufficient facts must be averred from which a court could draw an inference of fault. However, when it is considered what averments would have been necessary for the pursuers to have   9.2.26

---

[57] 1988 S.L.T. 662 at 664.
[58] *cf. Kerr v. Earl of Orkney* (1857) 20 D. 298.
[59] 1989 S.L.T. 837.
[60] 1991 S.L.T. 580.
[61] *ibid.* at 584.

succeeded in *Argyll* (they would have had to have specified what a proper system of maintenance amounted to and the way in which the defenders' activities fell short of this), the suspicion arises that the pleadings could not have differed much from those required in negligence. The major difference which can be deduced at this stage of analysis is the lack of any requirement in nuisance to aver the existence of a duty of care. This poses two problems: first, it makes nuisance appear an easy option for pleaders since an onerous requirement of pleadings may be circumvented by opting to claim in nuisance in preference to negligence; and, secondly, it suggests that negligence is the basis of liability in nuisance.

9.2.27   Indeed, the second point was the basis of a plea to the relevancy and subsequent reclaiming motion in *Kennedy v. Glenbelle*.[62] In this case a large opening had been made in a supporting wall in a basement flat, resulting in alleged damage to the other flats in the tenement. The case in nuisance was that the damage was caused by the second defenders, who instructed and directed hazardous works within the premises which they knew constituted an interference with the support enjoyed by each of the pursuers. The defenders argued that there was no difference between a case of nuisance and a case of negligence and that, in the absence of any averments regarding duty, the plea was irrelevant.

9.2.28   The First Division resolved the issue, founding *inter alia* on Lord Jauncey's dictum quoted above (para. 9.2.24). *Culpa* is required for liability, but may be established by means other than negligence. While negligence lies in not taking steps to avoid consequences which a defender should have foreseen would be likely to flow from one method of carrying out the operation, *culpa* may also be established where operations are carried out in the knowledge that harm will be the likely result.

9.2.29   The First Division in *Kennedy*, affirming the judgment of the Lord Ordinary (Abernethy), held that the pursuers had relevantly averred a deliberate act done in the knowledge that harm would result. Accordingly, the case in nuisance was allowed. *Kennedy* is significant because it places liability in nuisance, and the requirements of pleadings, firmly back within generally accepted notions of *culpa* in Scots law. In nuisance, there is no requirement to establish the existence of a duty owed by the defender to the pursuer. It follows that there is no requirement on pursuers to detail the precise way in which a duty has been breached. Nevertheless, pursuers must aver sufficient facts to allow a court to draw an inference of fault from the activities of defenders. Knowledge, actual or implied, on the part of defenders, that harm is the likely result of their activities, is crucial.

---

[62] n. 5 above.

Defences

It is clear from Lord Fraser's judgment in *RHM Bakeries Ltd*[62a] that defenders   9.2.30
may plead that the harm complained of was caused by a *damnum fatale* or
by third parties for whom the defender was not responsible. A source of
harm placed on a defender's land by another may yet give rise to liability
where the defender has adopted or continued the nuisance.[63] Where the
source of harm emanates from the activities of a number of different
operators, this fact does not furnish any individual with a defence since
liability arises where there is material contribution.[64] The right to complain
of a nuisance may be lost by operation of the negative prescription, *i.e.* 20
years' continuation.[65] A prescriptive right cannot be relied upon where,
within the prescriptive period, there has been an increase in the nuisance.[66]
The right to complain may also be lost by unequivocal acquiescence.[67]

Where a particular activity has been authorised by statute, the author of   9.2.31
interference amounting to nuisance may be furnished with a defence,
according to whether the nuisance complained of arises through the exercise
of a statutory duty or a statutory power. Liability may also depend upon the
terms of the statute relied upon. Some statutes contain an "exoneration
clause" restricting liability, whereas others contain a "nuisance clause"
preserving the common law. However, difficult issues of construction may
arise regarding the application of statutory provisions. In *Department of
Transport v. North West Water Authority*[68] the finding of Webster J., that the
defendants were liable to the plaintiffs in damages for the cost of road repairs
necessitated by a burst water main, was overturned by the House of Lords.
The fact that the defendants supplied water under pressure in the exercise
of a statutory duty meant that, in the absence of negligence on their part,
they were not liable for the consequences of the nuisance created by the
burst, notwithstanding section 18(2) of the Public Utilities Street Works
Act 1950 which stated *inter alia*: "nothing in the enactment ... shall
exonerate the undertakers from any action or other proceeding at the suit
... (i) of the street authority".[69]

The Court of Session has an equitable jurisdiction to make a declaratory   9.2.32
finding of nuisance, but to suspend the operation of interdict in circumstances
where the public interest in the continuation of an activity outweighs the
private interest invaded. A suspension of interdict does not ignore the

---

[62a] n. 15 above.
[63] *Broder v. Sailard* (1876) 2 Ch. D. 692; *Sedleigh-Denfield v. O'Callaghan* [1940] A.C. 880.
[64] *Duke of Buccleuch v. Cowan* (1866) 5 M. 214.
[65] Prescription and Limitation (Scotland) Act 1973, s. 8.
[66] *Webster v. Lord Advocate* (n. 47 above).
[67] See *Muirhead v. Glasgow Highland Society* (1864) 2 M. 420.
[68] [1984] A.C. 336.
[69] On the defence of statutory authority, see Whitty, *op. cit.*, n. 1, paras. 2110–2122.

infringed rights of the petitioner, but is intended to allow time for remedial measures to be taken. This power is exercised in accordance with the rule laid down by Lord McLaren in *Clippens Oil Co. v. Edinburgh and District Water Trustees*[70]:

> "I think, on consideration of the cases where this power has been exercised, it will be found that they all belong to one or other of two categories, viz., either (1) that the granting of immediate interdict would be attended with consequences to the rights of the respondents as injurious, or possibly more so, than the wrong that was complained of, or (2) again, because the effect of an immediate interdict would be to cause some great and immediate public inconvenience."

9.2.33   The court will not operate the rule without a finding on the facts. Thus, in *Ben Nevis Distillery (Fort William) Ltd v. The North British Aluminium Co. Ltd*[71] the reclaiming motion, on grounds of public interest, against the interlocutor of the Lord Ordinary (Birnam) allowing proof before answer, was refused. The public interest averred was substantial. It included the loss of 72 per cent of U.K. aluminium production with associated job losses. In *Webster v. Lord Advocate*[72] interdict was suspended for six months to allow the Edinburgh Tattoo to go ahead, but in that case there had been a finding of nuisance in respect of noise from the erection of scaffolding. The Lord Ordinary (Stott) also recognised that public interest was an appropriate consideration when weighing the balance of convenience in granting interim interdict.[73]

Distinguishing nuisance from negligence

9.2.34 Negligence consists in the breach of a duty where the defender's activities fall short of the standard required in circumstances where injury to others is foreseeable. In negligence it is necessary to establish the existence of a duty of care and to detail the way in which that duty has been breached. In nuisance there is no need to aver the existence of a duty, but the pursuer must aver sufficient facts from which a court can infer fault on the part of the defender. While negligence is restricted in scope to circumstances where a duty of care exists, nuisance is restricted in a different way. Unlike negligence, the law of nuisance is intimately connected with heritable property and only proprietary interests are protected. Possibly also, the harm must arise from the use made of, or activities carried out upon, neighbouring heritable property. Negligence is a failure to take care in circumstances

---

[70] (1897) 25 R. 370 at 383.
[71] 1948 S.C. 592.
[72] 1984 S.L.T. 13, 1985 S.L.T. 361.
[73] 1984 S.L.T. 13 at 14.

where care is required by law, whereas in nuisance liability arises either in respect of an act which could not have been undertaken without harm to the pursuer or in respect of an act deliberately done in the knowledge that harm to the pursuer would be the likely result.

Both grounds of action are highly relevant in the area of environmental 9.2.35 harm. Negligence is useful in that the possibility of liability may encourage safe behaviour in circumstances where activities are acknowledged to be hazardous. An example would be the voluntary withdrawal from agricultural use of particular fungicides. Negligence is less useful where there is doubt or controversy regarding the hazardous nature of a particular activity, since liability will be judged according to the state of knowledge regarding the harmfulness or otherwise of the activity at the time it is carried out.[74]

The law of nuisance can be mobilised only in restricted circumstances. 9.2.36 In common with negligence, it appears that it is not possible to recover damages in nuisance unless knowledge of likely harm can be attributed to the defender, otherwise fault cannot be established. However, the availability of interdict as a remedy renders nuisance a useful device in circumstances where parties are affected by environmental pollution in their own homes, or other premises. It is not necessary to prove fault in order to obtain interdict. Inasmuch as damages may be claimed in respect of loss suffered, it is apparent that there will be circumstances in which pursuers will advance alternative pleas of nuisance and negligence. This was the case in *Kennedy v. Glenbelle*. Indeed, given that the basis of the actions against Strathclyde Regional Council in both *RHM Bakeries* and *Argyll* appears to be an alleged failure to maintain, *i.e.* to take care, it is open to question whether these actions should have been brought in negligence rather than nuisance.

Liability for the escape from land of dangerous things

This category of wrongful behaviour is dealt with in English law under the rule 9.2.37 in *Rylands v. Fletcher*.[75] This case has been subject to numerous different interpretations. One is that it restated the medieval English rule that a man acts at his peril.[76] Thus, *Rylands* was cited in Scots cases as authority for the view that liability in nuisance was strict.[77] Another interpretation was that *Rylands* extended liability in nuisance from a continuing source of harm to one-off events.[78] Indeed, there is a long-standing view in England that *Rylands* was not part of the law of nuisance at all, but provided a separate category of liability

---

[74] *Roe v. Minister of Health* [1954] 2 Q.B. 66.
[75] (1868) L.R. 3 H.L.C. 330.
[76] Holdsworth, *History of English Law* (2nd ed., 1937), Vol. VIII, pp. 446–7.
[77] *e.g.* in *Western Silver Fox Ranch Ltd v. Ross and Cromarty C.C.*, 1940 S.C. 601.
[78] Newark, "The Boundaries of Nuisance" (1949) 65 L.Q.R. 480 at 488.

concerning non-natural use of land.[79] In England, the House of Lords in *Cambridge Water Co. v. Eastern Counties Leather plc*[80] significantly modified the way in which the rule in *Rylands* is understood. Liability is strict in that the defendant may be liable irrespective of how much care has been exercised. However, liability arises only in circumstances where harm to the plaintiff is reasonably foreseeable at the time the operation complained of is carried out.

9.2.38   In *RHM Bakeries* the House of Lords declared the view that *Rylands* formed part of Scots law to be "a heresy which ought to be extirpated".[81] However, this does not mean that persons harmed by such an escape have no means of redress in Scotland. Liability would rest on negligence or nuisance according to the circumstances in which the escape occurred. If a person brought something onto land which could escape and cause harm, no matter how much care was exercised, it is probable that liability would be in nuisance. The person would be at fault in bringing the thing there in the first place. However, in order to be remediable in nuisance it is probable that the escape would have to affect the pursuer's interest in his heritable property. On the other hand, if the thing brought, or the operation carried out, required special care in order to keep it safe, and that care was not adequately taken, and an escape occured which caused harm, then probably the ground of action would be negligence. There is no need in Scotland for a separate category in delict for liability for the escape of dangerous things. Lord Goff's judgment in *Cambridge Water* may be compared with the approach to liability for nuisance taken in Scotland by Lord Jauncey in *Noble's Trustees* and Lord President Hope in *Kennedy*.[82]

9.2.39   Where the escape is in the form of a flood resulting from the diversion of the natural course of a stream, liability is arguably strict, in the sense that damages may be awarded without proving fault, on the authority of *Caledonian Railway Co. v. Greenock Magistrates*,[83] about which Lord Fraser, in *RHM Bakeries*, said[84]: "It may be that that case should be regarded as laying down a special rule applicable only to the case of a person who interferes with the course of a natural stream. If so, it is contrary to a general principle of the law of Scotland and, in my opinion, the rule should not be extended beyond the precise facts of that case". This exception to the general rule was noted in *GA Estates Ltd v. Caviapen Trustees Ltd (No. 1)*[85] and in *Kennedy*.[86] However, it appears most unlikely that this special rule would survive close consideration in the House of Lords.

---

[79] Elements of this approach can be seen in some Scots cases, *e.g. Chalmers v. Dixon* (1876) 3 R. 461; *Giblin v. Lanarkshire C.C.*, 1927 S.L.T. 563. See further, Cameron (n. 24 above).

[80] [1994] A.C. 264; (1994) 6 J.E.L. 137.

[81] *RHM Bakeries (Scotland) Ltd v. Strathclyde R.C.*, 1985 S.L.T. 214 at 217.

[82] See paras. 9.2.24 and 9.2.28 above.

[83] 1917 S.C. (H.L.) 56.

[84] *RHM Bakeries* (n. 81 above), at 218.

[85] 1993 S.L.T. 1037 at 1041, *per* Lord Coulsfield.

[86] 1996 S.C.L.R. 411 at 414C, *per* Lord President Hope.

CONTRACT

Implied terms

The law of contract is relevant in some circumstances. For example, in 9.3.1 *Golden Sea Produce v. Scottish Nuclear plc*[87] the pursuers, a fish farming business, leased land from the defenders. Under the terms of the lease the pursuers were entitled to draw off water which the defenders had used for cooling their reactors. When the water became contaminated with chlorine the pursuers lost their entire stock of fish. In the Outer House the defenders were held liable to the pursuers for damages in respect of a breach of an implied term of the contract, that the water should be fit for the purposes of rearing fish.

Express terms: conventional nuisance

There is great scope for creating civil liability for environmental harm 9.3.2 through the use of contractual terms. Specific stipulations or prohibitions can be made in a variety of circumstances in a commercial context. For example, where a firm's activities are subject to regulation, contractors not subject to regulation can be made liable through the use of contractual terms. Equally, contracts for the sale or supply of goods may exclude the use of particular manufacturing processes or particular materials.

Further scope for restricting or eliminating polluting activities arises in 9.3.3 the context of contracts of land tenure. Bell states[88]: "But what is not at common law a nuisance may conventionally be declared so, in respect to some particular piece of ground or area." Probably this form of land use restriction, whereby feu charters would prohibit, for example, specified or unspecified forms of "noxious operation", was of greater practical importance before the advent of planning regulations. However, it remains the case that environmental legislation and planning restrictions may be supplemented by the inclusion of terms, particularly in leases. The advantage to lessors is the freedom to define their own terms, which need not necessarily coincide with either the common law or statute.

The expression "conventional nuisance" is not particularly useful. Where 9.3.4 restrictions have been expressed in terms of causing nuisance, the common law has applied to determine the existence or otherwise of the nuisance petitioned against.[89] In such cases, little or nothing was added by convention to the common law, although Bell states[90]:

---

[87] 1992 S.L.T. 942.
[88] Bell, *op. cit.*, n. 23, 974, under "Conventional Nuisance".
[89] See, *e.g. Anderson v. The Aberdeen Agricultural Hall Co. Ltd* (1879) 6 R. 901; *Manson v. Forrest* (1887) 14 R. 802.
[90] Bell, *op. cit.*, n. 23, 974.

> "The operations or works prohibited are not to be put to the test of what strictly is a nuisance at common law, but to be measured by the fair meaning of the parties as amounting to what is offensive in the circumstances and situation, or affecting the value or amenity of houses or property which the condition is intended to protect, or the comfort of persons living in them."

Where there is a clearly stated restriction, which is clearly breached, the law of contract provides remedies, and the law of delict does not have to come into play. In some circumstances a *jus quaesitum tertio* may arise allowing relief to neighbours who suffer the effects of pollution from activities carried on by a landholder in breach of landholding terms.[91]

STATUTORY NUISANCE

9.4.1 Civil liability in nuisance also arises under statute. While statutory bodies are empowered to identify and regulate specific sources of nuisance, individual citizens may also, in some instances, bring proceedings before the sheriff court.

9.4.2   Statutory regulation of nuisance is to be found in Part III of the Environmental Protection Act 1990 (EPA 1990), as amended by Schedule 17 to the Environment Act 1995 (EA 1995). The provisions in the Clean Air Act 1993, s. 17 relating to smoke nuisances have been repealed by EA 1995, Sched. 24. Equivalent provisions are now to be found in EPA 1990, s. 79(1)(b) and (3).[92]

9.4.3   Section 79(1) of EPA 1990 lists statutory nuisances as follows:

    (a) any premises in such a state as to be prejudicial to health or a nuisance;

    (b) smoke emitted from premises so as to be prejudicial to health or a nuisance;

    (c) fumes or gases emitted from premises so as to be prejudicial to health or a nuisance;

    (d) any dust, steam, smell or other effluvia arising on industrial trade or business premises so as to be prejudicial to health or a nuisance;

    (e) any accumulation or deposit which is prejudicial to health or a nuisance;

    (f) any animal kept in such a place or manner as to be prejudicial to health or a nuisance;

---

[91] *Ferguson v. McCulloch*, 1953 S.L.T. (Sh. Ct.) 113. In this case, both a nuisance at common law and breach of building restrictions in the feu charter were established.

[92] See paras. 8.3.2–13.

(g) noise emitted from premises so as to be prejudicial to health or a nuisance;

(ga) noise that is prejudicial to health or a nuisance and is emitted from or caused by a vehicle, machinery or equipment in a street or in Scotland, road;

(h) any other matter declared by any enactment to be a statutory nuisance.

Section 79(1) of EPA 1990 imposes a duty on the local authority to 9.4.4 detect statutory nuisances and, where complaints are brought, to take such steps as are reasonably practicable to investigate them. Where a statutory nuisance is found, the local authority is obliged to issue an abatement notice "requiring the abatement of the nuisance or prohibiting or restricting its occurrence or recurrence; requiring the execution of such works, and the taking of such other steps, as may be necessary for any of those purposes" (EPA 1990, s. 80(1)(a) and (b)). There is a right of appeal to the sheriff court against an abatement notice (EPA 1990, s. 80(3)). Contravention of an abatement notice constitutes an offence (EPA 1990, s. 80(4)). A defence, that the best practicable means were used to prevent or counteract the effects of the nuisance, operates in circumstances limited by section 80(8). A great variety of exceptions and qualifications to the circumstances defined in section 79(1) is listed in the succeeding subsections, along with a number of definitions. For example, section 79(1)(d) does not apply to steam emitted from a railway locomotive engine (EPA 1990, s. 79(5)).

Mobilisation of the law is not restricted to statutory bodies, but 9.4.5 "aggrieved persons" may make a summary application to the sheriff court under section 82 of EPA 1990. If the sheriff is satisfied that the nuisance exists, the court may make an order in terms similar to an abatement notice. In Scotland the court does not have the power enjoyed by magistrates' courts in England and Wales to impose a fine in these circumstances.

Civil liability also arises under the Control of Pollution Act 1974 9.4.6 (COPA 1974), s. 46 as substituted by the Water Act 1989, Sched. 23. Under this provision any person who causes or knowingly permits any poisonous, noxious or polluting matter to enter controlled water is liable to SEPA for the costs of operations carried out to clean up the pollution. This liability also arises where it appears to SEPA that pollution is likely to enter controlled water. The polluter may escape liability for meeting the cost of operations under section 46(3) if he can satisfy the court that the costs were incurred unnecessarily, or where the source of pollution is water from a mine abandoned before the end of 1999 (COPA 1974, s. 73(6)(a)).

Similarly, the costs of remedial treatment carried out by SEPA in respect 9.4.7 of offences under section 23(1)(a) or (c) of EPA 1990 may be recovered from the offender under section 27 of that Act.

9.4.8   Any person who deposits waste, or knowingly permits waste to be deposited so as to commit an offence under section 33(1) or 63(2) of EPA 1990 is liable for any damage caused under section 73(6) of the Act. Liability for damages does not arise under this section where the damage was due wholly to the fault of the person who suffered it, or where the person who suffered damage voluntarily assumed the risk (EPA 1990, s. 73(6)(b)). Offences under sections 33(1) and 63(2) concern the unauthorised or harmful depositing, treatment or disposal of waste.[93]

---

[93]   See para. 4.3.15.

CHAPTER TEN

NATURE CONSERVATION

INTRODUCTION

The law designed specifically for the purposes of nature conservation falls 10.1.1
into two categories. Certain laws aim to protect particular birds, animals
and plants from direct harm, making it an offence for people to kill, injure
or otherwise harm protected species. However, no matter how effective
such laws may be, they cannot secure the survival of a species in the wild if
it does not have the right habitat in which to live. Consequently, other laws
aim to secure the continued existence of the range of natural[1] habitats
necessary for species to survive in the wild. In most cases it has been the
loss of habitat rather than any deliberate intervention by mankind that has
caused the greatest harm to animal and plant life in this country, and which
continues to pose the greatest threat to the range and diversity of wildlife.

The law relating to nature conservation can be found in a range of 10.1.2
legislation — domestic and European.[2] The most important statute is the
Wildlife and Countryside Act 1981 (WCA 1981),[3] which lays down rules
for the protection of birds, animals and plants, and for some habitat. Two
European measures are also of great significance. The Directive on the
conservation of wild birds (the Wild Birds Directive)[4] was taken into account
in the framing of the 1981 Act, but the more recent Directive on the
conservation of natural habitats and of wild flora and fauna (the Habitats
and Species Directive)[5] has been implemented by means of the Conservation
(Natural Habitats etc.) Regulations 1994 (the 1994 Regulations),[6] which
overlie the existing provisions, creating two overlapping regimes. In addition
to WCA 1981, a range of individual statutes deal with particular species,
for example seals and deer, or with activities which have an impact on
wildlife, for example shooting and fishing, while the range of habitat

---

[1] Or, rather, semi-natural, as virtually all of Scotland's landscape shows signs of human
intervention at some stage in history.
[2] See, generally, Reid, *Nature Conservation Law* (1994).
[3] The 1981 Act has been amended several times.
[4] Directive 79/409.
[5] Directive 92/43.
[6] S.I. 1994 No. 2716.

designations is based on a wide variety of sources — domestic, European and international. The law in this field is, therefore, very fragmented.

10.1.3   Much of the responsibility for nature conservation matters lies with Scottish Natural Heritage (SNH), a body formed in 1992 to exercise the functions previously undertaken by the Nature Conservancy Council (and its short-lived successor, the Nature Conservancy Council for Scotland) and the Countryside Commission for Scotland.[7] SNH is responsible for the designation and management of nature reserves, the designation of sites of special scientific interest, for some other forms of habitat protection, and for licensing activities otherwise unlawful under the laws protecting individual species. The Secretary of State and SNH have a specific duty to exercise their powers so as to ensure compliance with the Habitats and Species Directive.[8]

10.1.4   Conservation law in the United Kingdom must also be seen in its broader international context. The United Kingdom is a party to several major treaties aimed at furthering the conservation of nature, including the Convention on the Conservation of European Wildlife and Natural Habitats (the Berne Convention 1979) which has been very influential in shaping E.C. law in this field. The Convention on Biological Diversity signed at the Rio Summit in 1992 has attracted further attention to this area, and has required the Government to address the issue more seriously and in a more co-ordinated way, for example through the introduction of an overall strategy, entitled *Biodiversity: The U.K. Action Plan*,[9] and the plans developed by the U.K. Biodiversity Steering Group.[10]

SPECIES PROTECTION

10.2.1 WCA 1981 contains most of the general provisions relating to species protection. A feature of the Act is the use of Schedules which categorise individual species entitled to greater or lesser protection than that provided by the general rules. In several places the Act also allows greater freedom of action to "authorised persons" — defined as the owner or occupier of the land concerned, or a person authorised by the owner or occupier, by the local authority or, in some cases, by SNH or a district salmon fisheries board (WCA 1981, s. 27). In most cases the Act also allows licences to be granted to permit otherwise prohibited acts, the licensing authority most commonly being SNH or the Secretary of State

[7]   Natural Heritage (Scotland) Act 1991, Pt. I.
[8]   1994 Regulations, reg. 3(2).
[9]   Cm. 2428 (1994).
[10] *Biodiversity: The U.K. Steering Group Report* (1995).

(WCA 1981, s. 16).[11] A smaller group of animals and plants enjoy further protection as European protected species under the Habitats and Species Directive, as implemented by the 1994 Regulations, which contain similar licensing provisions (under regulations 44–46).

Birds

General

Under WCA 1981 it is an offence intentionally to kill, injure or take any wild bird, to take, damage or destroy the nest of a wild bird while it is being built or in use, or to take or destroy the egg of a wild bird (WCA 1981, s. 1(1)). The definition of "wild bird" excludes poultry and game birds (WCA 1981, s. 27(1)), and birds shown to have been bred in captivity are also excluded (WCA 1981, s. 1(6)). Defences are provided for a range of circumstances, the onus frequently lying on the accused to establish them (WCA 1981, s. 4).[12] No offence is committed by acts which are the incidental result of a lawful operation and which could not reasonably have been avoided. Authorised persons have a defence for actions shown to have been necessary for preserving public health, public safety or air safety, or for preventing the spread of disease or serious damage to livestock, crops, growing timber, fisheries or inland waters. Statutory measures for agricultural pest control and animal health are permitted, as is mercy killing, the taking of injured birds in order to tend them (provided they are subsequently released), and the taking of some seabirds' eggs for human consumption (WCA 1981, s. 16(2)). Many methods of killing or taking birds are proscribed, including the use of poison, bird-lime, traps and snares (WCA 1981, s. 5); criminal liability extends to the setting of such devices in circumstances likely to cause harm, and to those who knowingly cause or permit their use.[13]

10.2.2

Possession of any wild bird, alive or dead, or of its eggs or anything derived from the bird, is an offence of strict liability (WCA 1981, s. 1(2)). It is a defence for the person in possession to establish that the bird was bred in captivity, or had come into his possession as the result of natural means or of conduct lawful under the 1981 Act or its predecessors (WCA 1981, s. 1(3) and (6)). The keeping of many species of bird is controlled by a registration and marking scheme (WCA 1981, s. 7). It is an offence to

10.2.3

---

[11] As amended by Wildlife and Countryside Act 1981 (Amendment) Regulations 1995 (S.I. 1995 No. 2825), reg. 3.

[12] *ibid.* reg. 2.

[13] Wildlife and Countryside (Amendment) Act 1991, s. 1.

sell, offer for sale or possess for sale wild birds or their eggs (WCA 1981, s. 6). Exceptions are allowed for controlled sales of live birds listed in Part I of Schedule 3 to the Act, and dead birds listed in Parts II and III of Schedule 3.

Protected species

10.2.4 More than 100 species of bird, which are listed in Schedule 1 to WCA 1981, enjoy enhanced protection, for example ospreys and kingfishers. It is an offence to disturb any of these birds while they are building their nests or are at or near their nests containing eggs or dependent young, or to disturb the dependent young of such birds (WCA 1981, s. 1(5)). The defences available to authorised persons do not apply in relation to these protected species (WCA 1981, s. 4(3)), and the penalties for harming or possessing such birds are significantly greater (WCA 1981, ss. 1(4) and 21).

Birds which can be hunted

10.2.5 Game birds fall outside the protection of the 1981 Act, but a number of other species may also be hunted, for example greylag geese. These are listed in Part I of Schedule 2 to the Act, and outside the close seasons laid down in the Act it is no offence to kill or to take such birds, or to injure them in the attempt to kill them (WCA 1981, s. 2). The Secretary of State can alter the close seasons and make orders protecting the birds during periods of temporary hardship.

10.2.6   Close seasons are prescribed for game birds, namely grouse (red and black), partridges, pheasant, ptarmigan, snipe, and probably capercailzie. As well as the permission of the person with the right to take game (usually the landowner) licences are required for the killing and taking of game birds and for their sale.[14] A range of offences exists to punish those trespassing on land to take game or found in unlawful possession of it.[15]

Pests

10.2.7 Provisions in the 1981 Act allow authorised persons to kill or take birds from the listed pest species (WCA 1981, s. 2(2) and Pt. II of Sched. 2), but such general permission was found to be in contravention of the Wild Birds Directive. There are now no such listed species, but essentially the same result is achieved in practice through the issue of general licences permitting authorised persons to take action to control certain species, for example herring gulls and feral pigeons.

---

[14] Game (Scotland) Act 1772; Game Licences Act 1860.
[15] *e.g.* Night Poaching Acts 1828 and 1844; Game (Scotland) Act 1832.

Animals

General

A number of other animals — mammals, reptiles, fish, insects and 10.2.8
invertebrates — are protected under the 1981 Act. These are listed in
Schedule 5 to the Act, and it is an offence intentionally to kill, injure or take
a wild animal of these species (WCA 1981, s. 9). Intentional damage,
disturbance or obstruction of a place used by the animal for shelter or
protection is also an offence, as is intentional disturbance of the animal in
such a place, unless the animal is found sheltering in a dwelling-house. As
with birds, several defences exist (WCA 1981, s. 10), covering the incidental
results of lawful operations, mercy killing and the tending of injured animals,
and action authorised for pest control and animal health purposes. Authorised
persons may also take action to prevent serious damage to livestock or
crops, but a licence from SNH must be sought if the need for such action
becomes apparent beforehand. Possession and sale of these animals, alive
or dead, or of anything derived from them, is a strict liability offence, subject
to similar defences to those available in relation to the possession of birds
and eggs (WCA 1981, s. 9).

A smaller group of animals, for example wild cats, otters and dolphins, is 10.2.9
given further protection as European protected species. The 1994 Regulations
list these in Schedule 2, and regulation 39 prohibits the deliberate killing,
capture or disturbance of these species and prohibits any action which damages
or destroys their breeding sites or resting places.[16] Possession and sale of the
animals or anything derived from them is also an offence. A slightly more
limited range of defences exists under regulation 40.

Lesser protection is given to species listed in Schedule 6 to the Act. The 10.2.10
law prohibits the killing or taking of these species by particular methods,
including the use of traps, snares, poisons, gas, nets, automatic weapons, or
dazzling devices (WCA 1981, s. 11). There is a parallel but not identical
provision based on the Habitats and Species Directive, protecting 17 species
from specified hunting methods (1994 Regulations, reg. 41 and Sched. 3).
Under the Wild Mammals (Protection) Act 1996 it is an offence to harm
any wild mammal with intent to inflict unnecessary suffering.

Bats

All the species of bat likely to occur in Scotland are listed in Schedules 5 10.2.11
and 6 to the 1981 Act, but they are further protected by limits to the defences

---

[16] The first element is essentially the same as under WCA 1981, except to the extent that
there is any difference between "intentional" and "deliberate" conduct, whereas the second
is a notable extension from the 1981 provisions as there is no longer a requirement for the
effect on the breeding or resting place to be intentional.

which normally cover the disturbance of creatures found in dwelling-houses and the killing or injuring of animals incidental to a lawful operation (WCA 1981, s. 10(5)). Only action taken to remove bats from living areas of a house is protected (therefore, disturbing bats found in the loft of a house is unlawful), and SNH must be notified and given an opportunity to advise on any intended action which is likely to affect bats (*e.g.* timber treatment of a known roosting place). Bats are also European protected species.

Badgers

10.2.12 As well as being protected under Schedules 5 and 6 to the 1981 Act, badgers are the subject of special legislation.[17] This largely repeats the prohibitions on killing, injuring, possessing and disturbing badgers, with special emphasis on prohibiting disturbance of their setts, but the onus of proof is reversed for some offences, so that an accused found in suspicious circumstances must prove that he was not attempting an unlawful act. Only firearms of the specified size and power can be used to kill badgers. There are special provisions for the licensing of activities affecting badgers and special sanctions in cases where dogs have been used to harm badgers.

Deer

10.2.13 Close seasons are laid down for the four species of deer in Scotland,[18] but killing or taking deer during the close season is lawful if authorised by the Deer Commission for Scotland or carried out by the occupier of arable land, improved pasture or enclosed woodland in order to avoid serious damage to crops, pasture, woodland or foodstuffs.[19] In most circumstances, a game licence is required before deer can be killed,[20] as well as permission of the landowner or other person who owns the right to take deer. Licences are not required for action authorised by the Commission,[21] nor for action taken by the occupier of enclosed land.[22] The only lawful method of killing a deer is by shooting with a firearm and ammunition of the prescribed form.[23] With limited exceptions, the killing of deer at night is unlawful.[24]

---

[17] Protection of Badgers Act 1992.

[18] Deer (Scotland) Act 1996, s. 5 and Sched. 6, para. 2; Deer (Close Seasons) (Scotland) Order 1984 (S.I. 1984 No. 76).

[19] Deer (Scotland) Act 1996, ss. 10, 26.

[20] Game Licences Act 1860, s. 4.

[21] Deer (Scotland) Act 1996, s. 38.

[22] Game Licences Act 1860, s. 5.

[23] Deer (Scotland) Act 1996, ss. 17(3), 21; Deer (Firearms) (Scotland) Order 1985 (S.I. 1985 No. 1168).

[24] Deer (Scotland) Act 1996, s. 18.

Part I of the Deer (Scotland) Act 1996 (DSA 1996) places the 10.2.14
conservation, control and sustainable management of deer under the
supervision of the Deer Commission for Scotland. Under section 10 of the
Act, the Commission can authorise the killing or removal of deer where
they are causing serious damage to the natural heritage or to crops, forestry
or farm animals (*e.g.* by serious overgrazing), or becoming a danger to
public safety. More general measures for the control of deer where they are
likely to cause harm of the above nature can be introduced by the
Commission through agreements with the relevant owners and occupiers
(DSA 1996, s. 7), or by order where agreements cannot be reached or are
not being carried out (DSA 1996, s. 8). If the measures required by a control
scheme order are not carried out, the Commission can take action itself and
recover the expenses from the defaulters (DSA 1996, s. 9).

Seals

Seals are protected under the Conservation of Seals Act 1970, which, under 10.2.15
section 1, prohibits the use of poison or certain classes of firearms and
ammunition to kill seals, and, under sections 2 and 3 prohibits the taking or
killing of seals outside the close seasons laid down for the two species of
seal found off Scotland. Close seasons can be extended by ministerial order.
Defences are available for mercy killing, taking an injured seal in order to
tend it, or harm done as the incidental result of a lawful action. It is also
lawful, under section 9 of the Act, for the person in possession of a fishing
net or tackle (or someone authorised by him) to kill or injure a seal in the
vicinity in order to prevent damage to the equipment or to fish caught in it.
Licences can be granted under section 10 for the taking or killing of seals.
Seals are also covered by the prohibition on using certain methods of killing
or taking under regulation 41 of and Schedule 3 to the 1994 Regulations.

Whales

All species of whales, dolphins and porpoises are protected under WCA 10.2.16
1981 and as European protected species, and it is an offence to catch any
species in British coastal waters.[25] In Scotland, it is also a specific offence
to drive ashore any of the smaller species of whale commonly known as
bottlenose or pilot whales.[26]

---

[25] Whaling Industry (Regulation) Act 1934, ss. 1, 2, as amended by the Fisheries Act 1981,
s. 35.
[26] Fisheries Act 1981 s. 36.

Fish

10.2.17 Fishing in Scotland, especially salmon fishing, has been subject to detailed legal regulation for centuries. The ownership of fishing rights, the permitted times and methods of fishing, and the powers of district salmon fishery boards are all the subject of legislation, augmented by byelaws for individual rivers.[27] Here it is possible to mention only a few of the most general provisions.

10.2.18   It is an offence to obstruct the passage of salmon smolt or fry or of mature salmon to the spawning grounds during the close season, or to injure any spawn, spawning bed or shallow where spawn may be, except as the incidental result of cleaning any lade or dam or of exercising proprietary rights over the bed of a watercourse.[28] The use of poison to kill fish is strictly prohibited, as is the use of explosive and electrical devices,[29] and the permitted methods of fishing are legally prescribed.[30] In addition, some species of fish are protected under Schedule 5 to WCA 1981; the sturgeon is a European protected species, and a further eight species (including the Atlantic salmon while in fresh water) are protected against certain methods of killing or taking under regulation 41 of and Schedule 3 to the 1994 Regulations.

10.2.19   The taking of shellfish is subject to legal control which specifies minimum sizes and close seasons and prohibits the landing or sale of crustaceans at vulnerable stages in their life cycle.[31] Marine fishing is the subject of an immense volume of regulatory legislation, at national and European level,[32] but in the exercise of ministerial powers, regard must be had to the conservation of marine flora and fauna.[33]

Plants

10.2.20 Under section 13 of WCA 1981 it is a criminal offence for anyone other than an authorised person intentionally to uproot any wild plant, which is defined as any plant growing wild and ordinarily found growing in a wild state in Great Britain. Almost 100 species of plant, listed in Schedule 8 to the Act, are given additional protection, in that it is an offence for anyone intentionally to pick, uproot or destroy any of these species. The sale of

---

[27] See Scott-Robinson, *The Law of Game, Salmon and Freshwater Fishing in Scotland* (1990).
[28] Salmon Fisheries (Scotland) Act 1868, s. 19.
[29] Salmon and Freshwater Fisheries (Protection) (Scotland) Act 1951, s. 4.
[30] *ibid.* s. 2, as amended by the Salmon Act 1986, s. 21.
[31] Sea Fisheries (Shellfish) Act 1967; Sea Fish (Conservation) Act 1967; Oyster Fisheries (Scotland) Act 1840; Mussel Fisheries (Scotland) Act 1847; Inshore Fishing (Scotland) Act 1994.
[32] See paras. 11.3.1–14.
[33] Sea Fisheries (Wildlife Conservation) Act 1992.

listed plants, or of anything derived from them, possession with a view to sale and advertisement of any sort are also offences. In all cases, however, there is a defence for any action which is the incidental result of a lawful operation and which could not reasonably have been avoided. Nine species are also European protected species under regulation 43 of the 1994 Regulations, which are protected by similar provisions, extending to all forms of collection and cutting.

Alien species

The introduction of alien species of animals and plants can be very damaging to native wildlife, and is subject to controls. Under section 14 of and Schedule 9 to WCA 1981 it is an offence to release or allow to escape into the wild any animal (from mammals and birds to fish and invertebrates) of a kind not ordinarily resident in or not a regular visitor to Great Britain, or any animal which is one of the listed species of aliens which have become established here, for example grey squirrels. Equally, it is an offence to plant to cause to grow in the wild any of the listed species of plant, for example giant hogweed. There is also a wealth of legislation on trade in endangered species and import and export controls operated for health reasons.[34]   10.2.21

HABITAT PROTECTION

Each of the following designations of land has been created for a different purpose and is governed by its own statutory provisions. The designations do not form an integrated system, and one piece of land can be covered by several designations. The precise effect of each designation will often depend on the byelaws made for a particular site, or on the terms of management agreements made by the conservation authorities with anyone with an interest in the land. In addition to any direct consequences, the presence of a formal designation may affect other features of the law, for example indicating that an environmental assessment should take place before permission is given for afforestation projects or other forms of development.[35]   10.3.1

In many of the designated areas, management agreements can be used to further the objectives of nature conservation. Under such agreements, the owners and occupiers of land receive payments from the conservation authorities in return for agreeing to manage their land in particular ways, either refraining from activities detrimental to the conservation value of   10.3.2

---

[34] See Reid, *Nature Conservation Law, op. cit.*, n. 1, pp. 234–245.
[35] See paras. 7.4.17–20.

land, or undertaking positive action to maintain or improve its value. The payments represent compensation for profit foregone or for expenses incurred, and can involve large sums.[36] Agreements are normally registrable in the Register of Sasines or Land Register, and, once registered, bind the successors in title to the original parties.[37] SNH enjoys a general power to enter management agreements to secure the conservation and enhancement of, or to foster the understanding or enjoyment of, the natural heritage in Scotland.[38]

European Sites

10.3.3 The strongest legal protection is offered to European sites, under the Habitats and Species Directive as implemented by the 1994 Regulations. European sites, which together form the Natura 2000 network of protected sites across the European Community, are sites of Community importance and special areas of conservation designated by the Commission and the Secretary of State respectively in accordance with the criteria laid out in the Directive (whether as protected habitat types or as the habitat of protected species) and special protection areas designated under the Wild Birds Directive.[39] The European Court of Justice has made it clear that Member States are under an obligation to designate all sites which meet the ecological criteria, regardless of conflicting interests in the sites,[40] and the Directive expressly provides for the Commission to propose sites which Member States have overlooked.[41] A public register of all such sites is maintained by the Secretary of State, with copies made available through planning authorities and SNH, whilst individual notification is given to owners and occupiers.[42]

10.3.4 The main tools adopted to secure protection for European sites are familiar from the previous domestic designations, and all of the sites will already have been designated as sites of special scientific interest (SSSIs).[43] A list of potentially damaging operations is notified to the owner and

---

[36] See, *e.g. Cameron v. Nature Conservancy Council*, 1991 S.L.T. (Lands Tr.) 81.
[37] *e.g.* Countryside Act 1968, s. 15.
[38] Countryside (Scotland) Act 1967, s. 49A, added by the Countryside (Scotland) Act 1981, s. 9, amended by the Natural Heritage (Scotland) Act 1991, Sched. 10.
[39] 1994 Regulations, reg. 10; the U.K.'s initial proposals for sites of Community importance and special areas of conservation were submitted in 1995, but the formal designation procedures may take several years.
[40] Case C–355/90, *Commission v. Spain* [1993] E.C.R. I–4221; Case C–44/95, *R. v. Secretary of State for the Environment, ex p. RSPB* [1997] 2 W.L.R. 123.
[41] Directive 92/43, Art 5.
[42] 1994 Regulations, regs. 11–15.
[43] Marine sites are treated differently and are discussed below with marine nature reserves at para. 10.3.12.

occupier, and it is an offence to carry out any of these without giving SNH prior notice, and either consent has been given or four months have passed. In contrast to the SSSI provisions, the list of operations can be amended in relation to European sites, and all previous consents must be reviewed and modified or withdrawn if incompatible with the duty to protect the site. To offer further protection for such sites, byelaws can be made and special nature conservation orders issued, under which it is an offence to carry out a potentially damaging operation without the consent of SNH. Management agreements can be made, and are likely to be the most common way of providing protection, but powers of compulsory purchase exist where such agreements cannot be reached or are broken.

Strict rules operate to limit the possibility of sites being harmed by   10.3.5
development of any sort.[44] Before any project which is likely to have a significant effect on a European site (whether or not it is on the site) can be given official permission, an assessment of its impact on the site must be carried out. If there is a negative assessment, the project can be approved only if there are no alternative solutions and if the project must be carried out for "imperative reasons of overriding public interest". If the site contains a priority species or habitat as listed in the Habitats and Species Directive, the only reasons which are acceptable are those which relate to human health, public safety or important environmental benefits, or which have been specifically approved by the European Commission. Existing permissions must be reviewed according to the same criteria when a site is designated, and modified or revoked as necessary. If overriding reasons justify projects damaging a site, compensatory measures must be taken to protect the overall coherence of Natura 2000. These rules are of general application, but specific provisions adapt them to fit in with particular regimes, such as the system of town and country planning (including rules on their application to cases of permitted development) and the mechanisms for approving roads, electricity works, pipelines and various pollution permits.[45]

Nature reserves

Nature reserves are land managed for the purpose of providing opportunities   10.3.6
for the study and preservation of the flora and fauna of Scotland and of geological and physiographical features of special interest.[46] Where the management of land as a nature reserve is considered expedient in the national interest, a reserve can be declared by SNH, which can lease or

---

[44] 1994 Regulations, regs. 48–53.
[45] *ibid.* regs. 54–68 (planning), 69–70 (roads), 71–74 (electricity), 75–78 (pipelines), 79–80 (transport and works), and 83–85 (pollution).
[46] National Parks and Access to the Countryside Act 1949, s. 15.

purchase the land or enter management agreements with those holding an interest in it.[47] A power of compulsory purchase exists where agreements cannot be entered on reasonable terms or where their terms are broken.[48] Land managed as a nature reserve by other bodies can also be brought within the statutory scheme.[49]

10.3.7   Once a reserve has been declared, SNH can make byelaws, including restrictions on access and prohibitions on any form of disturbance of the wildlife and natural features of the site.[50] Byelaws must be confirmed by the Secretary of State and cannot interfere with the rights of the owner or occupier (management agreements must be used if they are to be restricted) or of statutory undertakers. Compensation is available where the byelaws interfere with the exercise of rights vested in other people.

10.3.8   Local nature reserves can be created and managed in the same way by planning authorities where this is considered expedient in the interests of the locality.[51]

Marine nature reserves

10.3.9 Areas of the sea can be designated as marine nature reserves where it is considered expedient that they should be managed by SNH for the purpose of conserving flora, fauna and geological or physiographical features of special interest.[52] The standard restriction is to areas landward of the baselines used for measuring territorial waters, and seaward of these baselines for up to three nautical miles, but special orders can extend the reserves to any part of British territorial waters.

10.3.10   Marine nature reserves are designated by the Secretary of State on the application of SNH. The application and the proposed byelaws for the reserve must be advertised and notified to a range of public bodies likely to be affected, and objections and representations must be heard before the Secretary of State decides whether to make the designation, any designation being similarly advertised and notified. To date, no marine nature reserves have been designated in Scotland.

10.3.11   Once a reserve has been created, byelaws can be made by SNH, subject to the Secretary of State's confirmation, to restrict access to the reserve and to protect the wildlife therein.[53] However, the scope of the byelaws is restricted in many ways. Byelaws cannot restrict the right of passage of

---

[47] National Parks and Access to the Countryside Act 1949, s. 16.
[48] *ibid.* ss. 17–18.
[49] WCA 1981, s. 35.
[50] National Parks and Access to the Countryside Act 1949, s. 20.
[51] *ibid.* s. 21.
[52] WCA 1981, s. 36, as amended by the Territorial Sea Act 1987, s. 3 and Sched.
[53] *ibid.* s. 37.

vessels other than pleasure boats, and cannot prohibit pleasure boats from all of the reserve for the whole year, nor prohibit the discharge of any substance from a vessel.[54] Byelaws cannot interfere with the exercise of the statutory functions of the listed public bodies, which include local authorities, harbour boards, SEPA and district fisheries boards.

Some marine areas are also entitled to protection as European sites. 10.3.12 Powers under a wide range of legislation must be exercised so as to ensure compliance with the requirements of the Habitats and Species Directive.[55] Subject to the limitations applying for marine nature reserves, SNH can make byelaws for a site, and any of the authorities involved can establish a management scheme, but without any precedence or powers of compulsion over the other bodies concerned.[56] The intention is that through partnership, voluntary co-operation and the exercise of existing powers, the conservation interest of sites can be protected without the imposition of a mandatory management regime.

Sites of special scientific interest

Under WCA 1981 there is a duty on SNH to designate as a site of special 10.3.13 scientific interest (SSSI) land which is of special interest by reason of its flora, fauna or geological or physiographical features (WCA 1981, s. 28).[57] Every owner and occupier of the site, and the planning authority, must be notified; the notification must contain the reasons why the site is of special importance and a list of operations likely to damage its special features (potentially damaging operations). The notification takes effect at once, but will lapse after nine months unless confirmed by SNH after a consideration of any objections or representations made by those affected.

Where an objection relates to the grounds justifying the designation, the 10.3.14 case must be referred to the special advisory committee created by section 12 of the Natural Heritage (Scotland) Act 1991. Existing designations must also be referred to the committee if the owner or occupier makes representations that any of the grounds justifying designation are no longer valid. If such representations are made at the time of designation, a case can be referred to the committee at once, otherwise referral can occur only after 10 years from designation or the last consideration by the committee. The final decision, however, remains with SNH.

---

[54] See paras. 11.2.11–13.
[55] 1994 Regulations, reg. 3(3).
[56] *ibid.* regs. 33–36.
[57] As amended by the Wildlife and Countryside (Amendment) Act 1985, s. 2; Wildlife and Countryside (Service of Notices) Act 1985, s. 1; see *R. v. London Brick Property Ltd* [1996] J.P.L. 227.

10.3.15   If the owner or occupier wishes to carry out any of the potentially damaging operations which have been notified, written notice must be given to SNH; failure to do so is an offence.[58] It is a further offence to proceed with the operation within four months of this notice, unless the operation is authorised by consent from SNH, by an express grant of planning permission, or by the terms of a management agreement. Emergency operations are permitted provided SNH is given full details as soon as practicable. The four-month delay (which can be extended by agreement) is to allow SNH to consider and negotiate a management agreement or the making of a nature conservation order to secure the future of the site, and it is only through such further action that a potentially damaging operation can be prevented for longer than the four-month period.

10.3.16   Where a planning application relates to an SSSI, the planning authority will have to consult with SNH before reaching its decision, and an environmental assessment may be required. For SSSIs on agricultural land, if a farm capital grant is refused because of SNH's objections, a management agreement must be offered.[59]

Nature conservation orders

10.3.17 Nature conservation orders can be made by the Secretary of State in order to strengthen the protection given to a particular site.[60] The Secretary of State can take this step for the purposes of securing the survival in Great Britain of any kind of animal or plant, of complying with international obligations, or of conserving the wildlife or features of a site of national importance. Orders take effect immediately, but following public advertisement and notification to owners, occupiers and the planning authorities, the Secretary of State must consider whether to confirm the order, taking heed of any representations made and holding a local inquiry if necessary.

10.3.18   The effect of an order is much the same as for ordinary SSSIs, but with some modifications. It is a criminal offence for any person, not just the owner or occupier, to carry out any of the potentially damaging operations notified without informing SNH and waiting for the prescribed period, or gaining relevant consent. The period of delay is three months, but this is automatically extended to 12 months if SNH offers to acquire the person's interest in the land or to enter a management agreement. There is also a power of compulsory purchase for SNH if an agreement is not possible on reasonable terms. In the event of an offence being committed, the penalties are greater than for ordinary SSSIs, and the court has the power to order the offender to take restorative action.[61]

---

[58] WCA 1981, s. 28.
[59] *ibid.* s. 32.
[60] *ibid.* s. 29.
[61] *ibid.* s. 31.

Compensation is available for the loss in value of an agricultural unit 10.3.19
covered by an order, and for loss incurred (including abortive expenditure)
when the three-month delay is extended as a result of an offer to acquire
the land or enter a management agreement.[62]

Natural heritage areas

This new designation of land applies to areas which are of outstanding 10.3.20
value to the natural heritage of Scotland, and where special protection
measures are considered appropriate.[63] Areas are to be recommended by
SNH to the Secretary of State, who must advertise the proposal and listen
to any representations before deciding whether to make a designation order.
The legal effects of designation are minimal: planning authorities must
maintain a list of natural heritage areas in their area and must pay special
attention to the desirability of preserving or enhancing their character in
the exercise of powers under the planning legislation.[64]

It is intended, however, that an overall management statement should be 10.3.21
produced for each natural heritage area by SNH, acting in co-operation
with the public bodies and private interests involved. This statement will
then provide the basis for an integrated approach to the management of the
areas, with co-ordination between the various government departments and
other public bodies involved, augmented by the use of existing powers to
enter management agreements and to offer advice and assistance in order
to involve the private sector. Further legal measures, such as the designation
of SSSIs or the making of directions removing permitted development status
from some operations, might also be appropriate, but the emphasis should
be on voluntary co-operation. No natural heritage area has yet been
designated, although the underlying concept is being put into practice
through non-statutory arrangements, such as the Cairngorms Partnership.[65]

National scenic areas

National scenic areas are those which were designated by the Secretary of 10.3.22
State after consultation with the Countryside Commission for Scotland as
being areas of outstanding natural beauty in a national context, where special
protection measures are appropriate.[66] No new national scenic areas can be

---

[62] WCA 1981, s. 30.
[63] Natural Heritage (Scotland) Act 1991, s. 6.
[64] Town and Country Planning (Scotland) Act 1997, s. 264.
[65] *Common Sense and Sustainability: A Partnership for the Cairngorms* (Scottish Office, 1992); *The Cairngorms Partnership* (Scottish Office, 1994).
[66] Town and Country Planning (Scotland) Act 1972, s. 262C, added by the Housing and Planning Act 1986, Sched. 11.

created, but those which have already been designated continue in effect.[67] Within these areas, planning authorities must pay special attention to the desirability of preserving or enhancing the character or appearance of the areas. To this end the Secretary of State has made directions under the General Development Order[67a] to require express permission for some forms of development normally enjoying permitted development status, and consultation with SNH (as successor to the Countryside Commission) when considering some categories of application for planning permission.

Special protection areas

10.3.23 The provisions for special protection areas, designated under the Wild Birds Directive, have now been brought into line with those for special areas of conservation under the Habitats and Species Directive, and both are discussed above as European Sites. The criteria for designation are set out in the Wild Birds Directive, and the European Court of Justice has emphasised that if the ecological criteria for designation are met, then an area should be designated, regardless of any competing economic or social interests.[68]

Limestone pavement orders

10.3.24 Areas of limestone pavement, *i.e.* areas of limestone wholly or partly exposed on the surface of the ground and fissured by natural erosion, can be protected where they are of special interest by reason of their flora, fauna or geological or physiographical features.[69] SNH is under a duty to notify the relevant planning authority of any area meeting this test, and it is then the responsibility of the planning authority or the Secretary of State to make an order where the character or appearance of the land would be likely to be adversely affected by the removal or disturbance of the limestone. It is a criminal offence to remove or disturb limestone on designated land without reasonable excuse, for example an express grant of planning permission.

Areas of special protection

10.3.25 Areas of special protection are designed to provide additional protection for birds, and can be designated by the Secretary of State by means of statutory instrument only if there are no objections from the owners and

---

[67] Natural Heritage (Scotland) Act 1991, s. 6(9); Planning (Consequential Provisions) (Scotland) Act 1997, Sched. 3, para. 11.
[67a] See paras. 7.4.13–14.
[68] Case C–355/90, *Commission v. Spain* [1993] E.C.R. I–4221; Case C–44/95, *R. v. Secretary of State for the Environment, ex p. RSPB* [1997] 2 W.L.R. 123.
[69] WCA 1981, s. 34.

occupiers of the land affected. The orders designating areas can make it a criminal offence to kill or disturb any bird in the area, to damage any egg or nest, or to enter the area or part of it during all or part of the year. These restrictions do not affect the exercise of any vested right, and the owner or occupier continues to have the rights of an authorised person under the general law protecting birds.[70]

Environmentally sensitive areas

Environmentally sensitive areas can be created in areas where it is particularly desirable to achieve any of the following objectives and the maintenance or adoption of particular agricultural methods is likely to facilitate this: the conservation and enhancement of the natural beauty of the area; the conservation of the flora, fauna or geological or physiographical features of special interest; the protection of buildings or other subjects of archaeological, architectural or historical interest.[71] Areas are designated by means of statutory instruments made by the Secretary of State after consultations with SNH.   10.3.26

Within environmentally sensitive areas, any person with an interest in agricultural land can make an agreement with the Secretary of State that the land will be farmed in accordance with the agreement. The designation order may set out the rates of payment and other terms to apply to all agreements in the area. The owner of the land must be informed if anyone with a lesser interest seeks to enter such an agreement, and the Secretary of State is obliged to keep under review the effects of the agreements on the area as a whole.   10.3.27

Ramsar sites

The United Kingdom is a party to the Convention on Wetlands of International Importance especially as Waterfowl Habitat (the Ramsar Convention) signed in 1971, under which special protection is to be given to wetlands of international significance in terms of ecology, botany, zoology, limnology, or hydrology, especially in relation to birds. Wetlands are designated by the Secretary of State for inclusion in the List of Wetlands of International Importance maintained under the Convention. Sites in Scotland should already be protected as SSSIs or under nature conservation orders, but the obligations to promote the conservation of wetlands and to avoid, as far as possible, the loss of any wetland resource should strengthen the interests of nature conservation on such sites against proposals for   10.3.28

---

[70] WCA 1981, s. 3.
[71] Agriculture Act 1986, s. 18; following Art. 19 of EEC Regulation 797/85 on improving the efficiency of agricultural structures.

development, etc. If protected wetlands are damaged, new areas of habitat should be designated as a compensatory measure.

World Heritage sites

10.3.29 The World Heritage Convention was signed in 1972 under the auspices of UNESCO to provide international recognition of and assistance for the protection of monuments, buildings and sites which are the natural and man-made treasures of the world. Sites which are of outstanding universal value can be added to the World Heritage List, and the protection, conservation, preservation and transmission to future generations of the natural heritage in their territory is an obligation on all parties, to be carried out by active and effective measures. Only sites which already enjoy full legal protection, for example as nature reserves, are likely to be accepted for the List, and, once adopted, must be fully protected and conserved.

CHAPTER ELEVEN

MARINE ISSUES*

INTRODUCTION

It is impossible to start this chapter with a general overview of the system 11.1.1
of environmental regulation for the marine environment. There is no single
system to protect and preserve the marine environment, and no single body
entrusted with the protection, preservation, or environmental management
of the marine environment. Instead, numerous bodies and individuals are
given the authority and powers to deal with marine issues.

    With that in mind, this chapter is set out on a sector-by-sector basis, but 11.1.2
with certain sections dealt with on an issue basis. It is intended to throw the
spotlight on environmental issues which are not caught by the remit of
other chapters, but which are, nevertheless, important aspects of
environmental regulation within Scotland. An additional aim is to highlight
those actors with primary responsibility for, and obligations with regard to,
protection of the marine environment.

    Much of the basis for regulation of the marine environment within the 11.1.3
United Kingdom is to be found in international agreements. Numerous
agreements have been entered into and updated frequently in an effort to
ensure that the environment is protected. These, therefore, form the basis
of much of the national legislation discussed here, but it is on the national
legislation, rather than the international agreements, that this chapter focuses.

POLLUTION

There are three major sources of pollution of the marine environment: 11.2.1
pollution from ships, aircraft and offshore installations; dumping and
incineration at sea; and landbased sources, which covers run-off and
discharges and which is covered to a certain extent elsewhere (see Chapter
3), but is also touched upon in this chapter. Rather than tackling each
source on an individual basis, each will be considered, as appropriate,

---

* This chapter is based on the version provided for the previous edition by Jane Ryder, WS,
formerly a partner of Boyd Jameson, WS, and now Director of the Scottish Museums
Council. Her contribution is gratefully acknowledged.

under the following broad headings: prevention; control; liability; and compensation.

11.2.2   One major change which should be noted before proceeding further is that the geographical scope of much of the U.K. legislation and regulation on marine issues has been extended up to 200 nautical miles from the coast.[1] This extension has been prompted by the entry into force of the UN Convention on the Law of the Sea 1982, which came into force in 1994 and which allows coastal states to claim an area up to 200 nautical miles from their baselines, known as the Exclusive Economic Zone. The United Kingdom ratified the Convention in July 1997.

Prevention

Pollution from ships: oil pollution

11.2.3   The main method employed to prevent oil pollution from ships is detailed regulation of the construction, equipment and operation of vessels. These regulations are found in the International Convention for the Prevention of Pollution from Ships 1973 (MARPOL), which is a comprehensive Convention dealing with the prevention of several types of pollution. Annex I to MARPOL and the 1978 Protocol (referred to as MARPOL 1973/78), which cover oil pollution were implemented in the United Kingdom by the Merchant Shipping (Prevention of Oil Pollution) Order 1983,[2] and the Merchant Shipping (Prevention of Oil Pollution) Regulations 1983 and 1985, now consolidated in the Merchant Shipping (Prevention of Oil Pollution) Regulations 1996.[3]

11.2.4   The Regulations, besides containing detailed requirements on ship design and construction, also provide extensive powers of enforcement including powers of inspection, detention and denial of entry to U.K. ports or offshore terminals. Improvement notices and/or prohibition notices may also be used to prevent vessels from going to sea until the matters complained of are remedied. The owner and master of a vessel will both be liable for any contravention of the Regulations, and liable to potentially substantial fines.

---

[1]   See Fishery Limits Act 1976, s. 1; Merchant Shipping Act 1995, s. 129; Merchant Shipping (Prevention of Pollution) (Law of the Sea) Order 1996 (S.I. 1996 No. 282); and Merchant Shipping (Prevention of Pollution) (Limits) Regulations 1996 (S.I. 1996 No. 2188), and 1997 (S.I. 1997 No. 506).

[2]   S.I. 1983 No. 1106, made under powers contained in s. 20 of the Merchant Shipping Act 1979.

[3]   S.I.s 1983 No. 1398; 1985 No. 2040; and 1996 No. 2154, made under para. 3 of the 1983 Order.

In addition to regulations on vessel construction, equipment and operation, new regulations now impose an obligation on vessels (and the United Kingdom) to have plans for dealing with pollution emergencies. These regulations have their basis in the International Convention on Oil Pollution Preparedness, Response and Co-operation 1990 (OPRC Convention)[4] which came into force in 1995 and which requires all ships, offshore units and ports to have such plans at hand. The Convention was implemented in the United Kingdom by the Merchant Shipping Act 1995 and the Merchant Shipping (Prevention of Oil Pollution) Regulations 1996.[5]   11.2.5

Other pollution

Annex II to MARPOL is concerned with the control of pollution by noxious liquid substances in bulk. Annex II has been incorporated into U.K. law by the Merchant Shipping (Dangerous or Noxious Liquid Substances in Bulk) Regulations 1996,[6] and essentially creates a parallel regime under which the discharge of chemicals from tank cleaning or deballasting operations may be carried out.   11.2.6

Annex III to MARPOL lays down regulations for the prevention of pollution by harmful substances carried by sea in packaged forms, or in freight containers, portable tanks or road and rail tank wagons (*i.e.* otherwise than in bulk). Annex III has been implemented by the Merchant Shipping (Prevention and Control of Pollution) Order 1990,[7] and the Merchant Shipping (Dangerous Goods and Marine Pollutants) Regulations 1990.[8]   11.2.7

Annex IV to MARPOL regulates sewage, but is not yet in force. Meanwhile, the discharge of sewage effluent from ships within the territorial waters is exempt from the requirement to obtain discharge consents under the Control of Pollution Act 1974 (COPA 1974).[9] However, the Scottish Environment Protection Agency (SEPA) is required to arrange for the collection and disposal of waste from vessels in controlled waters which appear to require their waste collected (COPA 1974, s. 47).   11.2.8

Annex V to MARPOL deals with garbage — for which see the Merchant Shipping (Prevention of Pollution by Garbage) Order 1988,[10] the Merchant Shipping (Prevention of Pollution by Garbage) Regulations 1988,[11] the Merchant Shipping (Reception Facilities for Garbage) Regulations 1988,[12]   11.2.9

---

[4]   (1991) 30 I.L.M. 733.
[5]   S.I. 1996 No. 2154.
[6]   S.I. 1996 No. 3010.
[7]   S.I. 1990 No. 2595.
[8]   S.I. 1990 No. 2605.
[9]   COPA 1974, s. 32(4)(a); see paras. 3.7.13–14.
[10]   S.I. 1988 No. 2252.
[11]   S.I. 1988 No. 2292.
[12]   S.I. 1988 No. 2293.

and the Merchant Shipping (Prevention of Pollution by Garbage) (Amendment) Order 1993.[13] It is illegal for any vessel, including pleasure craft and oil platforms and drilling rigs, to throw anything overboard within three miles of the nearest land and in all inland waters, and within 12 miles, to throw overboard plastic, or (if not ground to less than 1") paper, glass or food. Moreover, the North Sea is now a "Special Area"[14] and there is a complete ban on dumping of all refuse, with the exception of food, which can be dumped, but not within 12 miles of land.[15]

Control

Dumping and incineration by vessels and aircraft

11.2.10 Dumping of materials is regulated by two international Conventions — the Convention for the Prevention of Marine Pollution by Dumping from Ships and Aircraft, Oslo 1972 (the Oslo Convention)[16] and the Convention on the Prevention of Marine Pollution by Dumping of Waste and other Matter, London 1972 (the London Convention). The Oslo and London Conventions are enacted into U.K. law by Part II of the Food and Environment Protection Act 1985, which applies to all ships in U.K. territorial waters. The Food and Environment Protection Act 1985 covers deposits in the sea by all British vessels, aircraft, offshore installations and hovercraft, and the granting of licences in respect of such dumping, and by all such craft within U.K. waters or which were loaded in the United Kingdom with the intention of dumping the load at sea.[17] Licences are required for such activities, unless the Secretary of State either specifically exempts the particular type of activity, or sets requirements through statutory instrument which are complied with by those dumping the materials at sea.

11.2.11   Both the Oslo and London Conventions list substances which are virtually prohibited from dumping (Annex I — the Black List, *e.g.* mercury and cadmium). Others may be dumped with a special permit (Annex II — the Grey List, *e.g.* pesticides and by-products, arsenic, lead, copper and zinc). Dumping of Annex I substances is only permitted if they are present as "trace contaminants", while Annex II substances must not be present in "significant quantities", a term which is defined as 0.1 per cent by weight. In addition, at the second North Sea Conference in 1989, it was agreed that

---

[13] S.I. 1993 No. 1581.
[14] S.I. 1993 No. 1681.
[15] Under S.I. 1993 No. 1681 and S.I. 1988 No. 2293.
[16] This Convention is to be replaced by the Paris Convention for the Protection of the Marine Environment of the North East Atlantic 1992, which will come into force 30 days after it has been ratified by all of the parties to the Oslo Convention, and all parties to the Paris Convention for the Prevention of Marine Pollution from Land-Based Sources.
[17] Food and Environment Protection Act 1985, s. 5.

annual loads of various chemical compounds (the Red List) be reduced by 50 to 70 per cent by 1995. A licence is also required for incineration of these Red List substances at sea. The Paris Convention goes further. It completely prohibits dumping and incineration at sea unless the material being dumped or incinerated is one of the express exceptions listed in Article 3 of Annex II. It is not yet, however, in force, nor has it been enacted into U.K. law.

In deciding whether to issue a licence to dump or incinerate waste at 11.2.12 sea, the licensing authority (in Scotland, the Secretary of State) must take into account the need to protect the marine environment and human health, and to prevent interference with legitimate uses at sea, for example, fishing or leisure activities.[18] Account must also be taken of alternative methods of disposal.

Intervention

There are three ways in which intervention to control pollution from 11.2.13 shipping incidents occurs. The first is the implementation of the vessel's plan to deal with pollution emergencies, outlined above (para. 11.2.5). The second, which will only come to the fore when the former has failed, is implementation of salvage operations. The third and final element is government intervention to control or limit likely pollution from shipping incidents.

Salvage

Where a pollution incident has occurred, the success or otherwise of any 11.2.14 salvage operation can have a major impact on the overall effect on the marine environment. Traditionally, the essence of salvage was that assistance was rendered on a voluntary basis to those in danger. The reward for salvage was based on the salvor's success in recovering the property in question, the rule being "no cure, no pay". That rule, however, has changed due to increasing public awareness of possible environmental damage from the escape of pollutant cargo and to recognition of the necessity to encourage investment in the larger, more sophisticated but costly tugs necessary to conduct salvage operations. In addition, shipowners have become increasingly concerned to ensure as little damage to the environment as possible from pollution, as they are liable for damage done by escaped cargo, for clean-up costs and/or for the costs associated with preventing damage. The cumulative effect of these pressures has been reflected in the International Convention on Salvage 1989 (which came into force in 1996)

---

[18] Food and Environment Protection Act 1985, s. 8(1).

and in amendments to the Lloyds Open Form (LOF) under which most professional salvage services are rendered.

International Convention on Salvage

11.2.15 The International Convention on Salvage is implemented in the United Kingdom by the Merchant Shipping Act 1995, s. 224 and Sched. 11; Part I of Schedule 11 simply reproduces the articles of the Convention.

11.2.16   The new emphasis on protection of the environment can be seen in two areas. The first is in relation to reward and reimbursement for salvage operations. In assessing the reward for salvage, account now has to be taken of "the skill and efforts of the salvors in preserving or minimising damage to the environment".[19] Salvors also now have a right to special compensation where efforts have been made to prevent damage to the environment; this is not, however, a right to remuneration, only to be reimbursed for the expenses of the operation.[20] This right arises where the salvor has not otherwise earned a reward for work done (Article 14(1) of the Convention, and Schedule 11 to the Merchant Shipping Act 1995). In addition, Article 14(2) provides for enhanced special compensation if the salvage operation has actually "prevented or minimised damage to the environment". Secondly, under Article 8 the salvor now specifically owes a duty to the owner of the vessel to exercise due care to prevent or minimise damage to the environment. Thus, the salvor's interest in preventing harm to the environment from pollution is both encouraged and required.

Lloyds Open Form 95 (LOF 95)

11.2.17 In keeping with the entry into force of the International Convention on Salvage, the industry has amended and updated LOF 90, with LOF 95. Unlike the pattern adopted by LOF 90, LOF 95 does not specifically adopt any part of the Convention. Instead, its terms are updated to take account of the new provisions found in the Convention, and it specifically includes, in clause 1(a)(ii), an obligation on the salvor to use his best endeavours "while performing the salvage services to prevent or minimise damage to the environment".

---

[19] Art. 13(1)(b) of the Convention, as reproduced in Sched. 11 to the Merchant Shipping Act 1995.

[20] *Semco Salvage and Marine Pte Ltd v. Lancer Navigation Co. Ltd (The Nagasaki Spirit)* [1996] 2 C.L. 667; and *Semco Salvage and Marine Pte Ltd v. Lancer Navigation Co. Ltd, The Times*, February 10, 1997 (H.L.).

Government intervention

When the Torrey Canyon ran aground off the Scilly Isles in 1967, the   11.2.18
Government eventually ordered the wreck to be bombed so as to destroy
the remaining oil by fire and avoid serious pollution to the coast. There was
considerable doubt as to the U.K.'s right to take such measures, since the
vessel was outside U.K. territorial waters, and this led eventually to the
International Convention Relating to Intervention on the High Seas of Oil
Pollution Casualties 1969. Article 1 allows parties to: "take such measures
on the high seas as may be necessary to prevent, mitigate or eliminate grave
and imminent danger to their coastline or related interests from pollution
or threat of pollution of the seas by oil following upon a maritime casualty".
Power to intervene was extended, by a 1973 Protocol, to a long list of
dangerous or noxious chemicals other than oil.

In the United Kingdom, the Secretary of State has power to direct   11.2.19
intervention measures to prevent or reduce oil pollution under section 137
of the Merchant Shipping Act 1995. Basically, these are that he may order
any steps to be taken in relation to the moving and/or unloading of the
vessel, or, where these measures are likely to be insufficient to prevent or
reduce pollution, require any action including the sinking or destruction of
the ship. These powers are to be augmented under the Merchant Shipping
and Maritime Security Act 1997.[21] At present, the Government can intervene
only where pollution is likely to occur "on a large scale", but the 1997 Act
reduces this requirement to where pollution is likely to be "significant".[22]

There is no right to compensation from the Government for damage or   11.2.20
loss caused by the exercise of the intervention powers, unless the action
taken was not reasonably necessary to prevent pollution or was
disproportionate.[23] However, the shipowner would usually be insured against
intervention damage.

Control by regulation: discharge consents

The measures discussed above relate to accidental and or occasional pollution.   11.2.21
Continuous discharge of pollutants is dealt with under COPA 1974.[24] It is an
offence under the Act to cause or knowingly permit the entry of "poisonous,
noxious or polluting matter" or any solid waste into controlled waters, which
includes the sea up to three nautical miles from the low water mark of ordinary
spring tides, or to cause or knowingly permit any trade effluent or sewage

---

[21] At the time of writing this Act is not in force.
[22] Merchant Shipping and Maritime Security Act 1997, s. 2.
[23] Merchant Shipping Act 1995, s. 138.
[24] See, generally, paras. 3.5.1–29.

effluent to be discharged into any controlled waters.[25] Offences under this section are committed when either coastal or inland waters are polluted.[26]

11.2.22   The definition of "poisonous, noxious or polluting matter" is broad, and includes suspended solids from quarries or chemical discharges. It may also include chemicals administered either directly or mixed with fish farm feed, although not necessarily organic waste products. A person is not, however, guilty of an offence under the Act if the entry or discharge is authorised by a discharge consent granted by SEPA, and is in accordance with the conditions, if any, to which the consent is subject.

11.2.23   Enforcement of the terms of discharge consents falls to SEPA. Where it believes that the holder of a discharge consent is contravening its terms SEPA can serve an enforcement notice detailing steps required to remedy the breach (COPA 1974, s. 49A). Such enforcement notices can, however, be appealed (COPA 1974, s. 49B). In addition, where it appears likely that an unauthorised discharge is about to occur, SEPA may, after consulting with the relevant individual, serve notice on them requiring them to prevent the discharge taking place (COPA 1974, s. 46A). The notice will specify the steps to be taken and the time in which they are to be taken.

Works within harbour areas

11.2.24   Certain works within harbour areas, for example dredging, can cause environmental harm. Such works may be subject to a requirement for authorisation. For example, dredging may require to be authorised in certain designated harbour areas under local Harbour or Conservancy Acts and may also require the consent of the Crown Estate Commissioners, while disposal of dredging soil must be licensed under the Food and Environment Protection Act 1985 unless carried out by harbour authorities in execution of harbour maintenance works, and deposit is made on the site of the works. Harbour works may also be subject to environmental assessment under the Harbour Works (Assessment of Environmental Effects) (No. 2) Regulations 1989, as amended.[27]

Liability and compensation for pollution damage

Oil pollution

11.2.25   The Torrey Canyon incident exposed other deficiencies in the existing law, including difficulties in proving fault or negligence, as well as the more

---

[25] COPA 1974, s. 30F.
[26] *Mackenzie v. Tractor Shovels Tawse Ltd*, 1992 S.C.C.R. 71.
[27] S.I. 1989 No. 424; and Harbour Works (Assessment of Environmental Effects) (Amendment) Regulations 1996 (S.I. 1996 No. 1946).

worrying fact that many shipowners were unable to pay the full amount of potential damages. The incident was a major stimulus to the development of parallel compensation and liability regimes, the first at governmental level, the second at industry level.

Liability for oil pollution

The first response on a governmental level was the International Convention on Civil Liability for Oil Pollution Damage 1969 (CLC), replaced by the International Convention on Civil Liability for Oil Pollution Damage 1992 (CLC 1992), now in force. The 1992 Convention is implemented by the Merchant Shipping Act 1995, Part VI, Chapter III, and is stricter than CLC. Like CLC, CLC 1992 imposes strict liability on the owner of a vessel, but it no longer applies only to discharges of persistent oils when the vessel is carrying a cargo of such oil. It also applies to all ships and all discharges of oil within 200 miles of states' coasts. The basic rule (as applied in the U.K.) is that the shipowner is liable: 11.2.26

    (a) for any damage caused in the area of the United Kingdom by contamination resulting from the discharge or escape;

    (b) for the cost of any measures reasonably taken after the discharge or escape begins for the purpose of preventing or reducing any such damage in the area of the United Kingdom;

    (c) for any damage caused in the area of the United Kingdom by any measures so taken;

    (d) in the case of tankers, for the cost of any measures reasonably taken to prevent or minimise damage in the area of the United Kingdom where damage is foreseen as a result of an occurrence.

In addition, costs related to redressing damage to the environment are now recoverable.

Tankers carrying over a set amount of oil in bulk as cargo must either be insured against liability for pollution, or have another security in place to meet liability for pollution damage (s. 163). There is a right of direct action against the insurer (s. 165(1)), although in any proceedings brought against the insurer it is a defence for the insurer to prove that the discharge or escape was due to the wilful misconduct of the owner (s. 165(2)). The owner, in turn, is entitled, provided there was no intent and that he did not act (or omit to act) recklessly, to limit his liability in accordance with the legislation. (This is a change from the former provisions under which the owner's right to limit liability was lost where there was "actual fault or privity".) 11.2.27

Compensation for oil pollution

To supplement the limited liability under CLC, the International Convention on the Establishment of an International Fund for Compensation for Oil 11.2.28

Pollution Damage 1971 (the Fund Convention 1971) was agreed under the auspices of the International Maritime Organisation (IMO). The Convention established a supplementary fund ("the Fund") to make additional payments to those who had suffered harm as a result of a pollution incident, where, due to limited liability, they could not recover all their costs or receive full compensation from those liable under CLC, or where no liability arose under CLC. The Fund Convention 1971 was replaced by the International Oil Pollution Compensation Fund (the Fund Convention 1992), which came into force in 1996. The Fund Convention 1992 simply updates the provisions of the Fund Convention 1971 and does not substantially change the system created by it.

11.2.29   The Fund is financed by the governments of signatory countries, which impose a levy on oil importers in their countries.

The industry response to oil pollution

11.2.30 At the time CLC was being negotiated, there was widespread concern in the tanker and oil industries over the length of time it would take for the then CLC and Fund Conventions to enter into force. Industry, therefore, evolved two voluntary schemes to ensure acceptable compensation in the interim. The Tanker Owners' Voluntary Agreement Concerning Liability for Oil Pollution (TOVALOP) was an agreement entered into by tanker owners and bare boat charterers under which the parties undertook to pay compensation, up to certain agreed limits, for oil pollution, even though they might not otherwise be legally liable. The Contract Regarding an Interim Supplement to Tanker Liability for Oil Pollution (CRISTAL) was intended to provide compensation supplementary to TOVALOP. Both came to an end in February 1997 having been superseded by the Fund Convention 1992 and CLC 1992.

11.2.31   The oil industry also entered into the Voluntary Offshore Pollution Liability Agreement in 1974, which covers pollution from offshore facilities used in connection with oil and gas exploration and exploitation. Those participating in the Agreement accept strict liability for pollution damage up to a limit, and agree to pay the costs of remedial measures, again, subject to a maximum limit on liability.

Other pollution

11.2.32 In May 1996 the Convention on Liability and Compensation in Connection with the Carriage of Hazardous and Noxious Substances by Sea (HNS) was adopted. It is to be given effect in the United Kingdom by section 14 of and Schedule 3 to the Merchant Shipping and Maritime Security Act 1997. The HNS Convention is designed to be complementary to the CLC 1992 and the Fund 1992 Conventions and adopts almost exactly the same approach and provisions. The materials covered by HNS are defined through reference

to various existing instruments, such as Annex II of MARPOL 73/78 and
the International Maritime Dangerous Goods (IMDG) Code.

HNS introduces strict liability for the shipowner and compulsory   11.2.33
insurance requirements. It also increases the limits of liability compared
with current regimes. As with the Fund 92 Convention, HNS creates its
own HNS Fund to meet situations where the shipowner's liability would
not meet the full costs of a pollution incident. Contributions are paid to the
HNS Fund on a similar basis to Fund 92, *i.e.* contributions are paid by
those receiving more than a certain quantity of hazardous and noxious
substances in one year. A difference between the two funds is that the HNS
Fund is divided into separate sectors: a general account and three specific
accounts for oil, liquefied natural gases of light hydrocarbons and liquefied
petroleum gases of light hydrocarbons.

Claims against the HNS Fund, or against individuals under HNS, must   11.2.34
be brought within three years of the date when the person suffering the
damage knew of it or ought reasonably to have known of it and, at the
latest, within 10 years of the incident happening, under Article 36.

FISH

Pollution of the marine environment is, without doubt, the major issue in   11.3.1
marine environmental sectors, but it is not the only issue. The other major
concern is, of course, fishing: the decline of stocks as a result of over-
fishing and pollution, and farming fish.

Prevention of harm

Shellfish

Shellfish are particularly susceptible to the effects of pollution. One major   11.3.2
source of pollution is the build-up of nutrients in coastal waters owing to
sewage disposal and agricultural run-off. Excessive nutrient input may be
evidenced by toxic alga blooms (these also occur naturally), which can
cause paralytic and less severe diarrhetic shellfish poisoning (PSP and DSP)
if bivalve molluscs, which have accumulated these toxins, are eaten.[28] Under
the powers conferred by section 1 of the Food and Environment Protection
Act 1985,[29] the Secretary of State has power to issue emergency prohibition
orders, prohibiting the fishing for, taking or removing of bivalve molluscs

---

[28] Scottish Office Consultation Paper of March 11, 1992, on the Urban Waste Treatment
Directive 91/271 and the Nitrates Directive 91/676.
[29] As amended by the Food Safety Act 1990, s. 15.

out of designated areas. The Secretary of State also has power to prohibit the deposit of shellfish in designated waters.[30]

Control

Fishing

11.3.3 All U.K. regulation of fishing should be based on European legislation because, under European law, the European Community has sole authority to regulate fishing.[31] In some instances, however, for example where emergency action is required, the European Community has delegated power to take action to the Member States.

Quotas

11.3.4 The decline in fish stocks has been of concern to commercial fishermen and independent conservationists alike, and commercial fishing is now subject to stringent quotas and effort limitation measures in an attempt to halt the decline. Each year the E.C. Fisheries Council sets quotas (total allowable catches (TACs)) for Member States (in the U.K.'s case after application of the Hague Preference which favours members of the Community particularly dependent on fishing).[32] There are different TACs for individual species. Each TAC is based on advice from the Scientific and Technical Committee for Fisheries, but consideration is also given to such matters as economic concerns and the needs of individual communities. This can mean that the TAC set for certain species may be more than environmental concerns would actually allow.

11.3.5   Member States allocate a TAC amongst individual fishermen by the issue of licences.[33] In the United Kingdom, these are issued by local fisheries offices, and almost all vessels are required to hold a licence for relevant species/areas. Although licences are issued to named fishermen/companies, a licence must be attached to a vessel, except with consent of the fisheries office. Any transfer of a licence must, therefore, be in conjunction with the sale of at least a share in the vessel. With the introduction of licences, attempts were made to restrict ownership of vessels (and, therefore, issue of licences) to U.K. nationals,[34] but the European Court of Justice has ruled

---

[30] Sea Fisheries (Shellfish) Act 1967.
[31] Act of Accession 1972, 1973 U.K.T.S. No. 1, Art. 102.
[32] Council Regulation 170/83.
[33] Sea Fish (Conservation) Act 1967; Sea Fish (Conservation) Act 1992.
[34] Merchant Shipping Act 1988; Merchant Shipping (Registration of Fishing Vessels) Regulations 1988 (S.I. 1988 No. 1926).

that this is incompatible with Community law.[35] Companies whose beneficial owners are E.C. nationals may, therefore, own British registered vessels, and participate in U.K. TACs, but all U.K. registered vessels (a) must fish under licence and (b) may be required to demonstrate that control is exercised from the United Kingdom and that there is a real connection with the United Kingdom.

Conditions for the issue, transfer and operation of licences (which include 11.3.6 reporting and may include other conditions, such as "tie-up" requirements)[36] are highly technical and complex, and not readily available in textbook form. In general, reference should be made to: (a) licences themselves, which must be aboard the vessel at all times; (b) Scottish Office press releases; (c) trade journals, such as *Scottish Fishing Weekly*; and (d) local fisheries officers. Where restrictions on fishing are breached by a British boat, the master, owner and (if applicable) charterer can all be prosecuted for the offence.[37] One point to note in relation to the transfer of licences is that the licences are tied to vessel capacity. Although vessel licences may be aggregated, limits may be placed on the percentage of the overall licence that may be transferred to the aggregating vessel (the remaining portion will be forfeited on transfer), or on the overall tonnage and/or engine capacity of that vessel and, from time to time, the Government may place a complete or partial ban on the transfer of licences. In addition, a vessel's licences may be revoked if the vessel has not fished for a certain period of time. The objective behind these provisions is to ensure that the Government has an accurate record of the operative capacity of the British fishing fleet which can be used to ensure that the appropriate licences are issued to enable the U.K.'s quotas to be met and not exceeded, nor under-utilised. It also provides a mechanism for reducing the overall capacity of the British fishing fleet.

In addition to the licensing controls outlined above, restrictions are also 11.3.7 placed on fishing in certain areas and on the use of certain types of gear.[38] While some of these restrictions are essentially permanent, others are introduced on a temporary basis.

Fish farms

Fish farming can also have a major impact on the marine environment. 11.3.8 Three main problems can arise: due to the numbers of fish kept in relatively

---

[35] Case C-221/89, *R. v. Secretary of State for Transport, ex p. Factortame Ltd (No. 3)* [1992] Q.B. 680.

[36] There are no "tie-up schemes" currently in operation.

[37] Sea Fishing (Enforcement of Community Quota Measures) Order 1996 (S.I. 1996 No. 247).

[38] Council Regulations 171/83 and 3094/86. See also *Procurator Fiscal, Stranraer v. Marshall*, 1991 S.C.C.R. 397.

confined spaces there is a greater likelihood of disease, which can spread to native populations; stocks can escape, which can lead to increased competition with local species for food and can lead to changes in the genetic make up of local stocks where interbreeding between the stocks occurs; and perhaps, of most immediate concern, there will be at least some pollution of the surrounding waters.

11.3.9   As the seabed and most of the foreshore are part of the Crown Estate, fish farmers must apply to the Crown Estate Commission for a lease of the area which the fish farm will occupy. The Environmental Assessment (Salmon Farming in Marine Waters) Regulations 1988,[39] which implement E.C. Directive 85/337, require that all applications to the Crown Estate for salmon farming leases must be submitted with a supplementary environmental statement if the proposed development is likely to have significant environmental effects because of its type, scale or location.[40] The special requirement extends to:

> (1)   marine salmon farming using fixed equipment within two kilometres of the coast; and
>
> (2)   projects over a certain size, with a lower threshold in certain sensitive areas.

11.3.10   Following receipt of an application, the Crown Estate Commissioners follow consultation procedures agreed with the Scottish Office. Consultees will include the general public, SEPA, planning authorities responsible for onshore development, and interested groups, including Scottish Natural Heritage. These procedures should ensure that impacts on the environment are kept to a minimum.

11.3.11   Where the proposal concerns the operation of a fish farm within certain harbours, a works licence must be obtained from the local harbour authorities.

11.3.12   In addition, all fish farms must be registered with the Scottish Office for disease control purposes, and certain diseases must be notified to the Scottish Office. Restrictions may be placed on movement of infected stock, and procedures are laid down for treatment and disposal.[41] Again, these should afford some protection to the environment.

11.3.13   Treatment of farmed fish can, in turn, give rise to one of the main pollution concerns: the introduction of drugs into the marine environment. All drugs used for treatment of fish are, by statutory definition, veterinary drugs for the purposes of the Medicines Acts 1968 and 1971. The Acts require that all veterinary medicines have a product licence covering sale, supply and

---

[39]   S.I. 1988 No. 1218.
[40]   See paras. 7.4.17–20.
[41]   See Diseases of Fish Acts 1937 and 1983, and Sea Fisheries (Shellfish) Act 1967.

manufacture, and the Veterinary Products Committee recommends to the licensing authority that it grants a licence only if it is satisfied that the product meets the required standards of safety, quality and efficiency. However, section 9(2) of the 1968 Act allows a vet to prescribe any medicine, licensed or unlicensed, for animals under his care as long as it is specially prepared to order. This means that any product, including unlicensed products, can be prescribed and can be introduced into the sea with potentially adverse effects on the marine environment.

There is also considerable concern over the use of pesticides, the environmental impact of which is, to say the least, uncertain. Classification as a pesticide or medicine depends upon the purpose to which the products are put: the same substance can be both medicine and pesticide, for example dichlorovos (the active ingredient in Nuvan). Pesticides as such are controlled by the Food and Environment Protection Act 1985, which contains powers to make regulations governing the maximum residue levels of pesticides in foods, but current regulations[42] do not include fish.

11.3.14

---

[42] Pesticides (Maximum Residue Levels in Food and Feeding Stuffs) Regulations 1994 (S.I. 1994 No. 1985). See para. 1.5.6.

CHAPTER TWELVE

EUROPEAN ENVIRONMENTAL LAW

INTRODUCTION

12.1.1 The European Community has achieved a considerable degree of success in developing a policy to protect and enhance an environment of widely different geographical, climatic and societal characteristics. At the same time, it has developed what appears to be an acceptable compromise between environmental protection and unconstrained economic development, the latter being one of the fundamental objectives of the originally purely economic community. Environmental policy for which the Treaty of Rome, in its unamended form, made no legal provision has been one of the most rapidly developing sectors of policy in the European Economic Community and now the European Union.

12.1.2 The reasons for this development (much of which has taken place within the decade) are several: first, the realisation that the increasingly serious problem of environmental damage cannot be adequately addressed at national level only — pollution is an international concern; secondly, one of the principal objectives of the Treaty of Rome is the continual improvement in the quality of life of the citizens of Europe (Preamble and Article 2), which demands the achievement of as clean an environment as possible in which to live and work; thirdly, the central objective of the Treaty of Rome is to establish a single Common Market with no barriers to trading on an equal footing throughout the Community (Article 2) — differences in standards of environmental control could seriously distort the concept of fair competition, and harmonisation of laws in this field is, therefore, essential; and finally, the Community itself has collectively been responsible for much of the pollution and contamination which has occurred in Europe, and it has a responsibility to its individual citizens to ensure that the efforts of Member States (upon whose individual laws the implementation of most European environmental policy depends) are effectively directed, co-ordinated and enforced.

12.1.3 Accordingly, the existence of an effective Community system of laws which will afford the environment a high level of protection, while at the same time promoting the internal market, is essential to the proper functioning of the Community. This was recognised by the European Commission when, in the Fourth Action Programme on the Environment

(1987–1992)[1] it emphasised that "the effective implementation of Community environmental legislation by all Member States will be of primary importance for the Community".

Relevance of E.C. environmental law

A knowledge of European environmental law and the policy which has 12.1.4 promoted it is essential to any consideration of Scottish environmental issues. This is partly because E.C. law is now a part of the law of Scotland and, as such, it is necessary to have an understanding of how Community rights and obligations are applied through our own laws. More importantly, it is essential to understand the purpose of the underlying policy, given that the courts in this country are required to interpret national law so as to ensure compliance with the Community policy in question. This "purposive" construction to be given to the national laws designed to give effect to directives was established in the House of Lords' decision in *Litster v. Forth Dry Dock & Engineering Co. Ltd.*[2] That case in fact dealt with employment law but, given the increasing incidence of U.K. legislation enacted specifically to implement E.C. environmental directives, it is likely that this approach will be adopted in any environmental decision in the near future. The judgment in *Kincardine & Deeside District Council v. Forestry Commissioners*[3] contains a clear indication that the courts will indeed adopt this approach.

DEVELOPMENT OF EUROPEAN ENVIRONMENTAL LAW

As originally enacted, the Treaty of Rome made no mention of the 12.2.1 environment and there was no formal environmental policy. In 1972 the UN Conference on the Environment at Stockholm highlighted the global concern over the damage being inflicted on the world and its ecosystems. Later in the same year the E.C. Summit Meeting in Paris recognised that the continuing encouragement of economic growth would require improvements in the quality of life.[4] The Commission was directed to formulate the first formal statement of Community environmental policy which, as well as addressing the overall aim of preventing, or at least greatly reducing, pollution, would recognise the need to achieve co-ordination amongst national governments on such aspects as:

---

[1] O.J. [1987] C 328/1.
[2] 1989 S.L.T. 540.
[3] 1992 S.L.T. 1180; 1991 S.C.L.R. 729; see commentary by Reid and Hunter in 1991 S.L.T. (News) 274.
[4] Meeting of Heads of State and of Government of the Enlarged Community, Cmnd. 5109 (Paris, October 1972).

(1) the planned use of scarce resources;

(2) the problem of transfrontier pollution;

(3) preventing distortion of competition where the cost of compliance with environmental legislation differs between Member States;

(4) the desire to promote similar living conditions throughout the Community;

(5) recognition that although extremely important *per se*, environmental policy is a critical element of economic development.

12.2.2   Having established a general policy, the Commission, wishing both to establish a programme of legislation to start the process of controlling further damage to the environment and, at the same time, to have the opportunity of reviewing progress, discussing changes in policy, etc., provided for an Environment Action Programme for the four-year period from 1973 to 1976.[5] This First Action Programme laid down the Commission's plans to cope with pollution of the atmosphere, of water and of land (particularly waste management). In addition, considerable emphasis was placed on the protection of natural habitats and wildlife.

12.2.3   The first programme was designed to focus the original primary aims of the Community into more identifiable plans to:

(1) reduce and prevent pollution and nuisances;

(2) improve the quality of life; and

(3) take action at Community level.

The First Action Programme was followed by a second,[6] third,[7] fourth,[8] and fifth[9] spanning the period 1977 to 2000.

12.2.4   The different action programmes had different emphases. The first and second were designed to produce a relatively speedy response to the worst effects of pollution; the third emphasised the concept of the preventative approach, while the fourth heralded a major change in the status of the environment in E.C. law; the fifth marks a further development in policy, away from prescriptive legislation towards voluntary action and market-based measures.

Treaty of Rome 1957

12.2.5   The Treaty of Rome 1957 did not specifically provide for the environment. The Paris Summit meeting based the environmental policy which it

---

[5] O.J. [1973] C 112/1.

[6] O.J. [1977] C 139/1.

[7] O.J. [1983] C 346/1.

[8] O.J. [1987] C 328/1.

[9] O.J. [1993] C 138/1.

established on the fact that the Preamble to the Treaty committed the signatories to *inter alia* "the constant improvement of the living and working conditions of their peoples". In addition, it was rapidly becoming clear that the absence of a "level playing-field" arising from the differing degrees of environmental regulation pertaining in different Member States could work against the principles of free trade and fair competition. With the rapidly developing importance of the environment as an international issue, this slightly contrived authority for action on the environment was replaced with formal recognition of environmental policy as an established part of the Treaty, in terms of the amendments introduced by the Single European Act in 1987 which provided, for the first time, an "Environment" Title (now, following further amendments introduced by the Maastricht Treaty, Title XVI) providing environmental policy with a proper legal basis.

Single European Act 1986

The Single European Act 1986 came into effect on July 1, 1987. It amended the Treaty of Rome in two important respects: 12.2.6

(1) by the introduction of a new environmental Title VII in Articles 130R to 130T. As well as putting environmental measures on a proper constitutional footing, this amendment required environmental issues to be a component of other E.C. policies and preserved the right of Member States to set higher standards provided they were compatible with the Treaty and did not amount to any restriction on trade;

(2) by adding Article 100A to the Treaty, which had the effect of providing a "green" alternative to Article 100 by allowing voting by qualified majority on measures designed to promote the establishment or functioning of the internal market. The Commission is required for such single market measures to take, as its base, a high level of protection to ensure that environmental issues are not subordinated to economic matters.

Title VII set out three principal objectives of environmental policy: 12.2.7

(1) to preserve, protect and improve the quality of the environment;
(2) to contribute towards the protection of human health; and
(3) to ensure prudent and rational utilisation of natural resources.

Title VII also enshrined in the Treaty of Rome the three cardinal principles of environmental action, as follows. 12.2.8

(1) *That preventative action should be taken:* there is considerable confusion between this principle and the precautionary approach introduced by the Maastricht Treaty. Some legal commentators believe that there is no difference between the two. Taking a

preventative approach is generally recognised as requiring legislation to control the acquisition, use, storage and disposal of
substances or the operation of industrial processes in advance of
the creation of environmental damage, rather than reactive legislation for the "clean up" after the event.

(2) *Environmental damage should be rectified at source:* this principle is founded on the recognition that environmental impairment will expand and increase, the further pollutants migrate
from their source. Action should, therefore, be taken as early
and as close to the source as possible.

(3) *The polluter should pay:* this is an elusive concept which policy
makers have been struggling to apply successfully. By and large,
it is society (which bears the costs of enforcement and monitoring) and the victims of environmental damage (who suffer personal injuries and property damage) that currently pay for
pollution. It is intended, however, that the environmental costs
of economic activity should fall on the operator, and that producers of waste or life-expired products should "internalise" the
costs of disposal into their design and production accounting.

The Treaty of European Union 1993 (the Maastricht Treaty)

12.2.9   The Maastricht Treaty continued the process by:

(1) introducing the concept of "sustainable and non-inflationary
growth respecting the environment" into the Treaty of Rome
(Article 2);

(2) laying down a requirement to aim at a high level of protection
for all environmental policies (Article 130R(2)) (previously restricted to single market issues);

(3) extending qualified majority voting in the European Council to
most items of environmental legislation with the exception of
those relating to fiscal matters, town and country planning and
measures affecting water and energy resources, where a unanimous vote is still required (Article 130S);

(4) introducing to European environmental policy the "precautionary principle" requiring action to be taken as soon as a realistic
risk of damage occurring has been identified, even if full, incontrovertible scientific proof has not been advanced. This principle could be said to represent a "just in case" approach (Article
130R(2));

(5) requiring the promotion of measures at international level to deal with
regional or worldwide environmental problems (Article 130R(1)).

12.2.10   At this point it would seem appropriate to consider the question of the
appropriate Article of the Treaty on which to base environmental legislation.

Prior to the Single European Act, legislation tended to be based either on Article 100 or Article 235: Article 100 provides "for the approximation of such provisions laid down by law, regulation or administrative action in Member States as directly affect the establishment or functioning of the common market". Thus, harmonisation of national laws to permit free movement of goods or include fair competition proved to be a relatively satisfactory basis for some aspects of environmental legislation (*e.g.* water quality) which had a direct bearing on the economic activity of the Common Market, and Article 100 was relied on in the early years to establish the Community environmental policy.

For aspects without a direct connection with the functioning of the market, Article 235 had to be used. A catch-all provision, Article 235 sanctions legislation where it is "necessary to attain in the course of the operation of the common market, one of the objectives of the Community", and where provision of the necessary powers is not made elsewhere in the Treaty. In a judgment in 1985 the European Court of Justice held that environmental protection was indeed an objective of the Treaty.[10]   12.2.11

As indicated above, the Single European Act amendments introduced new Articles 130R to 130T giving formal legislative recognition to environmental policy. These Articles provide a clear legal basis for legislation where the action proposed is specifically related to the environment. It is still possible to base legislation on Article 100A which reflects the original Article 100 of the Treaty in requiring legislation to have, as its objective, "the establishment and functioning of the internal market". The main distinction between the two has been that under Article 100A, also added by the Single European Act, proposed legislation can be adopted by a majority vote in the Council, whereas under Article 130S, unanimous agreement is required. Furthermore (and it is in this respect that most friction has arisen), the European Parliament has, under Article 100A, a considerable impact on the process of approving legislation whereas, under Article 130S the Council is required only to consult the Parliament.   12.2.12

The Commission has tended to favour Article 100A because it offers the European Parliament considerable scope for involvement in the process of legislation and emphasises the importance of Community law over that of Member States. Conversely, the Council has supported the basis provided by Article 130S because it gives Member States a greater degree of control and offers less opportunity for the Parliament and Commission to interfere.   12.2.13

This friction was brought to a head over the correct basis on which legislation was enacted to control pollution caused by waste from the titanium dioxide industry. The significance of Directive 89/428 on the control of waste from the titanium dioxide industry was that it sought to protect the   12.2.14

---

[10] Case 240/83 *Procureur de la République v. Association de défense des brûleurs d'huiles usagées* [1985] E.C.R. 531.

environment (for which Article 130 would be appropriate) and, at the same time, to harmonise laws relating to this industry throughout the European Community, thus promoting the internal market (for which Article 100A was designed). The European Court of Justice ruled in *E.C. Commission v. E.C. Council*[11] that while such a dual objective would normally require two directives to be issued (one under each Article), Article 100A could embrace both aims, whereas Article 130 was confined to legislation with the sole purpose of protecting the environment and, accordingly, Article 100A was the proper basis for the Directive. The principal result of this case (apart from the need to re-enact the Titanium Dioxide Directive and other directives which have been based on Article 130) is that if the Commission can demonstrate that the proposed new legislation is at least partly intended to avoid unfair competition it can be based on Article 100A which, because of the qualified majority voting requirement, will avoid the vetoing of the measure by any one Member State.

12.2.15   The confusion surrounding the appropriate basis for the introduction of new environmental legislation continued, notwithstanding the outcome of this "Titanium Dioxide case". To a considerable extent the matter has been resolved by the terms of the Maastricht Treaty. One of its potentially far-reaching provisions is the stipulation in Article 130R that "environmental protection requirements must be integrated into the definition and implementation of other Community policies". There has, however, been little or no reflection of this requirement *de facto*, and environmental issues continue to be subordinated to those of commerce and the wider "single market" economic concerns. In addition, the Community's objectives now require to include the promotion of "sustainable and non-inflationary growth respecting the Environment".

12.2.16   The principle of the adoption of environmental legislation by qualified majority voting has been extended to include all but a few areas of E.C. policy. Unanimous voting will still be required where there is a direct link to other policies which require unanimity, for example in respect of fiscal measures (including the carbon tax proposals — see para. 12.5.29), town and country planning and the supply of energy.

12.2.17   The European Parliament's powers in relation to environmental issues have been further strengthened by these developments. By and large, however, the only remaining area where the Parliament will have an explicit right of veto will be over the Community's Environmental Action Programmes.

12.2.18   The European Communities Act 1972 provides the legal basis for incorporation of E.C. law into the law of the United Kingdom. Section 2(1) enacts, in very wide terms, that all rights, powers, liabilities and restrictions under the Treaties and all remedies and procedures provided by them are

---

[11] Case C-300/89 [1991] E.C.R. I–2867.

without further enactment to be given legal effect in the United Kingdom. This means that any rights and liabilities which, under E.C. law, have immediate effect in the United Kingdom (*e.g.* regulations and directives with direct effect) have to be recognised by our national courts.

Apart from the few areas of environmental policy enacted by regulation, 12.2.19 the impact of E.C. environmental legislation on U.K. law is not immediately obvious, but it has had (and is increasingly having) a profound influence. Apart from direct compliance with directives through enactment of U.K. statutes, implementation is often achieved by means of statutory instruments or other forms of subordinate legislation, or merely by administrative action on the part of central government departments advising the regulatory bodies on action to be taken. There is no better example of the influence of E.C. aspects on the framing of national environmental policy than the Environmental Protection Act 1990. Many of the provisions of Part I on *inter alia* integrated pollution control, have been included to achieve compliance with the Air Framework Directive and the Large Combustion Plants Directive.[12] Throughout the Act there are requirements for information to be made publicly available — a direct response to the Freedom of Environmental Information Directive.[13]

THE INSTITUTIONS OF THE EUROPEAN COMMUNITY

The European Union

In 1993, the Treaty on European Union (the Maastricht Treaty) changed 12.3.1 the institutional nomenclature to the European Union from European Community or European Economic Community (EEC). The European Union (E.U.) is the term used to refer to all of the arrangements between the Member States, which in the fields of the Common Security and Foreign Policy and of Justice and Home Affairs operate in the same way as most international arrangements, relying on every state's agreement before action can be taken. It is the European Community (E.C.) which has the separate legal status, institutions and power to take decisions binding on Member States, and, in this chapter, E.C. will continue to be used to refer to the amalgam of 15 Member States. This accords with the current citational convention for legislation.

The Commission

The Commission is the starting-off point for all Community legislation and 12.3.2 is, in effect, the Community's "civil service". At its head is the President,

---

[12] Directives 84/360 and 88/609 respectively. See para. 12.5.15.
[13] Directive 90/313; see para. 12.5.26.

and there are currently 20 Commissioners who are appointed by the national governments and responsible for the work of one or more of the 23 Directorates-General, including DG XI, which deals with the environment, nuclear safety, and civil protection. The principal functions of the Commission are, first, to initiate legislation arising from proposals made by the appropriate Commissioner and, secondly, to monitor and enforce implementation of and compliance with existing legislation by Member States as part of its overall task as guardian of the E.C. Treaties.

The Council

12.3.3 The Council is made up of one minister from each of the Member States, headed by a Presidency which rotates every six months. Its membership varies according to the matter under discussion. The Council debates proposals for legislation submitted to it by the Commission, and can adopt, amend or reject any proposal put to it. If national differences are likely to emerge at any point in the process of Community law-making, these will be focused in the Council. The dichotomy between the narrower interests of the Member States and the greater good of the Community is reflected in the requirement that the Council, in its deliberations, should seek the highest common denominator as between the Community and the Member States. Depending on the basis for action adopted for proposed legislation, voting in the Council requires to be either unanimous or by qualified majority.[14]

The European Parliament

12.3.4 Members of the European Parliament are directly elected by the citizens of each Member State but, strictly speaking, the Parliament is not a legislative body. After the accession in 1995 of Austria, Finland and Sweden, the number of members rose from 567 to 626. Although its powers of supervision over the Commission were increased by the Single European Act and the Maastricht Treaty, its main function is as a consultative and advisory link in the process and formulation of laws. Its opinion must be sought by the Commission and Council before any proposed legislation can be adopted, and it has the right to put forward amendments.[15]

12.3.5 The powers of the European Parliament have been progressively strengthened by both the Single European Act and the Maastricht Treaty. Under the Treaty of Rome, the Parliament had no rights other than to be consulted (on the basis of a single reading of a draft measure). This "consultation" procedure was replaced, following the passing of the Single

---

[14] See paras. 12.2.12 and 12.2.16.
[15] EC Treaty, Art. 149(2) (as added by the Single European Act).

European Act, by the so called "co-operation procedure", which further increased the Parliament's influence over the Commission's legislative powers and entitled it to reject or amend proposals on which the Commission and the Council had reached consensus (a "common position"), although the Parliament could, ultimately, be overruled. The process was further developed by the Maastricht Treaty to the extent that, on a rejection of a common position by the Parliament (or the rejection by the Council of Parliament's amendments to a common position), a Conciliation Committee (staffed equally by Parliament and Council) will try to reach agreement. Under this "co-decision" procedure, the Parliament has an ultimate veto which can result in the proposal for legislation lapsing.

European Court of Justice

The European Court of Justice, which is situated in Luxembourg and whose   12.3.6
members (15 judges and nine Advocates-General) are appointed by national governments, is the highest authority on matters of Community law. It seeks to provide independent and consistent interpretation of E.C. legislation, undistracted by the influence of national courts, which must follow its rulings. A Court of First Instance was established by the Single European Act to assist in the reduction of the backlog of cases. Decisions of the court have considerable influence on the development of policy within the Community. One notable example in recent years has been the establishment at the hands of the court of the doctrine of "direct effect" which will be referred to later.[16]

The Economic and Social Committee

The Economic and Social Committee is a consultative body whose opinion   12.3.7
on proposals for new legislation is sought by the Commission. Many of its members are technical experts and representatives of different industries, small businesses and general consumers. The Committee has considerable influence, particularly in environmental matters where the end result of new controls on industry and commerce are important.

The European Environment Agency

The European Environment Agency was established in 1990 and, after much   12.3.8
wrangling, its headquarters are established in Copenhagen, Denmark. It is not a true regulatory agency in the sense of, for example, the Scottish Environment Protection Agency (SEPA), although it may eventually be given

---

[16] See paras. 12.4.6 *et seq.*

wider powers. At present, the Agency acts mainly as an information and monitoring centre, providing the Member States with "objective, reliable and comparable" information on the state of the European environment to enable them to honour their obligations under the Treaty in respect of environmental protection.

IMPLEMENTATION OF ENVIRONMENTAL POLICY

Legal instruments

12.4.1 The principal instruments used to translate environmental policy into legislation are regulations and directives. Article 189 of the Treaty of Rome also provides for the use of decisions, recommendations and opinions, but these are seldom seen in the field of environmental policy, although decisions (which are binding in their entirety on those to whom they are addressed) have been used, mainly to implement international conventions.

12.4.2   Regulations introduce directly applicable law, *i.e.* they require no legislation on the part of Member States to implement them and legal rights and responsibilities are created as soon as they are passed. Directives, on the other hand, are binding only in respect of the results to be achieved. National governments have freedom to determine how these results are to be obtained. They have less choice, however, as to the time of implementation, each directive having a set date for compliance.

12.4.3   Directives have tended to be the principal instruments used for the translation of environmental policy into law. This is partly because Article 100 (on which the majority of environmental policy has, to date, been based) specifies directives as the means by which approximation of laws is to be achieved. Furthermore, there are few areas of environmental policy where an immediately binding and uniform result can be readily obtained, such is the variety of social, climatic and regulatory backgrounds throughout the Community.

12.4.4   Regulations, which traditionally have tended to be used for such areas as agricultural policy where immediate implementation is essential, have also been used in the environmental field on a few occasions. Regulation 3322/88 requires Community-wide action on the part of manufacturers to reduce CFC production by 50 per cent by the year 2000.[17] Another example is Regulation 1210/90 establishing the European Environment Agency.

12.4.5   In the environmental field, a "blurring" can be discerned in the distinction between regulations and directives arising out of the use made of the directives. Environmental controls increasingly require emission or discharge standards to be met, and many directives are now framed to include

---

[17] See also para. 12.5.13.

details of limits and concentrations as well as provisions for monitoring and analysis to ensure that they will be adhered to. A directive containing such requirements which give Member States comparatively little flexibility as to their application is much more akin to a regulation than a framework directive which, by definition, establishes only a broad outline, requiring, for its complete implementation, one or more subsidiary or daughter directives.

Doctrine of Direct Effect

Until recently, environmental policy enacted by directives has required 12.4.6 national legislation to make available to individual citizens the rights and obligations of that policy. The European Court of Justice has, however, developed a doctrine resulting in such underlying rights and responsibilities being immediately enforceable before national courts. Hitherto, non-compliance with a directive has not been a matter which an individual citizen has been able to raise. Instead, it has been an issue to be resolved between the Commission and the Member State guilty of the infringement. Following the establishment, in recent years, of what is known as the doctrine of "direct effect", it is now possible for an individual, or, for example, an environmental pressure group in an action against the Government (or a government agency) to rely on provisions of a directive even if the provisions have not been implemented under the national law (see para. 2.8.10).

The doctrine of direct effect, which is entirely judge-made, has been 12.4.7 developed over a number of years, and is particularly appropriate to issues of environmental policy, much of which is enacted by directives. The doctrine was relied upon in a recent case in Scotland involving environmental assessment.[18]

Two aspects restrict the availability of the doctrine of direct effect. (1) 12.4.8 The doctrine cannot be invoked in respect of every provision of a directive. The obligation being relied upon must be "clear and unambiguous", so that provisions according a Member State a large degree of discretion will not be accorded direct effect.[19] (2) The doctrine is not available as a remedy in cases where the parties to the dispute are private individuals. One of the parties must be an "emanation of the state" which would, in Scotland, appear to include not only the obvious examples of the Scottish Office itself, but also its Environment Department, local authorities, SEPA, etc.[20]

---

[18] *Kincardine and Deeside D.C. v. Forestry Commissioners*, 1991 S.C.L.R. 729.

[19] Case 8/81 *Becker v. Finanzamt Münster-Innenstadt* [1982] E.C.R. 53.

[20] Case 152/84 *Marshall v. Southampton and South-West Hampshire Area Health Authority (Teaching)* [1986] E.C.R. 723, [1986] Q.B. 401; Case 188/89 *Foster v. British Gas* [1991] Q.B. 405. The *obiter* comments in *Guthrie v. Scottish Environment Protection Agency*, 1997 G.W.D. 6–244 that a local authority is not an "agency of government" in this sense are clearly wrong.

Compliance

12.4.9 A lack of consistent implementation and compliance in all Member States has tarnished, to some extent, the image of E.C. law as an effective self-sufficient legal system. This is particularly true in the case of the environment. The general public's increasing concern with the quality of life itself ensures that delayed implementation and infringements will be accorded maximum publicity. The Commission, although aware of the problem, has not matched its enthusiasm for promoting environmental laws with any determination to enforce them. There has been an increasing number of cases before the European Court of Justice brought by the Commission for failure on the part of a Member State to translate European law into its own national system.[21] What is of much greater importance for the protection of the environment is the failure to ensure that the various technical standards, for example in relation to air and water quality, are, in fact, being met.

12.4.10   The Commission has recognised that there are weaknesses in the current state of implementation and enforcement of E.C. environmental law and, with a view to addressing this problem, it issued, in October 1996, a Communication to the Council and European Parliament on implementing Community environmental law. This is designed to provoke widespread discussion not only on reinforcing the existing system by making fuller use of Articles 169 and 171 (infringement proceedings and financial penalties), but also by exploring new areas for action. These may include strengthening Member States' inspection and monitoring powers, standardisation of local complaints mechanisms within Member States, and encouraging greater access to justice, particularly by non-governmental organisations and individual citizens, as distinct from public authorities.

Complaints procedure

12.4.11 It remains to be seen whether these initiatives produce any improvement in the record of compliance. As indicated above, the only way of drawing attention to incomplete or inconsistent enforcement has been to persuade the Commission (if it has not already pursued the matter — the Commission is required by terms of Article 155 of the Treaty to ensure that Community

---

[21] There are many examples involving most of the Member States. A representative sample includes Case C-361/88 *E.C. Commission v. Germany* [1991] E.C.R. I-2567, for failure to implement Directive 80/779 on air quality values for sulphur dioxide; Case C-56/90 *E.C. Commission v. United Kingdom* [1994] 1 C.M.L.R. 769, for failure to implement Directive 76/160 concerning bathing water quality; Case C-355/90 *Commission v. Spain* [1993] E.C.R. I-4221, for failure to implement Directive 79/409 concerning conservation of wild birds.

law is observed) to commence infringement proceedings against the government of the transgressing Member State. Until recently, lobbying the Commission has been the only way in which individual citizens can take practical steps to seek redress. However, the case of *Francovich and Bonifaci v. Italy*[23] has established that (in some circumstances at least) my E.C. citizen may take his national government to the Court of Justice for non-implementation of E.C. laws. Indeed, in some circumstances citizens may claim damages from the Member State if they suffer loss as a result of the state's failure to give effect to a directive in national law.

There is an established complaints procedure which can be initiated by an individual, an association or a corporate body. Although this can be a cumbersome and lengthy process, complaints will be dealt with eventually. Very few complaints get to the stage where the Member State is actually brought to court. It is much more likely that the Commission will, during earlier stages in the complaint, bring pressure to bear on the Member State to comply. Even if the Commission's case is found by the court to be justified there was (before the Maastricht Treaty) no effective sanction that the court could apply. An amendment to Article 171 of the Treaty of Rome gives the European Court of Justice power to impose a lump sum or penalty payment on a Member State which fails to comply with the court's judgment. There is no redress available to a complainant who considers that the Commission has not dealt with his complaint fully, although allegations of maladministration can be investigated by the Ombudsman appointed by the European Parliament under Article 138E. 12.4.12

SPECIFIC ENVIRONMENTAL LEGISLATION

It is not possible in the space of one chapter to do more than give a very brief outline of some of the specific areas of environmental control for which there is legislation in force, in draft or still just anticipated. In addition to the very recent developments in the integrated approach to pollution control, emphasis is on the three principal media of water, air and land (waste), with more brief comments on noise pollution and the protection of wildlife and, finally, a brief reference to aspects of publicity and economic control of environmental issues. 12.5.1

Integrated pollution prevention and control

Directive 96/61 on integrated pollution prevention and control was adopted on October 30, 1996 with an implementation date three years later in 1999. This measure (reflecting existing systems in some Member States, including 12.5.2

---

[23] Cases C-6/90 and C-9/90 [1991] E.C.R. I-5357.

the United Kingdom) will replace the current system of separate authorisations for different forms of emissions or discharges. The Directive is based on a prescribed list of industrial operations and is likely to have major implications beyond the administrative changes it will introduce. The requirement for old-fashioned facilities to upgrade (admittedly over a period of time) will impose considerable strains on some industries.

Water

12.5.3 Control over pollution of water was one of the earliest areas of environmental concern, the first proposal in this respect being introduced in 1973. The 25 or so relevant directives have, until recently, been divided into two principal areas of protection: first, general control over discharges to the aquatic environment; and, secondly, the setting of specific standards for the quality of water according to its uses (*e.g.* bathing water and drinking water) and related source controls, namely surface water, ground water, etc. In addition, an action programme concerning marine oil pollution has been established.

12.5.4   The most significant legislation under the first area of protection above is the framework Directive 76/464 on substances discharged into the aquatic environment (the Dangerous Substances Directive). This Directive established a system of prior authorisation for discharges of dangerous substances on the so called "Black" or "Grey" Lists and gave birth to a series of "daughter" directives setting limit values on individual toxic substances, for example mercury, cadmium, dieldrin, hexachlorobenzene, etc. The U.K. Red List (substances prescribed for prior authorisation under Part I of the Environmental Protection Act 1990) is similar but not identical to the Black List.[24]

12.5.5   E.C. policy on the discharge of dangerous substances has proceeded along the dual approach of, on the one hand, setting Community-wide limits for the maximum concentration of substances that can be released and, on the other hand, establishing standards based on the quality of the waters receiving those discharges. This twin-track basis has given rise to considerable conflict in the past, as the United Kingdom has been the only Member State to support the second approach. The hiatus was, to some extent, resolved by the framework Directive which gives priority to discharge standards, but also acknowledges the need for the receiving water quality test, which compromise has been repeated in some of the more recent derivative directives.

12.5.6   In addition, measures have been taken to reduce damage to the aquatic environment by controlling the output from specific industries. An example

---

[24] See para. 5.3.2.

of these are directives designed to limit the dumping at sea of ferrous sulphate waste from the titanium dioxide industry.[25]

Of the directives setting quality objectives for different uses of water, Directive 76/160 on bathing water and Directive 80/778 on drinking water have attracted considerable attention in recent years as a result of the persistent failure of many of the U.K.'s designated beaches to meet the required standards, and the reporting of the U.K. Government to the European Court for excessive nitrate and lead levels in drinking water (the affected supply points for the latter being mainly in Scotland). *E.C. Commission v. United Kingdom*[26] resulted in the United Kingdom being held not to have taken adequate steps to enforce the standards required under the Directive. 12.5.7

A further measure relating to water pollution control with far-reaching consequences is Directive 91/271 on municipal waste water treatment, which requires the secondary treatment of most sewage discharges (including industrial trade effluent), with additional restrictions for outfalls in particularly sensitive areas. It also bans, as from 1998, the dumping at sea of sewage sludge (the residue from sewage treatment works). This has major implications for the newly established water authorities, which now have responsibility for the provision of sewerage services. Directive 90/415 (requiring standards to be met from 1993 onwards) is a further directive of the framework Directive, and applies the same twin-track approach to other dangerous substances, for example trichlorobenzene. 12.5.8

In the 20 years since the passing of the Directive on dangerous substances it has become apparent that E.C. policy on the control of water pollution has not been as effective as it might have been. Comparatively few of the substances identified for control by the use of daughter directives were made subject to regulations, and the legislation itself had become very complex and piecemeal. Many of the standards and parameters in the water directives had become out of date. Proposals were published in 1994 for a directive to improve the ecological quality of surface waters, but this has itself been set aside by proposals for a framework directive on water resources, which arose following a public hearing held by the European Parliament in June 1995 to consider a more integrated approach to water resource management. The proposals will apply to both surface and ground water, and are likely to utilise both emission limits and environmental quality objectives in their approach to discharge controls. 12.5.9

---

[25] Directives 78/176; 83/29; 82/883 and 89/428. Following the annulment of Directive 89/428 by the European Court of Justice, a new directive was required, Directive 92/112.
[26] Case C-337/89 [1992] E.C.R. I-6103.

Air

12.5.10 Control over atmospheric emissions is probably the sector of European environmental policy which has received the most publicity. The problems of acid rain, climate change (global warming) and ozone depletion feature prominently in any research into those aspects of environmental damage giving most cause for concern. Initially, the policy was to legislate to protect human health, but more recent directives recognise the need to have regard to the wider environment. There are many directives controlling air pollution, several of which interact and overlap, but, essentially, the directives fall into three main groups: those setting quality standards for different products; those dealing with air quality standards for specific gases; and those controlling emissions from vehicles and industrial plants.

12.5.11   Some of the earliest initiatives fall into the first category. In 1975 Directive 75/716 fixed the maximum sulphur content of gas oils, and in 1978 Directive 78/611 set limits on the lead content of petrol. Directive 85/210 was adopted in 1985 in which the emphasis is on the promotion and availability of unleaded petrol as distinct from preventing the distortion of trade in petrol (and motor vehicles) from differing limits on lead concentration.

12.5.12   Air quality standards for sulphur dioxide and suspended particulates (smoke) were set in 1980 in Directive 80/779 (with amendments in 1989) and for nitrogen dioxide in 1985 in Directive 85/203; nitrogen dioxide is considered to be one of the main constituents of acid rain. The concentration of lead in the air is dealt with by Directive 82/884. Directive 92/72 concerns air pollution by ground level ozone.

12.5.13   Chlorofluorocarbons (CFCs) are not air pollutants in the traditional sense, in that they are non-toxic and not directly injurious to human health. However, the damage they cause to the upper atmosphere ozone layer now seems incontrovertible. Action was taken in 1980 and 1982 when Decision 80/372/EEC[27] and Decision 82/795/EEC[28] limited the production of CFCs and reduced their use in aerosols. These were followed by the Community's signing of the Montreal Convention in 1988 (implemented by Regulation 3322/88), imposing a commitment to a 50 per cent reduction in the use of CFCs by the year 2000. Further legislation both tightened controls over consumption and importation of ozone-depleting substances, and consolidated existing legislation. In 1994, Regulation 3093/94 was passed to impose progressive reductions on the use of hydrobromofluorocarbons (HCFCs), one of the main substitutes for CFCs.

---

[27] Council Decision 80/372/EEC of March 26, 1980 concerning chlorofluorocarbons in the environment: O.J. [1980] L90/45.

[28] Council Decision 82/795/EEC of November 15, 1982 on the consolidation of precautionary measures concerning fluorocarbons in the environment: O.J. [1982] L329/29.

There has been a series of directives on measures to be taken to reduce 12.5.14
air pollution from motorvehicle engines, both petrol and diesel.[29] As well
as the moves to reduce damage caused by lead in petrol (the "clean air"
initiatives requiring, *e.g.* all new cars to run on lead free petrol by specified
dates), limit values for other exhaust gases such as carbon monoxide,
nitrogen oxide and unburnt hydrocarbons have been set and standards for
private diesel cars were laid down in 1988. Limits were progressively
lowered for passenger cars in 1991, 1993, and 1994, with similar reductions
for trucks and other commercial vehicles. As with legislation in respect of
other forms of pollution, the fragmented approach to the regulation of
atmospheric emissions from motorvehicles has not resulted in air quality
targets being met and, with this in mind, the E.C. Commission adopted, in
June 1996, proposals for a radical revision of current standards. The
Commission claims that this "auto oil" proposal will produce the cleanest
air quality standards in the world by the year 2010.

Alarm over the damage being caused to the forests of Germany and 12.5.15
Scandinavia resulted in the adoption of directives on combating air pollution
from industrial plants. The 1984 Air Framework Directive 84/360 was a
more general measure requiring certain categories of plant to have prior
authorisation before being able to operate, while Directive 88/609 and
Directive 94/66 limit the emission of sulphur dioxide and the nitrogen oxides
from large combustion plants. It was the requirement to implement these
Directives which was partly responsible for the enactment of Part 1 of the
Environmental Protection Act 1990. Waste incinerators are major
contributors to industrial air pollution and Directives 89/369 and 89/429
set out exacting standards for new and existing plant. The legislation has
had a marked effect in Scotland, where several municipal waste incinerators
have failed to meet the required standards, and have been closed down.

Two other directives will have important implications for E.C. air quality 12.5.16
standards. The Directive on integrated pollution prevent and control has
already been mentioned (see para. 12.5.2), and, when it comes into force in
1999, should assist in the reduction of atmospheric emissions from
prescribed types of industrial operation. Directive 96/62 on ambient air
quality assessment and management sets limit values for a range of air
pollutants. This framework control is designed to implement an overall
strategy to reduce the harmful effects of air pollution which, despite (or
perhaps because of) the many but disparate existing laws, has clearly not
been improving. As well as E.C.-wide limits on emissions the Directive
also sets "alert thresholds" the exceedance of which, because of particular
geographical or climatic circumstances, could be dangerous to health, even
on brief exposure.

---

[29] See paras. 2.7.1 *et seq.*

Waste

12.5.17 Estimates of the annual production of waste throughout the Community vary considerably, but the overall tonnage certainly exceeds 1.5 billion tonnes, 22 million tonnes of which is of a hazardous nature. A shortage of sites for landfill disposal coupled with increasing concern regarding the movement of hazardous waste within the Community (especially following completion of the internal market) has resulted in an increasing number of legal measures on waste control. E.C. policy on waste is largely based on three precepts: concentration on the recycling or reuse of recoverable waste; reduction in the amount of waste produced; and the proper management and disposal (including transport) of non-recoverable waste. These, along with other principles, were embodied in an E.C. *Strategy for Waste Management*, published in 1989, which remains the principal statement of policy in this area.

12.5.18   The Waste Framework Directive 75/442 required Member States to take action in respect of household and toxic waste in these general areas, including the preparation of plans for waste disposal and recycling and the licensing of persons handling waste. Daughter directives, stemming from Directive 75/442, tightened the control over toxic waste (Directive 78/319) and polychlorinated biphenyls (PCBs) (Directive 76/403). A new framework Directive 91/156, with a compliance date of April 1, 1993, replacing much of Directive 75/442, redefines, and in so doing strengthens, many of the earlier measures, laying particular emphasis on Member States (and thus the Community at large) achieving self-sufficiency in the disposal of waste. It also attempts to clarify the vexed question of the definition of "waste", and has been responsible for the incorporation into the U.K. waste management regulations of the defined term "directive waste" and the subsequent amendment of the main statutory definition (see para. 4.2.1).

12.5.19   Increasing quantities of dangerous and intractable waste arisings in the European Community have led to the adoption of several directives dealing with hazardous waste. Directive 78/319, the first to deal with the more general forms of toxic waste (as distinct from dangerous chemicals on which earlier policy had concentrated), was found, in practice, to be inadequate and was eventually repealed in June 1995 by Directive 91/689. This measure replaces the general definition of "toxic and dangerous waste" by a series of annexes setting out a generic classification of what is now referred to as "hazardous waste". It is on this categorisation that the U.K. Special Waste Regulations are based.[29a] Much of the Directive relates to the identification, recording and monitoring of hazardous waste movements.

12.5.20   The increasing problems, both environmental and political, of the transfrontier shipment of hazardous waste and its effective disposal have

---

[29a] Special Waste Regulations 1996 (S.I. 1996 No. 972).

prompted an increasing portfolio of Community legislation, largely to fulfil its obligations under international law, in particular the Basle Convention on the Control of Transboundary Movements of Hazardous Waste in 1989. The 1978 Directive 78/319 on toxic waste made no provision for the transport of waste between Member (and non-Member) States. This was rectified by Directive 84/631, which established a system of monitoring and control based on the consignment note procedure, and introduced requirements for labelling and packaging of waste. Regulation 259/93 was issued to implement the Convention's requirements, updating the E.C. law on transfrontier shipment of hazardous waste to the extent that there is now a complete ban on the trade in hazardous waste (for final disposal) between Member States and third party developing countries. There is now considerable pressure to extend this to waste destined for recycling.

Other measures related to the issue of waste reduction and its safe disposal include the following.   12.5.21

(1) Directive 91/157 restricting the marketing of batteries. This requires national plans to be drawn up for the collection and recycling of waste batteries and imposes limits on the quantities of heavy metals such as mercury and cadmium in different types of battery.

(2) A directive was proposed in 1991 and amended in 1993 on the landfill of waste, setting design standards and establishing controls over monitoring of landfill gas and providing for aftercare and restoration. After a lengthy period of gestation the directive was, in effect, stillborn when the Council rejected virtually all of the Parliament's amendments. The Commission is, however, determined not to give up on this initiative, and a new proposal for an amended draft directive has recently been issued.[30] One of the directive's main requirements would be a staged reduction in the amount of biodegradable municipal waste that could be disposed of by landfill — a measure designed to reduce the incidence of methane generation.

(3) Directive 94/62 on packaging and packaging waste sets Member States targets for recovery and recycling of packaging, and requires conformity with various standards in respect of manufacture, recyclability, etc. The U.K. "producer responsibility" regulations (see paras. 4.6.1–3) derive their effect from this measure.

(4) A draft directive has been prepared on civil liability for damage caused by waste.[31] The draft, which has now been amended sev-

---

[30] COM (96) 647.
[31] Initial proposal O.J. [1989] C 251/3, revised O.J. [1991] C 192/6.

eral times, would impose strict, joint and several liability on producers of waste for damage to persons and property and "impairment to the environment". This measure has been overtaken by wide-ranging discussion on the possibility of legislation to harmonise rules on more general liability for environmental damage from all causes (not just waste). A discussion paper was issued by the Commission in 1993, followed by several public hearings and the commissioning of further technical papers. As this chapter was being prepared, the latest pronouncement was that, rather than proceed directly to a proposal for legislation, a White Paper is to be issued for further consultation.[32]

Noise pollution

12.5.22 Pollution from noise (both in the workplace and from different vehicles and appliances) is an area of environmental control which the European Community has paid less attention to than other forms of pollution. Indeed, many Member States have more comprehensive national coverage of this aspect than the Community itself. However, as the concept of harm to man's senses extends the traditional definition of environmental pollution, so will this become of increasing concern. To date, the Commission has tackled the problem of noise pollution from the standpoint of the levels of noise emitted by different products, attempting to ensure that free circulation of goods is not inhibited by varying standards applied in different Member States. Accordingly, maximum noise levels for aircraft, four-wheeled vehicles (including tractors), motor cycles, lawnmowers and even household appliances have been laid down by a series of directives.[33] It may be the case that the Commission will progress to considering the problem of general ambient noise quality as an integral component of environmental protection. Directive 86/188 on the protection of workers from the risk of noise in the workplace could, perhaps, be regarded as a move in that direction, although based on the Community's social, rather than strictly environmental programme.

Protection of wildlife and countryside

12.5.23 In contrast to the preceding section, the protection of wildlife and countryside is an area of E.C. endeavour which has attracted much public interest and support, and one where European environmental policy is closely linked to

---

[32] See "Bjerregaard poised for fresh move on environmental liability" (1996) 260 *ENDS Report* 38.

[33] Directives 89/629 (aircraft); 74/151 (tractors); 84/538 (lawnmowers) and 86/594 (household appliances) (see para. 8.4.17).

action at the international level. Fauna, particularly migratory wild birds and marine mammals such as whales, seals, etc., are no respecters of national boundaries, and several important treaties and directives have been issued with a view to regulating numbers, protecting habitats and prohibiting trade in those species most at risk of extinction (see Chapter 10).

Directive 79/409 on the conservation of wild birds is one of the most 12.5.24 important landmarks in the development of this aspect of E.C. environmental policy. It was enacted as a direct result of public outcry at the indiscriminate killing and capturing (in several of the Community's Member States) of migrating wild birds, and lays down rules not only for the overall protection of many species but also regulates methods of hunting and the preservation of habitats. The Commission's determination to enforce this measure has been demonstrated on several occasions; one notable Scottish example being the priority accorded to the protection of wild geese at Duich Moss in Islay over the competing interests of the whisky industry which sought to destroy the peat moss on which the geese were accustomed to graze.

Directive 92/43 on the conservation of natural habitats and of wild fauna 12.5.25 and flora is potentially of much greater importance. This is because it exerts control over a much wider range of species and habitats, but also because it puts in place a framework of compulsorily designated sites of particular importance in respect of the biodiversity, not only of each Member State, but also of the wider Community and beyond (see paras. 10.3.3–5).

General measures designed to assist in achieving environmental protection.

If market forces are to play their part along with legislative regulation in 12.5.26 implementing the environmental policy of the European Community, it is essential that the public is given comprehensive access to information on environmental matters to enable informed choices to be made including, for example, the initiating of action to bring to heel regulatory agencies which are deemed to have been lax in enforcement. Directive 90/313 on the freedom of environmental information requires Member States to make information on environmental matters held by public authorities available to the public.

Directive 85/337 on the assessment of the effects of certain public and 12.5.27 private projects on the environment requires an environmental statement to be prepared as a prerequisite to the development of a project if it is included on one of two Annexes (see paras. 7.4.17–20). Annex 1 (where an assessment is mandatory) includes proposals likely to have a major impact on the environment, for example oil refineries, nuclear reactors and airports. A project listed under Annex 2 may require an assessment where it is likely to have a significant effect on the environment. It has been a lack of clarity of that definition and a general vagueness in other aspects that has resulted in very uneven enforcement of the Directive throughout the Community. As a result of this, an amending Directive 97/11, has been made which should ensure a more uniform approach. The Commission has also signalled its wish to see environmental assessment being extended to include not only projects but also plans and programmes by publishing a proposal for a directive to require such assessment of the policy framework upon which more detailed development proposals are based.

12.5.28   Another initiative designed to encourage environmental protection on the part of business and industry is Regulation 1836/93 on the Eco-Management and Audit Scheme (EMAS). Firms which take part in the Scheme are required to set an environmental policy in terms of standards prescribed in the Regulation and, thereafter, an environmental audit of the firm's activities (covering everything from regulatory compliance to waste stream management) is carried out. Compliance with the Regulation requirements must then be verified by an independent verifier who is accredited by the Member State's internal system. Advertisement to the public of a firm's certificate of compliance with EMAS is anticipated to provide the necessary incentive to participate in the Scheme.

12.5.29   In the longer term, the Commission has also been considering the use of economic and fiscal matters as a method of achieving some degree of harmony between economic growth and environmental protection. Pollution taxes on carbon dioxide and other gases, deposit refund schemes and tradeable emission permits are all areas which may expect considerable future attention from the Community.

CONCLUSION

12.6.1 As this short review has shown, E.C. environmental law is of considerable scope, diversity and importance for the future of the Community. Its effectiveness is subject to the same shortcomings in terms of compliance and enforcement which are found in our own national system. Nevertheless, there is no denying that its development as a system of laws separate from, but interacting with, those of its Member States has resulted in considerable achievements in the field of environmental protection, and it will continue to be a critical element in the functioning and future refinement of the new internal market.

12.6.2   However, the story is not one of complete success. European environmental policy is at a crucial stage in its development. It is certainly the case that the major pollution problems which have affected the Community for the last 20 or 30 years have been legislated for. Notwithstanding over 200 pieces of legislation, the current (Fifth) Community Action Programme on the Environment speaks of a "slow but relentless deterioration of the general state of the environment of the Community". Furthermore, major problems are likely to arise as the European Community progresses towards accession of aspirant Eastern European states, where current environmental standards are either nonexistent or at a very low level. The ever-present tension within the European Community between the sectoral interests of the economy and the environment seems likely to persist, although there is some hope that the current renegotiation of the Maastricht Treaty may result in policy in other sectors, such as agriculture and transport, being specifically required to reflect environmental issues rather than merely having regard to them.

For those with an interest in or practising environmental law in Scotland, knowledge of European environmental law and policy is essential. This is not merely because it is part of and prevails over our national law and requires to be brought into the equation when interpreting "local" provisions; more importantly, as the full measure of damage to planet Earth becomes clear, as environmental issues assume increasing importance internationally, and as the costs of responding to environmental liability mount, commerce and industry will be required to include environmental aspects in their longer-term strategic planning. Given the political importance of the European Community in the world order, and the willingness of the Commission (unhindered by electoral considerations) to propose radical solutions, it is to Brussels that lawyers (who in the environmental field will have to become increasingly anticipative in their advice) will look for the majority of new environmental legal initiatives. 12.6.3

FURTHER READING

General

Ball and Bell, *Environmental Law* (4th ed., 1997)
Burnett-Hall, *Environmental Law* (1995)
Hughes, *Environmental Law* (3rd ed., 1996)
Leeson, *Environmental Law* (1995)
Malcolm, *A Guidebook to Environmental Law* (reissued as *Introduction to Environmental Law*) (1994)
Mumma, *Environmental Law — Meeting U.K. and E.C. requirements* (1995)
Murley (ed.), *Pollution Handbook 1997* (1997)
Tromans (with Nash and Poustie), *The Environment Acts 1990–1995* (1996)
The Laws of Scotland: Stair Memorial Encyclopaedia (1987) (and Cumulative Supplement), especially *Environment* (Vol. 9), *Fisheries and Game* (Vol. 11), *Nuisance* (Vol. 14), *Public Health* (Vol. 19), *Town and Country Planning* (Vol. 23), *Water and Water Rights* and *Water Supply* (Vol. 25)
Garner's Environmental Law (looseleaf) (1976)
Encyclopaedia of Environmental Law (looseleaf) (1993)

Scottish Planning and Environmental Law (six issues per year)
ENDS Report (monthly)
Journal of Environmental Law (two issues per year)
Environmental Law and Management (six issues per year)

This Common Inheritance: Britain's Environmental Strategy, Cm. 1200 (1990) and *Annual Reports*, Cm. 1655 (1991); Cm. 2068 (1992); Cm. 2549 (1994); Cm. 2822 (1995); Cm. 3188 (1996); Cm. 3556 (1997)
Department of the Environment, *The U.K. Environment* (1993)
Sustainable Development: The U.K. Strategy, Cm. 2426 (1994)

Air

Department of the Environment/Scottish Office, *Improving Air Quality: Meeting the Challenge* (1995)
Department of the Environment/Scottish Office, *The U.K. National Air Quality Strategy — Consultation Draft* (1996)
Department of the Environment/Scottish Office, *The U.K. National Air Quality Strategy*, Cm. 3587 (1997)
Transport — The Way Forward: the Government's response to the Transport Debate, Cm. 3234 (1996)

Royal Commission on Environmental Pollution, *Air Pollution Control: An Integrated Approach* (5th Report), Cmnd. 6371 (1976)

Royal Commission on Environmental Pollution, *Lead in the Environment* (9th Report), Cmnd. 8852 (1983)

Royal Commission on Environmental Pollution, *Tackling Pollution: Experience and Prospects* (10th Report), Cmnd. 9149 (1984)

Royal Commission on Environmental Pollution, *Transport and the Environment* (18th Report), Cm. 2672 (1994).

Scottish Office, *Keeping Scotland Moving, A Scottish Transport Green Paper*, Cm. 3565 (1997)

Water

Ferguson, *The Law of Water and Water Rights in Scotland* (1907)

The Laws of Scotland: Stair Memorial Encyclopaedia, Water and Water Rights and *Water Supply* (Vol. 25) (1989)

Waste

Bates, *U.K. Waste Law* (1992)

Garbutt, *Waste Management Law* (2nd ed., 1994)

Cheyne and Purdue, "Fitting Definition to Purpose and the Search for a Satisfactory Definition of Waste" (1995) 7 J.E.L. 149

Pocklington, "Waste Holder Liability" [1996] 8 E.L.M. 101

Department of the Environment, *Waste Management Paper No. 4: The Licensing of Waste Management Facilities* (1994)

Department of the Environment, *Waste Management Paper No. 26A: Landfill Completion* (1993)

Scottish Environment Protection Agency, *Draft National Waste Strategy: Scotland* (1997)

Making Waste Work — A Strategy for England and Wales, Cm. 3040 (1995)

Planning

Collar, *Planning* (1994)

Henderson (ed.), *Scottish Planning Sourcebook* (revised, 1996)

Henderson and O'Carroll, *Town and Country Planning in Scotland: Powers and Procedures* (1994)

McAllister and McMaster, *Scottish Planning Law: An Introduction* (1994)

Young, *Scottish Planning Appeals* (1991)

Young and Rowan Robinson, *Scottish Planning Law and Procedure* (1985)

Scottish Planning Encyclopaedia (ed. the Hon. Lord Gill) (1996)

The Laws of Scotland: Stair Memorial Encyclopaedia, Town and Country Planning (Vol. 23) (1988)

Noise

The Laws of Scotland: Stair Memorial Encyclopaedia, Environment (Vol. 9) (1988)
Adams and McManus, *Noise and Noise Law* (1994)
Hawke, *Environmental Health Law* (1995)
McManus, *Environmental Health Law in Scotland* (1989), Chap. 3
McManus, *Environmental Health Law* (1994), Chap. 3
Murley (ed.), *Pollution Handbook 1997* (1997), Chap 3.
Penn, *Noise Control* (2nd ed., 1995)
This Common Inheritance: Britain's Environmental Strategy, Cm. 1200 (1990), Pt. 4
United Kingdom Environmental Health Action Plan, Cm. 3323 (1996), Chap. 3.7

Civil liability

The Laws of Scotland: Stair Memorial Encyclopaedia (1988), *Nuisance* (Vol. 14)
Reid, "The Basis of Liability in Nuisance", 1997 J.R. 162
Pugh and Day, *Pollution and Personal Injury — Toxic Torts II* (1995)

Nature conservation

Reid, *Nature Conservation Law* (1994)
Fry, *A Manual of Nature Conservation Law* (1996)
Garner and Jones, *Countryside Law* (3rd ed., 1997)
Lyster, *International Wildlife Law* (1985)
Parkes and Thornley, *Fair Game* (1989)
Scott Robinson, *The Law of Game, Salmon and Freshwater Fisheries in Scotland* (1990)
Biodiversity: The U.K. Action Plan, Cm. 2428 (1994)
Biodiversity: The U.K. Steering Group Report (1995)

Marine issues

Bates, *United Kingdom Marine Pollution Law* (1985)
Brice, *Maritime Law of Salvage* (1983)
Darling and Smith, *LOF 90 and The New Salvage Convention* (1991)
Gaskell, Debattista and Swatton, *Chorley & Giles, Shipping Law* (8th ed., 1987)
Holden, *The Common Fisheries Policy: Origin, Evaluation and Future* (1994)
Howarth, *The Law of Aquaculture* (1990)
Karagiannakos, *Fisheries Management in the European Union* (1995)
Steel and Rose, *Kennedy's Law of Salvage* (5th ed., 1985)

Scottish Office, *Guidance on the Location of Marine Fish Farms* (Consultative Draft, December 1991)

European environmental law

Towards Sustainability: E.C. programme of policy and action in relation to the environment and sustainable development: O.J. [1993] C 138/5
Freestone, *Environmental Protection in E.C. Law* (1993)
Haigh, *Environmental Policy — E.C. and Britain* (looseleaf) (1992)
Holder (ed.) *The Impact of E.C. Environmental Law in the United Kingdom* (1997)
Johnson and Corcelle, *The Environmental Policy of the European Communities* (2nd ed., 1995)
Kiss, *Manual of European Environmental Law* (1993)
Krämer, *EEC Treaty and Environmental Protection* (2nd ed., 1994)
Krämer, *Focus on European Environmental Law* (1992)
Salter, *European Environmental Law* (looseleaf) (1996)
Somsen (ed.), *Protecting the European Environment: Enforcing E.C. Environmental Law* (1996)
Ziegler, *Trade and Environment Law in the E.C.* (1996)

INDEX

Agriculture
controlled water, entry of matter into, 3.5.18, 3.7.2
silage, slurry and oil, pollution by, 3.7.3

Air pollution
acid rain, creation of, 2.1.4
air quality management. *See* Air quality management
Beaver Committee, 2.1.1
chimney heights, control of, 2.6.10–2.6.12
dark smoke,
  charge of emitting, defences to, 2.6.4–2.6.6
  control of, 2.6.2, 2.6.3
  emission, prohibition of, 2.6.3
  inadvertent emission of, 2.6.6
  locomotive engine, from, 2.6.5
  meaning, 2.6.3
  premises emitting, 2.6.3
European law. *See* European environmental law
furnaces,
  arrestment equipment on, 2.6.9
  grit and dust from, 2.6.8
  prohibited material, burning, 2.6.11
  smoke from, 2.6.7
greenhouse effect, 2.1.6
industrial, control of, 2.4.1, 2.4.2
integrated control, 2.1.11
international measures, 2.1.4–2.1.7
legislation,
  Clean Air Acts, 2.1.2
  consolidation, 2.1.12
  development of, 2.1.1–2.1.3
  early, 2.1.1
  European Community, 2.1.8–2.1.10
  international measures, 2.1.4–2.1.7
  recent developments, 2.1.11, 2.1.12
  standards employed,
    emission, 2.8.4, 2.8.5
    process, 2.8.2, 2.8.3
    product, 2.8.12
    quality, 2.8.6–2.8.11
local control, 2.1.11
nauseous or offensive emissions, control of, 2.1.2

ozone depletion, threat of, 2.1.5
regulations, 2.1.2
regulatory bodies,
  development of, 2.2.1, 2.2.2
  H.M. Alkali Inspectorate, 2.2.1
  H.M. Industrial Pollution Inspectorate, 2.2.1
  integrated control, for, 2.2.2
  local authorities, 2.2.4
  Secretary of State, 2.2.5
  SEPA. *See* Scottish Environment Protection Agency
smoke, by,
  cable burning, 2.6.18
  chimney heights, control of, 2.6.10–2.6.12
  colliery bings, burning, 2.6.19
  control of, 2.6.1, 2.6.2
  control orders and areas, 2.6.13–2.6.16
  dark. *See* dark smoke,
  fireplaces, adaptation of, 2.6.16
  furnaces, from, 2.6.7
  meaning, 2.6.1
  straw and stubble burning, 2.6.17
statutory nuisance, as, 2.5.1
straw and stubble burning, by, 2.6.17
sustainable development strategies, 2.1.7
transboundary problem of, 2.1.3
vehicle emissions,
  control, need for, 2.7.1
  economic instruments, control by, 2.7.6, 2.7.7
  fuel content, 2.7.2, 2.7.3
  motor vehicles, type approval, construction and use of, 2.7.4, 2.7.5
  unleaded petrol, vehicles running on, 2.7.5

Air quality management
Directive, approach of, 2.8.8, 2.8.9
local,
  action plan, 2.3.7
  assessment of quality, 2.3.7
  local authorities, role of, 2.3.6
  management areas (AQMAs), 2.3.6, 2.3.7

251

ST